Reading

Reading Comprehension

English

Spelling

TABLE OF CONTENTS

Over 10 Million Copies in Print!

COMPREHENSIVE CURRICULUM
of Basic Skills

GRADE 2

Math

Reading

Reading Comprehension

English

Writing

Thinking Kids®
Carson-Dellosa Publishing LLC
Greensboro, North Carolina

Thinking Kids®
Carson-Dellosa Publishing LLC
P.O. Box 35665
Greensboro, NC 27425 USA

© 2016 Carson-Dellosa Publishing LLC. Except as permitted under the United States Copyright Act, no part of this publication may be reproduced, stored, or distributed in any form or by any means (mechanically, electronically, recording, etc.) without the prior written consent of Carson-Dellosa Publishing LLC. Thinking Kids® is an imprint of Carson-Dellosa Publishing LLC.

Printed in the USA • All rights reserved.   ISBN 978-1-4838-2411-6
09-210191151

READING

All About Me!

Directions: Fill in the blanks to tell all about you!

Name _____
    (First)   (Last)

Address _____

City _____ State _____

Phone number _____

Age _____

Places I have visited: _____

_____

_____

_____

My favorite vacation: _____

_____

_____

_____

Beginning Consonants: *B, C, D, F, G, H,* and *J*

Directions: Fill in the beginning consonant for each word.

Example: _c_ at

__b__ ox

__j__ acket

__g__ oat

__h__ ouse

__d__ og

__f__ ire

Beginning Consonants: *K, L, M, N, P, Q,* and *R*

Directions: Write the letter that makes the beginning sound for each picture.

Beginning Consonants: *K, L, M, N, P, Q,* and *R*

Directions: Fill in the beginning consonant for each word.

Example: __r__ose

 __M__oney

__q__uilt

__L__ion

__P__an

__K__ey

__N__ose

Name _____

Beginning Consonants: *S, T, V, W, X, Y,* and *Z*

Directions: Write the letter that makes the beginning sound for each picture.

Beginning Consonants: *S, T, V, W, X, Y,* and *Z*

Directions: Fill in the beginning consonant for each word.

Example: __s__ ock

 ipper

__T__ able

__X__ ray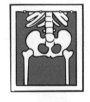

__V__ ase

__Y__ olk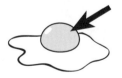

__W__ and

Name _____

Ending Consonants: *B*, *D*, *F*, and *G*

Directions: Fill in the ending consonant for each word.

ma __n__

cu __b__

roo __f__

do __g__

be __d__

bi __b__

Ending Consonants: *K*, *L*, *M*, *N*, *P*, and *R*

Directions: Fill in the ending consonant for each word.

nai __l__

ca __n__

gu __m__

ca __r__

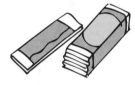

truc __k__

ca __p__

pai __t__

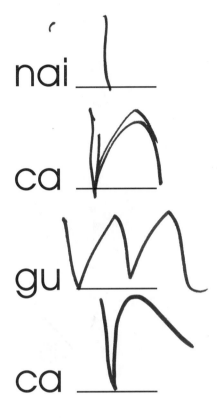

Ending Consonants: *S*, *T*, and *X*

Directions: Fill in the ending consonant for each word.

ca __t__

bo __x__

bu __s__

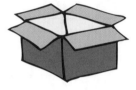

fo __x__

boa __t__

ma __t__

Consonant Blends

Consonant blends are two or three consonant letters in a word whose sounds combine, or blend. **Examples: br, fr, gr, pr, tr**

Directions: Look at each picture. Say its name. Write the blend you hear at the beginning of each word.

Blends: *fl*, *br*, *pl*, *sk*, and *sn*

Directions: Look at the pictures, and say their names. Write the letters for the beginning sound in each word.

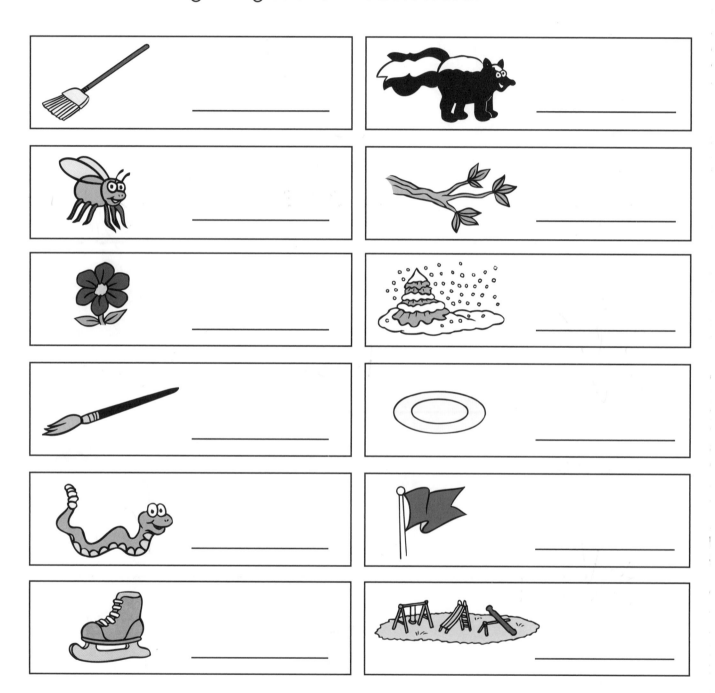

Blends: *bl*, *cl*, *cr*, and *sl*

Directions: Look at the pictures, and say their names. Write the letters for the beginning sound in each word.

____own

____anket

____ayon

____ock

____ide

____oud

____ed

____ab

____ocodile

Name _____

Consonant Blends

Directions: Write a word from the word box to answer each riddle.

| clock | glass | blow | climb | slipper |
| sleep | gloves | clap | blocks | flashlight |

1. You need me when the lights go out.
   What am I? _____

2. People use me to tell the time.
   What am I? _____

3. You put me on your hands in the winter
   to keep them warm. **What am I?** _____

4. Cinderella lost one like me at midnight.
   What am I? _____

5. This is what you do with your hands when
   you are pleased. **What is it?** _____

6. You can do this with a whistle or with
   bubble gum. **What is it?** _____

7. These are what you might use to build a
   castle when you are playing.
   What are they? _____

8. You do this to get to the top of a hill.
   What is it? _____

9. This is what you use to drink water or milk.
   What is it? _____

10. You do this at night with your eyes closed.
    What is it? _____

Name _____

Consonant Blends

Consonant blends can be made up of three letters whose sounds combine. **Examples: spl, scr**

Directions: Read the words in the box. Write a word from the word box to finish each sentence. Circle the consonant blend in each word. **Hint:** There are three letters in each blend.

splash	screen	spray	street	scream
screw	sprain	split	strong	string

1. Did you _~~sprain~~_ your ankle?

2. I tied a _~~string~~_ to my tooth to help pull it out.

3. I have many friends who live on my _~~street~~_.

4. We always _~~scream~~_ when we ride the roller coaster.

5. A _~~screen~~_ helps keep bugs out of the house.

6. It is fun to _~~splash~~_ in the water.

7. My father uses an ax to _~~split~~_ the firewood.

8. We will need a _~~screw~~_ to fix the chair.

9. You must be very _~~strong~~_ to lift this heavy box.

10. The firefighters _~~spray~~_ the fire with water.

Comprehensive Curriculum - **Grade 2**

Consonant Teams

Consonant teams are two or three consonant letters that have a single sound. **Examples: sh** and **tch**

Directions: Write each word from the word box next to its picture. Underline the consonant team in each word. Circle the consonant team in each word in the box.

bench	match	shoe	thimble
shell	brush	peach	watch
whale	teeth	chair	wheel

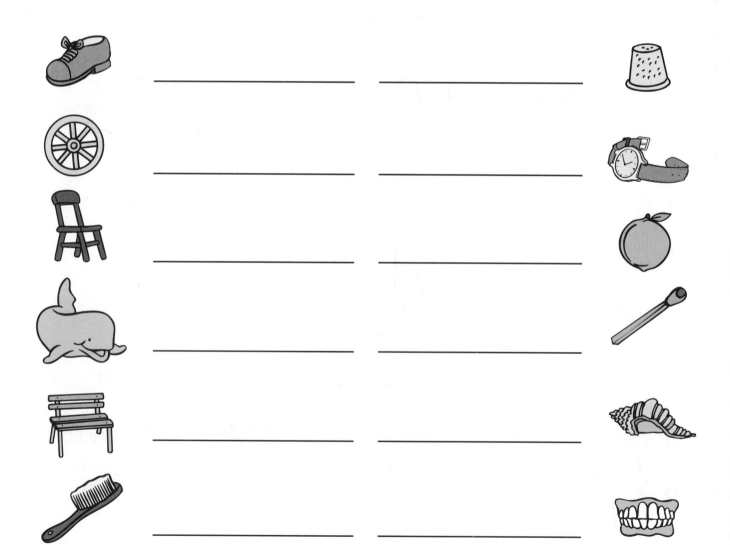

Consonant Teams: *sh*, *ch*, *wh*, and *th*

Directions: Look at the first picture in each row. Circle the pictures that have the same sound.

whistle

shoe

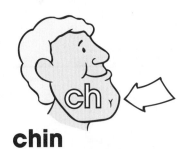
chin

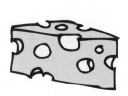

thumb

Consonant Teams: *sh*, *ch*, *wh*, and *th*

Directions: Look at the pictures, and say the words. Write the first two letters of the word on the line below each picture.

_____

_____

_____

_____

_____

_____

_____

_____

_____

Consonant Blends and Teams

Directions: Circle the consonant team in each word that is in the word box. Write a word from the word box to finish each sentence.

trash	splash	chain
shut	chicken	catch
ship	when	patch
	which	

1. My _____ won't lay eggs.

2. I put a _____ on my bicycle so nobody can take it.

3. We watched the big _____ dock and let off its passengers.

4. It is my job to take out the _____ .

5. I have to wear a _____ over my eye until it is better.

6. The baby likes to _____ in the bathtub.

7. Can you _____ the ball with one hand?

8. Please _____ the windows before it rains.

9. _____ are we going to leave for school?

10. I don't know _____ of these books is mine.

Consonant Blends and Teams

Directions: Look at the words in the word box. Write all of the words that end with the **ng** sound in the column under the picture of the **ring**. Write all of the words that end with the **nk** sound under the picture of the **sink**. Finish the sentences with words from the word box.

| strong | rank | bring | bank | honk | hang | thank |
| long | hunk | song | stung | bunk | sang | junk |

_____   _____

_____   _____

_____   _____

_____   _____

_____   _____

1. _____ your horn when you get to my house.

2. He was _____ by a bee.

3. We are going to put our money in a _____.

4. I want to _____ you for the birthday present.

5. My brother and I sleep in _____ beds.

Silent Letters

Some words have letters you can't hear at all, such as the **gh** in **night**, the **w** in **wrong**, the **l** in **walk**, the **k** in **knee**, the **b** in **climb**, and the **t** in **listen**.

Directions: Look at the words in the word box. Write the word under its picture. Underline the silent letters.

knife	light	calf	wrench	lamb	eight
wrist	whistle	comb	thumb	knob	knee

_____ _____ _____ _____

_____ _____ _____ _____

_____ _____ _____ _____

Comprehensive Curriculum - **Grade 2**

Review

Directions: Read the story. Circle the consonant teams, consonant blends, and silent letters in the underlined words. Be sure to check for more than one team in a word! One has been done for you.

One day last (sp)ri(ng), my family went on a picnic. My father picked out a <u>pretty</u> <u>spot</u> next to a <u>stream.</u> <u>While</u> my <u>brother</u> and I <u>climbed</u> a <u>tree</u>, my mother <u>spread</u> out a <u>sheet</u> and <u>placed</u> the food on it. But before we could eat, a <u>skunk</u> <u>walked</u> out of the woods! Mother <u>screamed</u> and <u>scared</u> the skunk. It <u>sprayed</u> us with a terrible <u>smell!</u> Now, we <u>think</u> it is a funny <u>story</u>. But <u>that</u> day, we ran!

Directions: Write the words with three-letter blends on the lines.

_____   _____   _____

_____   _____

Name _____

Hard and Soft C

When **c** is followed by **e**, **i**, or **y**, it usually has a **soft** sound. The soft **c** sounds like **s**. For example, **c**ircle and fen**c**e. When **c** is followed by **a** or **u**, it usually has a **hard** sound. The **hard c** sounds like **k**, as in **c**up or **c**art.

Directions: Read the words in the word box. Write the words in the correct lists. One word will be in both. Write a word from the word box to finish each sentence.

Words with soft c	**Words with hard c**
<u>pencil</u>	_____
_____	_____
_____	_____
_____	_____
_____	_____

pencil	cookie
dance	cent
popcorn	circus
carrot	mice
tractor	card

1. Another word for a penny is a _____.

2. A cat likes to chase _____.

3. You will see animals and clowns at the _____.

4. Will you please sharpen my _____?

Name _____

Hard and Soft *G*

When **g** is followed by **e**, **i**, or **y**, it usually has a **soft** sound. The soft **g** sounds like **j**. **Example:** chan**g**e and **g**entle. When **g** is followed by **a**, **o**, or **u**, it usually has a **hard** sound, like the **g** in **g**o or **g**ate.

Directions: Read the words in the word box. Write the words in the correct lists. Write a word from the box to finish each sentence.

engine	glove	cage	magic	frog
giant	flag	large	glass	goose

Words with soft g

engine

_____

_____

_____

_____

Words with hard g

_____

_____

_____

_____

1. Our bird lives in a _____.

2. Pulling a rabbit from a hat is a good _____ trick.

3. A car needs an _____ to run.

4. A _____ is a huge person.

5. An elephant is a very _____ animal.

Hard and Soft C and G

Directions: Look at the **c** and **g** words at the bottom of the page. Cut them out, and glue them in the correct box below.

soft sound	hard sound

cut ✂ -

jug	gem	giant	crayon
grass	goat	grow	age
juice	face	engine	cart

Page is blank for cutting exercise on previous page.

Short Vowels

Vowels can make **short** or **long** sounds. The short **a** sounds like the **a** in **cat**. The short **e** is like the **e** in **leg**. The short **i** sounds like the **i** in **pig**. The short **o** sounds like the **o** in **box**. The short **u** sounds like the **u** in **cup**.

Directions: Look at each picture. Write the missing short vowel.

p __ p

n __ t

s __ ck

__ x

l __ ps

h __ t

f __ x

t __ nt

p __ n

Short Vowels

Vowels can make **short** or **long** sounds. The short **a** sounds like the **a** in **cat**. The short **e** is like the **e** in **leg**. The short **i** sounds like the **i** in **pig**. The short **o** sounds like the **o** in **box**. The short **u** is like the **u** in **cup**.

Directions: Look at the pictures. Their names all have short vowel sounds. But the vowels are missing! Fill in the missing vowels in each word.

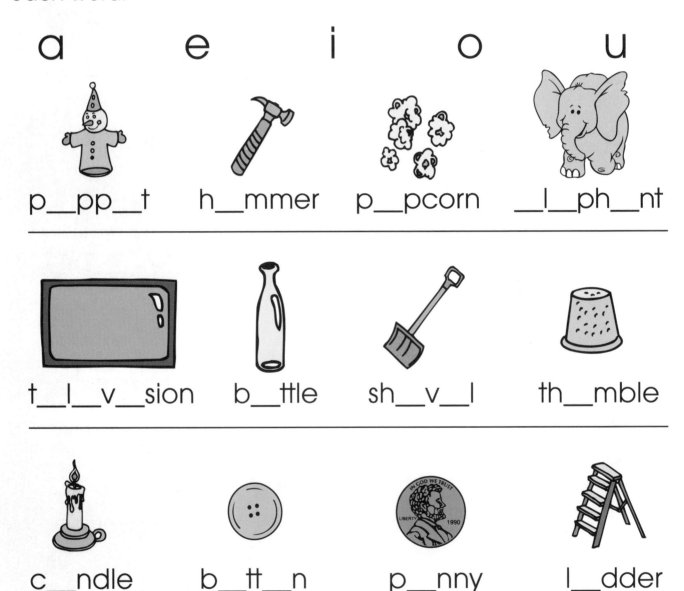

a   e   i   o   u

p__pp__t   h__mmer   p__pcorn   __l__ph__nt

t__l__v__sion   b__ttle   sh__v__l   th__mble

c__ndle   b__tt__n   p__nny   l__dder

Short Vowels

Directions: Cut out the giant vowels. Decorate them with pictures or words that have the short vowel sound.

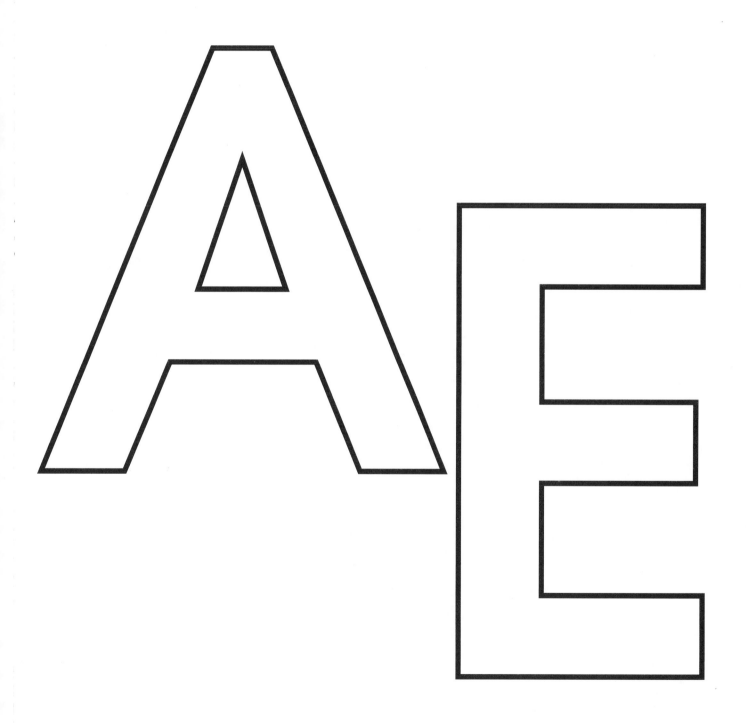

Page is blank for cutting exercise on previous page.

Short Vowels

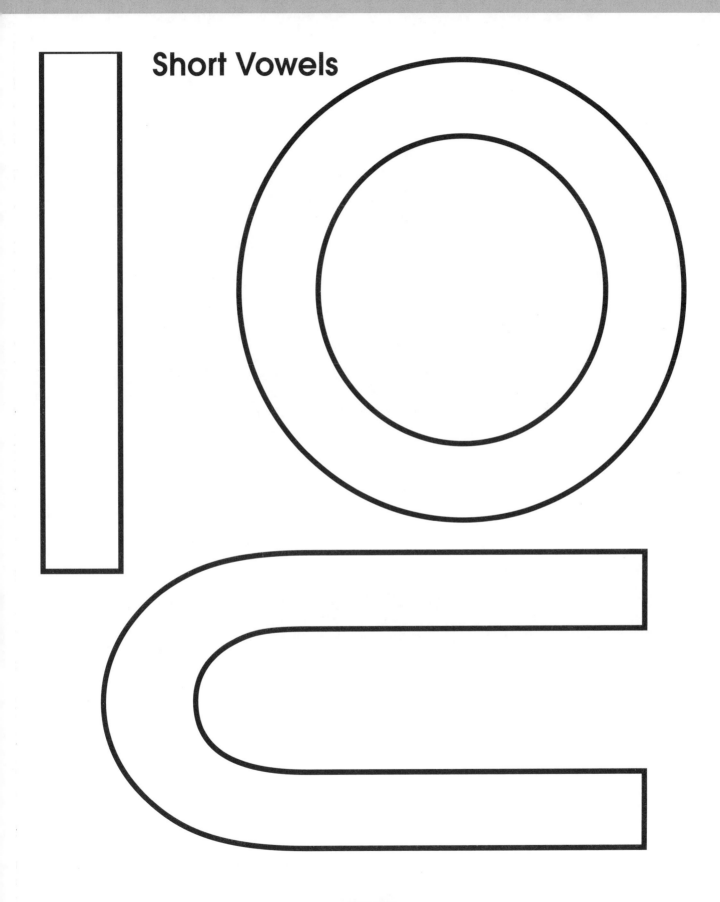

Page is blank for cutting exercise on previous page.

Super Silent *E*

Long vowel sounds have the same sound as their names. When a **Super Silent e** appears at the end of a word, you can't hear it, but it makes the other vowel have a long sound. For example: **tub** has a **short** vowel sound, and **tube** has a **long** vowel sound.

Directions: Look at the following pictures. Decide if the word has a short or long vowel sound. Circle the correct word. Watch for the **Super Silent e**!

can   cane   tub   tube   rob   robe   rat   rate

pin   pine   cap   cape   not   note   pan   pane

slid   slide   dim   dime   tap   tape   cub   cube

Name _____

Long Vowels

Long vowels have the same sound as their names. When a **Super Silent e** comes at the end of a word, you can't hear it, but it changes the short vowel sound to a long vowel sound.

Example: rope, skate, cute, line

Directions: Say the name of the pictures. Listen for the long vowel sounds. Write the missing long vowel sound under each picture.

c __ ke

h __ ke

n __ se

__ pe

c __ be

gr __ pe

r __ ke

b __ ne

k __ te

Review

Directions: Read the words in each box. Cross out the word that does not belong.

long vowels	short vowels
cube	man
cup	pet
rake	fix
me	ice
long vowels	**short vowels**
soap	cat
seed	pin
read	rain
mat	frog

Directions: Write **short** or **long** to label the words in each box.

_____ vowels	_____ vowels
hose	frog
take	hot
bead	sled
cube	lap
eat	block
see	sit

Name _____

R-Controlled Vowels

When a vowel is followed by the letter **r**, it has a different sound.

Example: he and **her**

Directions: Write a word from the word box to finish each sentence. Notice the sound of the vowel followed by an **r**.

park	chair	horse	bark	bird
hurt	girl	hair	store	ears

1. A dog likes to ___bark___.

2. You buy food at a ___store___.

3. Children like to play at the ___park___.

4. An animal you can ride is a ___horse___.

5. You hear with your ___ears___.

6. A robin is a kind of ___bird___.

7. If you fall down, you might get ___hurt___.

8. The opposite of a boy is a ___girl___.

9. You comb and brush your ___hair___.

10. You sit down on a ___chair___.

Name _____

READING

R-Controlled Words

R-controlled vowel words are words in which the **r** that comes after the vowel changes the sound of the vowel. **Examples:** bird, star, burn

Directions: Write the correct word in the sentences below.

horse	purple
jar	bird
dirt	turtle

1. Jelly comes in one of these. _____

2. This creature has feathers and can fly. _____

3. This animal lives in a shell. _____

4. This animal can pull wagons. _____

5. If you mix water and this,
   you will have mud. _____

6. This color starts with the letter **p**. _____

Comprehensive Curriculum - **Grade 2**

Name _____

R-Controlled Vowels

Directions: Answer the riddles below. You will need to complete the words with the correct vowel followed by **r**.

1. I am something you may use to eat.
   What am I?   f_____k

2. My word names the opposite of tall.
   What am I?   sh_____t

3. I can be seen high in the sky. I twinkle.
   What am I?   st_____

4. I am a kind of clothing a girl might wear.
   What am I?   sk_____t

5. My word tells what a group of cows is
   called. What am I?   h_____d

6. I am part of your body. What am I?   _____m

Double Vowel Words

Usually when two vowels appear together, the first one says its name and the second one is silent.
Example: b<u>e</u>an

Directions: Unscramble the double vowel words below. Write the correct word on the line.

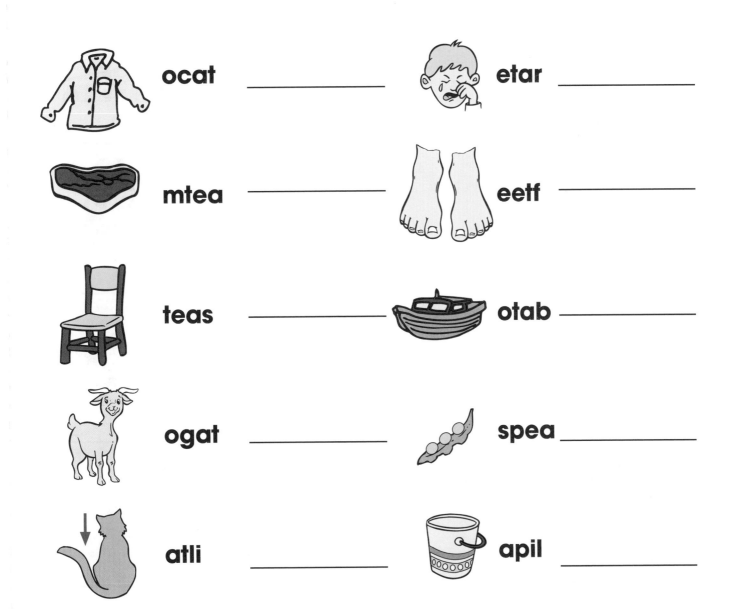

ocat _____

etar _____

mtea _____

eetf _____

teas _____

otab _____

ogat _____

spea _____

atli _____

apil _____

Vowel Teams

The vowel teams **ou** and **ow** can have the same sound. You can hear it in the words **clown** and **cloud**. The vowel teams **au** and **aw** have the same sound. You hear it in the words **because** and **law**.

Directions: Look at the pictures. Write the correct vowel team to complete the words. The first one is done for you. You may need to use a dictionary to help you with the correct spelling.

auto

cl_____n

h_____se

fl_____er

s_____

_____l

p_____der

m_____th

j_____

p_____

m_____se

cl_____d

Vowel Teams

The vowel team **ea** can have a short **e** sound, like in **head**, or a long **e** sound, like in **bead**. An **ea** followed by an **r** makes a sound like the one in **ear** or like the one in **heard**.

Directions: Read the story. Listen for the sound **ea** makes in the bold words.

Have you ever **read** a book or **heard** a story about a **bear**? You might have **learned** that bears sleep through the winter. Some bears may sleep the whole **season**. Sometimes, they look almost **dead**! But they are very much alive. As the cold winter passes and the spring **weather** comes **near**, they wake up. After such a nice rest, they must be **ready** to **eat** a **really** big **meal**!

words with long **ea**	words with short **ea**	**ea** followed by **r**
_____	_____	_____
_____	_____	_____
_____	_____	_____
_____	_____	_____

Vowel Teams

The vowel team **ie** makes the long **e** sound, as in **believe**. The team **ei** also makes the long **e** sound, as in **either**. But, **ei** can also make a long **a** sound, as in **vein**. The teams **eigh** and **ey** also make the long **a** sound.

Directions: Circle the words with the long **a** sound.

neighbor   veil

receive   reindeer

reign   ceiling

Directions: Finish the sentences with words from the word box.

| chief | sleigh | obey | weigh | thief | field | ceiling |

1. Eight reindeer pull Santa's _____ .

2. Rules are for us to _____ .

3. The bird got out of its cage and flew up to the _____ .

4. The leader of a tribe is the _____ .

5. How much do you _____ ?

6. They caught the _____ who took my bike.

7. Corn grows in a _____ .

Vowel Teams: *oi, oy, ou,* and *ow*

Directions: Look at the first picture in each row. Circle the pictures that have the same sound.

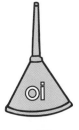
oil

toy

couch

howl

Comprehensive Curriculum - **Grade 2**

Vowel Teams: *ai* and *ee*

Directions: Write in the vowel team **ai** or **ee** to complete each word.

r ___ ___ n

f ___ ___ d

s ___ ___ d

p ___ ___ l

s ___ ___ l

cr ___ ___ k

Review

Directions: Read the story. Fill in the blanks with words from the word box.

cookies	Joe	bowl	tooth	flour	Layla
spoon	eats	enjoys	round	boy	chewy

Do you like to cook? I know a _____ named

_____ who loves to cook. When Joe has a sweet

_____, he makes healthy and tasty _____.

He puts _____ and applesauce in a _____

and stirs it with a _____. Then, he adds butter,

oatmeal, raisins, and eggs. He makes cookies that are

_____ and _____. Now is the part he

_____ the most: Joe _____ the cookies.

He shares them with his sister, _____.

Y as a Vowel

When **y** comes at the end of a word, it is a vowel. When **y** is the only vowel at the end of a one-syllable word, it has the sound of a long **i** (as in **my**). When **y** is the only vowel at the end of a word with more than one syllable, it has the sound of long **e** (as in **baby**).

Directions: Look at the words in the word box. If the word has the sound of long **i**, write it under the word **my**. If the word has the sound of long **e**, write it under the word **baby**. Write the word from the word box that answers each riddle.

happy	penny	fry	try	sleepy	dry
bunny	why	windy	sky	party	fly

my   **baby**

_____   _____

_____   _____

_____   _____

_____   _____

_____   _____

1. It takes five of these to make a nickel.   _____

2. You might call it a rabbit.   _____

3. It is often blue, and you can see it if you look up. _____

4. You might have one of these on your birthday.   _____

5. It is the opposite of wet.   _____

6. You might use this word to ask a question.   _____

Name _____

Y as a Vowel

Directions: Read the rhyming story. Choose words from the box to fill in the blanks.

Larry	Mary
money	funny
honey	bunny

_____ and _____ are friends.

Larry is selling _____ . Mary needs _____

to buy the honey. "I want to feed it to my _____ ," said

Mary. Larry laughed and said, "That is _____ . Everyone

knows that bunnies do not eat honey."

Y as a Vowel

Directions: Read the story. Choose words from the box to fill in the blanks.

try	my	Why	cry	shy	fly

Sam is very _____. Ann asks, "Would you like to

_____ my kite?" Sam starts to _____ .

Ann asks, "_____ are you crying?"

Sam says, "I am afraid to _____ ."

"Oh, _____ ! You are a good kite flyer," cries Ann.

School Words

pencil	teacher	crayons
recess	lunchbox	play
fun	math	

Directions: Fill in the blanks with a word from the word box.

1. I need to sharpen my _____.

2. I like to _____ at recess.

3. School is _____!

4. My _____ helps me learn.

5. I need to color the picture with _____.

6. I play kickball at _____.

7. My sandwich is in my _____.

8. In _____, I can add and subtract.

Days of the Week

Directions: Write the day of the week that answers each question.

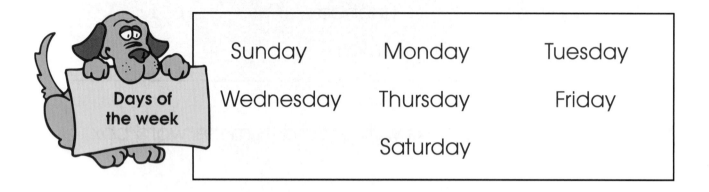

Sunday	Monday	Tuesday
Wednesday	Thursday	Friday
	Saturday	

1. What is the first day of the week?

   _____

2. What is the last day of the week?

   _____

3. What day comes after Tuesday?

   _____

4. What day comes between Wednesday and Friday?

   _____

5. What is the third day of the week?

   _____

6. What day comes before Saturday?

   _____

7. What day comes after Sunday?

   _____

Compound Words

Compound words are two words that are put together to make one new word.

Directions: Help the cook brew her stew. Mix words from the first column with words from the second column to make new words. Write your new words on the lines at the bottom.

grand	brows
snow	light
eye	stairs
down	string
rose	book
shoe	mother
note	ball
moon	bud

1. _____

2. _____

3. _____

4. _____

5. _____

6. _____

7. _____

8. _____

Name _____

Compound Words

Directions: Read the sentences. Fill in the blank with a compound word from the box.

raincoat	bedroom	lunchbox	hallway	sandbox

1. A box with sand is a

_____.

2. The way through a hall is a

_____.

3. A box for lunch is a

_____.

4. A coat for the rain is a

_____.

5. A room with a bed is a

_____.

Compound Words

Directions: Cut out the words below. Glue them together in the box to make compound words.

COMPOUND WORDS

Can you think of any more compound words?

sun	air	mail	ball
box	room	water	guard
foot	screen	class	flower
plane	sun	melon	body

Page is blank for cutting exercise on previous page.

Compound Words

Directions: Draw a line under the compound word in each sentence. On the line, write the two words that make up the compound word.

1. A firetruck came to help put out the fire.

_____

2. I will be nine years old on my next birthday.

_____

3. We built a treehouse in the oak tree.

_____

4. Dad put a scarecrow in his garden.

_____

5. It is fun to make footprints in the snow.

_____

6. I like to read the comics in the newspaper.

_____

7. Cowboys ride horses and use lassos.

_____

Name _____

Contractions

Contractions are a short way to write two words.

Examples: it is = **it's, is not** = **isn't, I have** = **I've**

Directions: Draw a line from each word pair to its contraction.

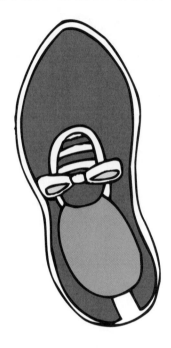 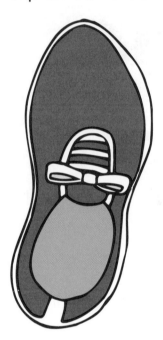

I am	she's
it is	they're
you are	we're
we are	he's
they are	I'm
she is	it's
he is	you're

Contractions

Directions: Circle the contraction that should replace the underlined words.

Example: were not = **weren't**

1. The boy <u>was not</u> sad.
    wasn't   weren't

2. We <u>were not</u> working.
    wasn't   weren't

3. Jen and Caleb <u>have not</u> eaten lunch yet.
        haven't   hasn't

4. The mouse <u>has not</u> been here.
        haven't   hasn't

Name _____

Contractions

Directions: Match the words with their contractions.

would not	I've
was not	he'll
he will	wouldn't
could not	wasn't
I have	couldn't

Directions: Make the words at the end of each line into contractions to complete the sentences.

1. He _____ know the answer.　　**did not**

2. _____ a long way home.　　**It is**

3. _____ my house.　　**Here is**

4. _____ not going to school today.　　**We are**

5. _____ take the bus home tomorrow.　　**They will**

Contractions

Directions: Cut out the broken hearts, and put them together to show what two words make each contraction. Glue them over the contraction.

cut ✂ -

Page is blank for cutting exercise on previous page.

Syllables

Words are made up of parts called **syllables**. Each syllable has a vowel sound. One way to count syllables is to clap as you say the word.

Example: cat   1 clap   1 syllable

table   2 claps   2 syllables

butterfly   3 claps   3 syllables

Directions: "Clap out" the words below. Write how many syllables each word has.

movie _____   dog _____

piano _____   basket _____

tree _____   swimmer _____

bicycle _____   rainbow _____

sun _____   paper _____

cabinet _____   picture _____

football _____   run _____

television _____   enter _____

Name _____

Syllables

Dividing a word into syllables can help you read a new word. You also might use syllables when you are writing if you run out of space on a line. Many words contain two consonants that are next to each other. A word can usually be divided between the consonants.

Directions: Divide each word into two syllables. The first one is done for you.

kitten   <u>   kit   ten   </u>

lumber   _____

batter   _____

winter   _____

funny   _____

harder   _____

dirty   _____

sister   _____

little   _____

dinner   _____

Syllables

One way to help you read a word you don't know is to divide it into parts called **syllables**. Every syllable has a vowel sound.

Directions: Say the words. Write the number of syllables. The first one is done for you.

straw • ber • ry

bird   _____1_____   rabbit   _____

apple   _____   elephant _____

balloon   _____   family   _____

basketball   _____   fence   _____

breakfast   _____   ladder   _____

block   _____   open   _____

candy   _____   puddle   _____

popcorn   _____   Saturday _____

yellow   _____   wind   _____

understand _____   butterfly _____

Syllables

When a double consonant is used in the middle of a word, the word can usually be divided between the consonants.

Directions: Look at the words in the word box. Divide each word into two syllables. Leave space between each syllable. One is done for you.

butter	puppy	kitten	yellow
dinner	chatter	ladder	happy
pillow	letter	mitten	summer

__but   ter__

_____   _____   _____

_____   _____   _____

_____   _____   _____

Many words are divided between two consonants that are not alike.

Directions: Look at the words in the word box. Divide each word into two syllables. One is done for you.

window	doctor	number	carpet
mister	winter	pencil	candle
barber	sister	picture	under

__win   dow__

_____   _____   _____

_____   _____   _____

_____   _____   _____

Syllables

Directions: Write 1 or 2 on the line to tell how many syllables are in each word. If the word has 2 syllables, draw a line between the syllables. **Example: sup|per**

dog _____

bedroom _____

slipper _____

tree _____

batter _____

chair _____

fish _____

master _____

timber _____

cat _____

street _____

chalk _____

blanket _____

marker _____

brush _____

rabbit _____

Haiku

A **haiku** is a form of Japanese poetry. Most haiku are about nature.

first line – 5 syllables
second line – 7 syllables
third line – 5 syllables

Example: The squirrel is brown.
He lives in a great big tree.
He eats nuts all day.

Directions: Write your own haiku. Draw a picture to go with it.

_____

_____

_____

Suffixes

A **suffix** is a letter or group of letters that is added to the end of a word to change its meaning.

Directions: Add the suffixes to the root words to make new words. Use your new words to complete the sentences.

help + ful = _____

care + less = _____

build + er = _____

talk + ed = _____

love + ly = _____

loud + er = _____

1. My mother _____ to my teacher about my homework.

2. The radio was _____ than the television.

3. Madison is always _____ to her mother.

4. A _____ put a new garage on our house.

5. The flowers are _____ .

6. It is _____ to cross the street without looking both ways.

Name _____

Suffixes

An **ing** at the end of an action word shows that the action is happening now. An **ed** at the end shows that the action happened in the past.

Directions: Look at the words in the word box. Underline the root word in each one. Write a word to complete each sentence.

| snowing | wished | played | looking | crying |
| talking | walked | eating | going | doing |

1. We like to play. We _____ yesterday.

2. Is that snow? Yes, it is _____.

3. Do you want to go with me? No, I am _____ with my friend.

4. The baby will cry if we leave. The baby is _____.

5. We will walk home from school. We _____ to school this morning.

6. Did you wish for a new bike? Yes, I _____ for one.

7. Who is doing the dishes? I am _____ them.

8. Did you talk to your friend? Yes, we are _____ now.

9. Will you look at my book? I am _____ at it now.

10. I like to eat pizza. We are _____ it for lunch.

Suffixes

Directions: Write a word from the word box next to its root word.

coming	running	sitting
lived	rained	swimming
visited	carried	racing
hurried		

run _____   come _____

live _____   carry _____

hurry _____   race _____

swim _____   rain _____

visit _____   sit _____

Directions: Write a word from the word box to finish each sentence.

1. I _____ my grandmother during vacation.

2. Ava went _____ at the lake with her cousin.

3. Tyson _____ the heavy package for his mother.

4. It _____ and stormed all weekend.

5. Cars go very fast when they are _____ .

Suffixes

Directions: Read the story. Underline the words that end with **est**, **ed**, or **ing**. On the lines below, write the root word for each word you underlined.

The funniest book I ever read was about a girl named Nan. Nan did everything backward. She even spelled her name backward. Nan slept in the day and played at night. She dried her hair before washing it. She turned on the light after she finished her book—which she read from the back to the front! When it rained, Nan waited until she was inside before opening her umbrella. She even walked backward. The silliest part: The only thing Nan did forward was back up!

1. _____   6. _____   11. _____

2. _____   7. _____   12. _____

3. _____   8. _____   13. _____

4. _____   9. _____

5. _____   10. _____

Prefixes: The Three Rs

A **prefix** is a letter or group of letters that is added to the beginning of a word to change its meaning. The prefix **re** means "again."

Directions: Read the story. Then, follow the instructions.

   Kim wants to find ways she can help our planet. She studies the "three Rs"—reduce, reuse, and recycle. **Reduce** means "to make less." Both **reuse** and **recycle** mean "to use again."

Add **re** to the beginning of each word below. Use the new words to complete the sentences.

_____ build   _____ fill

_____ read   _____ tell

_____ write   _____ run

1. The race was a tie, so Sanj and Mia had to _____ it.

2. The block wall fell down, so Simon had to _____ it.

3. The water bottle was empty, so Luna had to _____ it.

4. Javier wrote a good story, but he wanted to _____ it to make it better.

5. The teacher told a story, and students had to _____ it.

6. Toni didn't understand the directions, so she had to

   _____ them.

Prefixes

Directions: Read the story. Change Unlucky Sam to Lucky Sam by removing the **un** prefix from the **bold** words. Write the new words in the new story.

Unlucky Sam

Sam was **unhappy** about a lot of things in his life. His parents were **uncaring**. His teacher was **unfair**. His big sister was **unkind**. His neighbors were **unfriendly**. He was **unhealthy**, too! How could one boy be as **unlucky** as Sam?

Lucky Sam

Sam was _____ about a lot of things in his life. His parents were _____ . His teacher was _____ . His big sister was _____ . His neighbors were _____ . He was _____, too! How could one boy be as _____ as Sam?

Prefixes

Directions: Change the meaning of the sentences by adding the prefixes to the **bold** words.

The boy was **lucky** because he guessed the answer **correctly**.

The boy was (un)_____ because he guessed the

answer (in)_____ .

When Jada **behaved**, she felt **happy**.

When Jada (mis) _____ ,

she felt (un)_____ .

Mike wore his jacket **buttoned** because the dance was **formal**.

Mike wore his jacket (un)_____ because the dance

was (in)_____ .

Cameron **understood** because he was **familiar** with the book.

Cameron (mis) _____ because he was

(un)_____ with the book.

Prefixes

Directions: Read the story. Change the story by removing the prefix **re** from the **bold** words. Write the new words in the new story.

Repete is a **rewriter** who has to **redo** every story. He has to **rethink** up the ideas. He has to **rewrite** the sentences. He has to **redraw** the pictures. He even has to **retype** the pages. Who will **repay** **Repete** for all the work he **redoes**?

_____ is a _____ who has to

_____ every story. He has to _____

up the ideas. He has to _____ the sentences.

He has to _____ the pictures.

He even has to _____ the pages.

Who will _____ _____ for all the

work he _____ ?

Review

Directions: Read each sentence. Look at the words in **bold**. Circle the prefix, and write the root word on the line.

1. The **preview** of the movie was funny.   _____

2. We always drink **nonfat** milk.   _____

3. We will have to **reschedule** the trip.   _____

4. Are you tired of **reruns** on television?   _____

5. I have **outgrown** my new shoes already.   _____

6. You must have **misplaced** the papers.   _____

7. Police **enforce** the laws of the city.   _____

8. I **disliked** that book.   _____

9. The boy **distrusted** the big dog.   _____

10. Try to **enjoy** yourself at the party.   _____

11. Please try to keep the cat **inside** the house.   _____

12. That song is total **nonsense**!   _____

13. We will **replace** any parts that we lost.   _____

14. Can you help me **unzip** this jacket?   _____

15. Let's **rework** today's arithmetic problems.   _____

Parts of a Book

A book has many parts. The **title** is the name of the book. The **author** is the person who wrote the words. The **illustrator** is the person who drew the pictures. The **table of contents** is located at the beginning to list what is in the book. The **glossary** is a little dictionary in the back to help you with unfamiliar words. Books are often divided into smaller sections of information called **chapters**.

Directions: Look at one of your books. Write the parts you see below.

The title of my book is _____

The author is _____

The illustrator is _____

My book has a table of contents.   Yes or No

My book has a glossary.   Yes or No

My book is divided into chapters.   Yes or No

READING COMPREHENSION

Directions
1. Take boat out of box.
2. Add sail.
3. Tighten with wrench.
4. Have fun!

Recalling Details: Nikki's Pets

Directions: Read about Nikki's pets. Then, answer the questions.

Nikki has two cats, Tiger and Sniffer, and two dogs, Spot and Wiggles. Tiger is an orange striped cat who likes to sleep under a big tree and pretend she is a real tiger. Sniffer is a gray cat who likes to sniff the flowers in Nikki's garden. Spot is a Dalmatian with many black spots. Wiggles is a big, furry brown dog who wiggles all over when he is happy.

1. Which dog is brown and furry? _Wiggles_

2. What color is Tiger? _Orange_

3. What kind of dog is Spot? _Dalmatian_

4. Which cat likes to sniff flowers? _Sniffer_

5. Where does Tiger like to sleep? _under the_

6. Who wiggles all over when he is happy? _Wiggles_

Recalling Details: Pet Pests

Directions: Read the story. Then, answer the questions.

Sometimes, Marvin and Mugsy scratch and itch. Maggie knows that fleas or ticks are insect pests to her pets. Their bites are painful. Fleas suck the blood of animals. They don't have wings, but they can jump.Ticks are very flat, suck blood, and are related to spiders. They like to hide in dogs' ears. That is why Maggie checks Marvin and Mugsy every week for fleas and ticks.

1. What is a pest? _____

_____

2. List three facts about fleas.

   a) _____

   b) _____

   c) _____

3. List three facts about ticks.

   a) _____

   b) _____

   c) _____

Reading for Details

Directions: Read the story about baby animals. Answer the questions with words from the story.

Baby cats are called kittens. They love to play and drink lots of milk. A baby dog is a puppy. Puppies chew on old shoes. They run and bark. A lamb is a baby sheep. Lambs eat grass. A baby duck is called a duckling. Ducklings swim with their wide, webbed feet. Foals are baby horses. A foal can walk the day it is born! A baby goat is a kid. Some people call children kids, too!

1. A baby cat is called a _____.

2. A baby dog is a _____.

3. A _____ is a baby sheep.

4. _____ swim with their webbed feet.

5. A _____ can walk the day it is born.

6. A baby goat is a _____.

Reading for Details

Directions: Read the story about bike safety. Answer the questions below the story.

Mike has a red bike. He likes his bike. Mike wears a helmet. Mike wears knee pads and elbow pads. They keep him safe. Mike stops at signs. Mike looks both ways. Mike is safe on his bike.

1. What color is Mike's bike? _____

2. Which sentence in the story tells why Mike wears pads and a helmet? Write it here.

   _____

3. What else does Mike do to keep safe?

   He _____ at signs and _____ both ways.

Reading for Details

Directions: Read the story about different kinds of transportation. Answer the questions with words from the story.

People use many kinds of transportation. Boats float on the water. Some people fish in a boat. Airplanes fly in the sky. Flying in a plane is a fast way to get somewhere. Trains run on a track. The first car is the engine. The last car is the caboose. Some people even sleep in beds on a train! A car has four wheels. Most people have a car. A car rides on roads. A bus can hold many people. A bus rides on roads. Most children ride a bus to school.

1. A boat floats on the _____.

2. If you want to get somewhere fast, which form of transportation would you use? _____.

3. The first car on a train is called an engine, and the last car is a

   _____ .

4. _____ ride on a bus.

5. A _____ has four wheels.

Following Directions

Directions: Read the story. Answer the questions. Try the recipe.

Cows Give Us Milk

Cows live on a farm. The farmer milks the cow to get milk. Many things are made from milk. We make ice cream, sour cream, cottage cheese, and butter from milk. Butter is fun to make! You can learn to make your own butter. First, you need cream. Put the cream in a jar and shake it. Then, you need to pour off the liquid. Next, you put the butter in a bowl. Add a little salt and stir! Finally, spread it on crackers and eat!

1. What animal gives us milk?_____

2. What 4 things are made from milk?

_____ _____ _____ _____

3. What did the story teach you to make?_____

4. Put the steps in order. Place 1, 2, 3, or 4 by each sentence.

_____ Spread the butter on crackers and eat!

_____ Shake cream in a jar.

_____ Start with cream.

_____ Add salt to the butter.

Following Directions: Parrot Art

Directions: Draw the missing parts on each parrot.

1. Draw the parrot's eye.

2. Draw the parrot's tail.

3. Draw the parrot' s beak.

4. Draw the parrot's wings.

Following Directions: How to Treat a Ladybug

Directions: Read about how to treat ladybugs. Then, follow the instructions.

Ladybugs are shy. If you see a ladybug, sit very still. Hold out your arm. Maybe the ladybug will fly to you. If it does, talk softly. Do not touch it. It will fly away when it is ready.

1. Complete the directions on how to treat a ladybug.

   a. Sit very still.

   b. _____

   c. Talk softly.

   d. _____

2. Ladybugs are red. They have black spots. Color the ladybug.

Following Directions: Insect Art

Directions: Read about insects. Then, follow the instructions.

All insects have these body parts:

Head at the front

Thorax in the middle

Abdomen at the back

Six *legs*—three on each side of the thorax

Two *eyes* on the head

Two *antennae* attached to the head

Some insects also have *wings.*

Draw your favorite insect. Include all the body parts listed above.

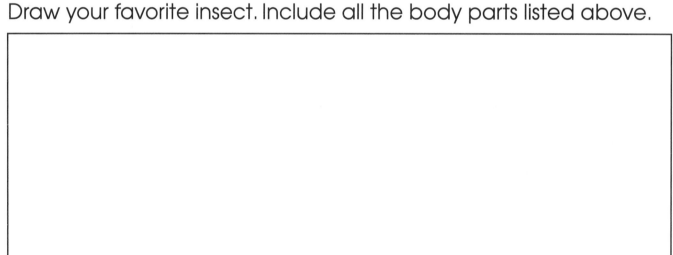

Sequencing: Packing Bags

Directions: Read about packing bags. Then, number the objects in the order they should be packed.

Cans are heavy. Put them in first. Then, put in boxes. Now, put in the apple. Put the bread in last.

Sequencing: 1, 2, 3, 4!

Directions: Write numbers by each sentence to show the order of the story.

The pool is empty. _____   Ben plays in the pool. _____

Ben gets out. _____   Ben fills the pool. _____

Sequencing/Predicting: A Game for Cats

Directions: Read about what cats like. Then, follow the instructions.

Cats like to play with paper bags. Pull a paper bag open. Take everything out. Now, lay the bag on its side.

1. Write 1, 2, and 3 to put the pictures in order.

2. In box 4, draw what you think the cat will do.

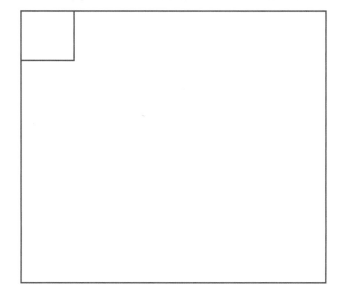

Sequencing: Story Events

Spencer likes to make new friends. Today, he made friends with the dog in the picture.

Directions: Number the sentences in order to find out what Spencer did today.

_____ Spencer kissed his mother good-bye.

_____ Spencer saw the new dog next door.

_____ Spencer went outside.

_____ Spencer said hello.

_____ Spencer got dressed and ate breakfast.

_____ Spencer woke up.

Sequencing: Yo-Yo Trick

Directions: Read about the yo-yo trick.

Wind up the yo-yo string. Hold the yo-yo in your hand. Now, hold your palm up. Throw the yo-yo downward on the string. Hold your palm down. Now, swing the yo-yo forward. Make it "walk." This yo-yo trick is called "walk the dog."

Directions: Number the directions in order.

_____ Swing the yo-yo forward, and make it "walk."

_____ Hold your palm up, and drop the yo-yo.

_____ Turn your palm down as the yo-yo reaches the ground.

Sequencing: Make a Hat

Mrs. Posey made a new hat, but she forgot how she did it. When she tried to tell her friend, she got all mixed up.

Directions: Read Mrs. Posey's story. Write her story on the lines in the order you think it happened. Then, color the picture.

I glued flowers on it. Then, I bought this straw hat. Now, I am wearing my hat. Then, I added ribbon around the flowers. I tried on many hats at the store.

The real story:

_____

_____

_____

_____

_____

_____

_____

Sequencing: Follow a Recipe

Here is a recipe for guacamole. When you use a recipe, you must follow the directions carefully. The sentences below are not in the correct order.

Directions: Write number 1 to show what you would do first. Then, number each step to show the correct sequence.

_____ Cut the avocado in half, and squeeze the flesh into a bowl.

_____ Eat and enjoy!

_____ Add lime juice, salt, and garlic powder to the mashed avocado.

_____ First, wash the avocado.

_____ Mix all the ingredients together, and serve with corn chips.

_____ Mash the avocado in the bowl with a fork until only a few small chunks remain.

Try the recipe with an adult.

Do you like to cook? _____

Sequencing: Follow a Recipe

Alana and Marcus are hungry for a snack. They want to make nacho chips and cheese. The steps they need to follow are all mixed up.

Directions: Read the steps. Number them in 1, 2, 3 order. Then, color the picture.

_____ Bake the chips in the oven for 2 minutes.

_____ Get a cookie sheet to bake on.

_____ Get out the nacho chips and cheese.

_____ Eat the nachos.

_____ Put the chips on the cookie sheet.

_____ Put grated cheese on the chips.

Sequencing: Making a Snowman

Directions: Read about how to make a snowman. Then, follow the instructions.

It is fun to make a snowman. First, find things for the snowman's eyes and nose. Dress warmly. Then, go outdoors. Roll a big snowball. Then, roll another to put on top of it. Now, roll a small snowball for the head. Put on the snowman's face.

1. Number the pictures in order.

2. Write two things to do before going outdoors.

a) _____

b) _____

Sequencing: Baking a Cake

Directions: Read about baking a cake.
Then, write the missing steps.

Dylan, Dana, and Dad are baking a
cake. Dad turns on the oven. Dana opens
the cake mix. Dylan adds the eggs. Dad
pours in the water. Dana stirs the batter.
Dylan pours the batter into a cake pan.
Dad puts it in the oven.

1. Turn on the oven.

2. _____

3. Add the eggs.

4. _____

5. Stir the batter.

6. _____

7. _____

Sequencing: Story Events

Mari was sick yesterday.

Directions: Number the events in 1, 2, 3 order to tell the story about Mari.

_____ She went to the doctor's office.

_____ Mari felt much better.

_____ Mari felt very hot and tired.

_____ Mari's mother went to the drugstore.

_____ The doctor wrote down something.

_____ The doctor looked in Mari's ears.

_____ Mari took a pill.

_____ The doctor gave Mari's mother the piece of paper.

_____ Mari drank some water with her pill.

Sequencing: Making a Card

Directions: Read about how to make a card. Then, follow the instructions.

You will need scissors, glue, old greeting cards, and colored paper. First, look at all your old cards. Then, cut out what you like. Now, fold the colored paper in half. Glue the cut-outs to the front of your card. Write your name inside.

1. Write the steps in order for making a card.

a) Look at all your old cards.

b) _____

c) _____

d) _____

e) _____

Sequencing: Making Clay

Directions: Read about making clay. Then, follow the instructions.

It is fun to work with clay. Here is what you need to make it:

1 cup salt
2 cups flour
3/4 cup water

Mix the salt and flour. Then, add the water. DO NOT eat the clay. It tastes bad. Use your hands to mix and mix. Now, roll it out. What can you make with your clay?

1. Circle the main idea:

   Do not eat clay.

   Mix salt, flour, and water to make clay.

2. Write the steps for making clay.

   a. _____

   b. _____

   c. Mix the clay.

   d. _____

3. Write why you should not eat clay. _____

_____

Sequencing: Play a Game

Children all around the world like to play games. Think about your favorite game. Maybe you could teach your friends to play it.

Directions: Write, in order, how to play your game.

_____

_____

_____

_____

_____

_____

_____

Directions: Draw a picture of you playing your favorite game.

Sequencing: A Visit to the Zoo

Directions: Read the story. Then, follow the instructions.

One Saturday morning in May, Olivia and Anna went to the zoo. First, they bought tickets to get into the zoo. Second, they visited the Gorilla Garden and had fun watching the gorillas stare at them. Then, they went to Tiger Town and watched the tigers as they slept in the sunshine. Fourth, they went to Hippo Haven and laughed at the hippos cooling off in their pool. Next, they visited Snake Station and learned about poisonous and nonpoisonous snakes. It was noon, and they were hungry, so they ate lunch at Parrot Patio.

Write **first**, **second**, **third**, **fourth**, **fifth**, and **sixth** to put the events in order.

_____ They went to Hippo Haven.

_____ Olivia and Anna bought zoo tickets.

_____ They watched the tigers sleep.

_____ They ate lunch at Parrot Patio.

_____ The gorillas stared at them.

_____ They learned about poisonous and nonpoisonous snakes.

Sequencing: Why Does It Rain?

Directions: Read about rain. Then, follow the instructions.

Clouds are made of little drops of ice and water. They push and bang into each other. Then, they join together to make bigger drops and begin to fall. More raindrops cling to them. They become heavy and fall quickly to the ground.

Write **first**, **second**, **third**, **fourth**, and **fifth** to put the events in order.

_____ More raindrops cling to them.

_____ Clouds are made of little drops of ice and water.

_____ They join together and make bigger drops that begin to fall.

_____ The drops of ice and water bang into each other.

_____ The drops become heavy and fall quickly to the ground.

Sequencing: Make a Pencil Holder

Directions: Read how to make a pencil holder. Then, follow the instructions.

You can use "junk" to make a pencil holder! First, you need a clean can with one end removed. Make sure there are no sharp edges. Then, you need glue, scissors, and paper. Find colorful paper, such as wrapping paper, wallpaper, or construction paper. Cut the paper to fit the can. Glue the paper around the can. Decorate your can with glitter, buttons, and stickers. Then, put your pencils inside!

Write **first, second, third, fourth, fifth, sixth**, and **seventh** to put the steps in order.

_____ Make sure there are no sharp edges.

_____ Get glue, scissors, and paper.

_____ Cut the paper to fit the can.

_____ Put your pencils in the can!

_____ Glue colorful paper to the can.

_____ Remove one end of a clean can.

_____ Decorate the can with glitter and stickers.

Tracking: Where Does She Go?

Every morning when Ivana wakes up, she goes somewhere. Find out where she goes.

Directions:
Read the sentences. Follow the instructions.

1. On Monday, Ivana needs bread. Use a red crayon to mark her path from her house to the place she buys bread. Where does she go? _____

2. On Tuesday, Ivana wants to read books. Use a green crayon to mark her path. Where does she go? _____

3. On Wednesday, Ivana wants to swing. Use a yellow crayon to mark her path. Where does she go? _____

4. On Thursday, Ivana wants to buy stamps. Use a black crayon to mark her path. Where does she go? _____

5. On Friday, Ivana wants to get money. Use a purple crayon to mark her path. Where does she go? _____

Tracking: Sequencing

Directions: Look at the paths you drew for Ivana on page 108. Number, in order, the places that she went each day. Draw a line to connect the place with the day of the week.

_____ Bank   Monday

_____ Park   Tuesday

_____ Library   Wednesday

_____ Bakery   Thursday

_____ Post Office   Friday

Tracking: With a Map

Greg and Tess walk to and from school together each day. After school, they stop at the park to play. Then, they go home.

Directions: Read the sentences. Draw Greg's path in red and Tess's path in blue.

Greg starts at his home.
He walks to school.
When he leaves school, he stops at the park.
Then, he goes home.
Tess goes the same places that Greg goes.
Some of their paths will be the same.

Name _____

Tracking: With a Map

Directions: Study the map of the United States. Follow the instructions.

1. Draw a star on the state where you live.
2. Draw a line from your state to the Atlantic Ocean.
3. Draw a triangle in the Gulf of Mexico.
4. Draw a circle in the Pacific Ocean.
5. Color each state that borders your state a different color.

CANADA

Pacific Ocean

Atlantic Ocean

Gulf of Mexico

N
W ← → E
S

Comprehensive Curriculum - **Grade 2**

Tracking: Alternate Paths

Look at Spotty Dog's home. Look at the paths he takes to the oven and the back door. The numbers by each path show how many steps Spotty must take to get there.

Directions: Follow the instructions.

1. Spotty Dog's casserole is done. Trace Spotty's path from his chair to the oven.

2. How many steps does Spotty take? _____

3. While Spotty is looking in his oven, he hears a noise in the backyard. Trace Spotty's path to the door.

4. How many steps has Spotty taken in all? _____

5. Spotty goes back to his chair. How many steps must he take? _____

6. How many steps has he taken in all? _____

7. Spotty's path has made a shape. What shape is it? _____

Same/Different: Objects

Directions: Look at the pictures. Draw an **X** on the picture in each row that is different.

Same/Different: Stuffed Animals

Kate and Oralia like to collect and trade stuffed animals.

Directions: Draw two stuffed animals that are alike and two that are different.

Same/Different: Shell Homes

Directions: Read about shells. Then, answer the questions.

Shells are the homes of some animals. Snails live in shells on land. Clams live in shells in the water. Clam shells open. Snail shells stay closed. Both shells keep the animals safe.

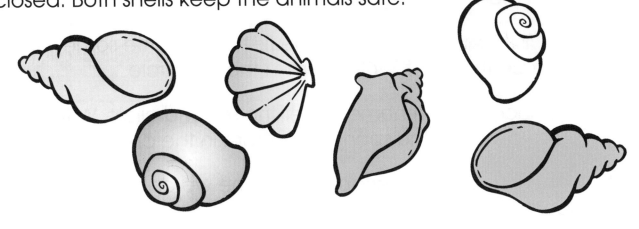

1. (Circle the correct answer.) Snails live in shells

   in the water.   on land.

2. (Circle the correct answer.)
   Clam shells are different from snail shells because

   they open.

   they stay closed.

3. Write one way all shells are the same. _____

   _____

Same/Different: Venn Diagram

A **Venn diagram** is a diagram that shows how two things are the same and different.

Directions: Choose two outdoor sports. Then, follow the instructions to complete the Venn diagram.

1. Write the first sport name under the first circle. Write some words that describe the sport. Write them in the first circle.

2. Write the second sport name under the second circle. Write some words that describe the sport. Write them in the circle.

3. Where the two circles overlap, write some words that describe both sports.

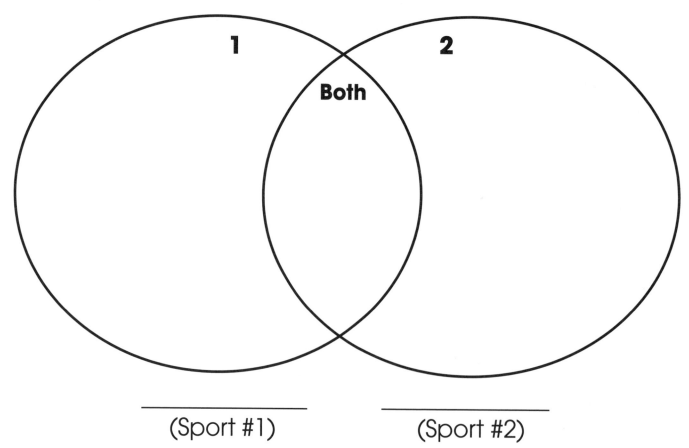

(Sport #1)   (Sport #2)

Same/Different: Dina and Dina

Directions: Read the story. Then, complete the Venn diagram, telling how Dina, the duck, is the same or different than Dina, the girl.

One day in the library, Dina found a story about a duck named Dina!

My name is Dina. I am a duck, and I like to swim. When I am not swimming, I walk on land or fly. I have two feet and two eyes. My feathers keep me warm. Ducks can be different colors. I am gray, brown, and black. I really like being a duck. It is fun.

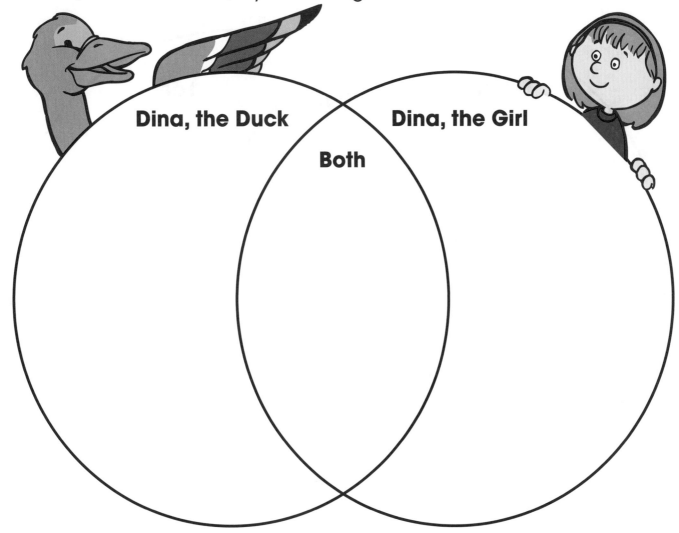

Dina, the Duck

Both

Dina, the Girl

Same/Different: Emma and Lee Have Fun

Directions: Read about Emma and Lee. Then, write how they are the same and different in the Venn diagram.

Emma and Lee like to play ball. They like to jump rope. Lee likes to play a card game called "Old Maid." Emma likes to play a card game called "Go Fish." What do you do to have fun?

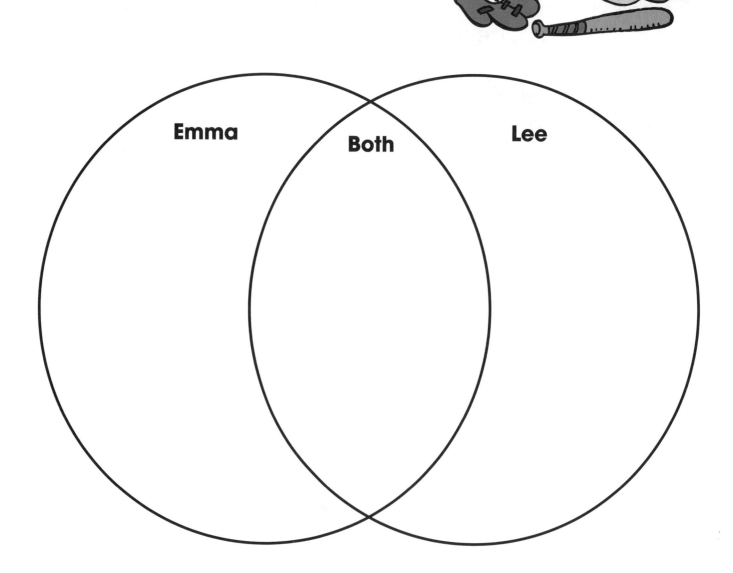

Emma   Both   Lee

Same/Different: Cats and Tigers

Directions: Read about cats and tigers. Then, complete the Venn diagram, telling how they are the same and different.

Tigers are a kind of cat. Pet cats and tigers both have fur. Pet cats are small and tame. Tigers are large and wild.

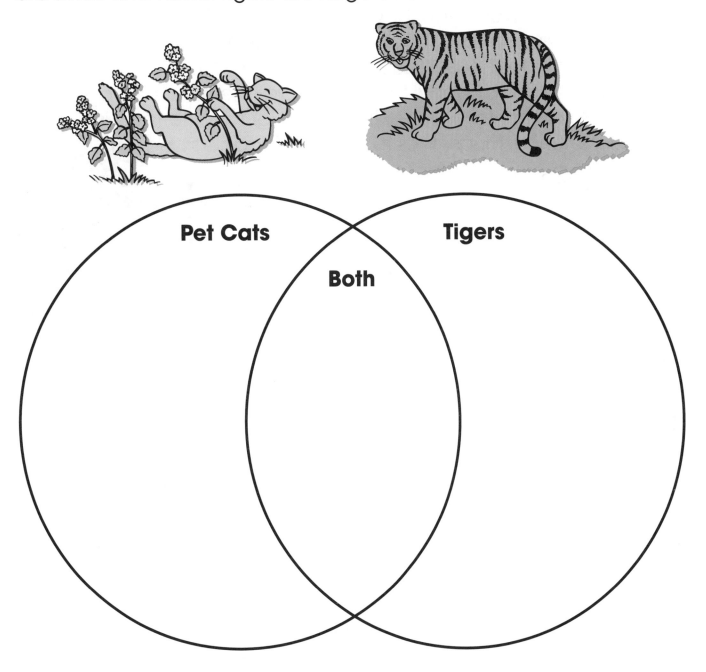

Pet Cats   **Tigers**

Both

Comprehensive Curriculum - **Grade 2**

Same/Different: Marvin and Mugsy

Directions: Read about Marvin and Mugsy. Then, complete the Venn diagram, telling how they are the same and different.

Maggie has two dogs, Marvin and Mugsy. Marvin is a black-and-white spotted Dalmatian. Marvin likes to run after balls in the backyard. His favorite food is Canine Crunchy Crunch. Maggie likes to take Marvin for walks, because dogs need exercise. Marvin loves to sleep in his doghouse. Mugsy is a big, furry brown dog who wiggles when she is happy. Since she is big, she needs lots of exercise. Maggie takes her for walks in the park. Her favorite food is Canine Crunchy Crunch. Mugsy likes to sleep on Maggie's bed.

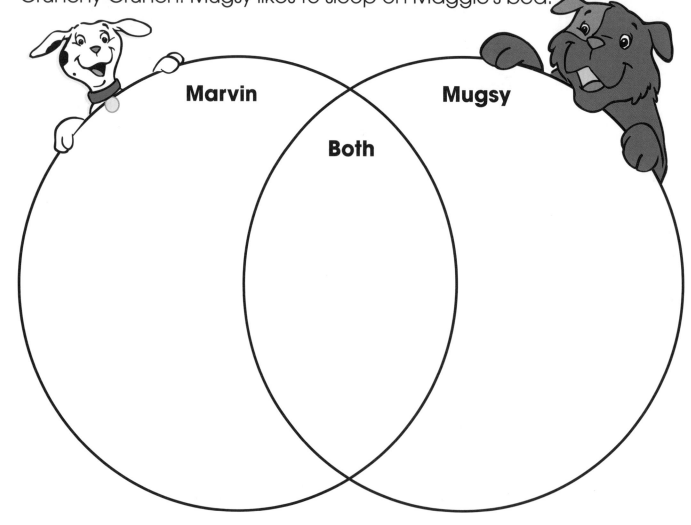

Marvin   Both   Mugsy

Same/Different: Bluebirds and Parrots

Directions: Read about parrots and bluebirds. Then, complete the Venn diagram, telling how they are the same and different.

Bluebirds and parrots are both birds. Bluebirds and parrots can fly. They both have beaks. Parrots can live inside a cage. Bluebirds must live outdoors.

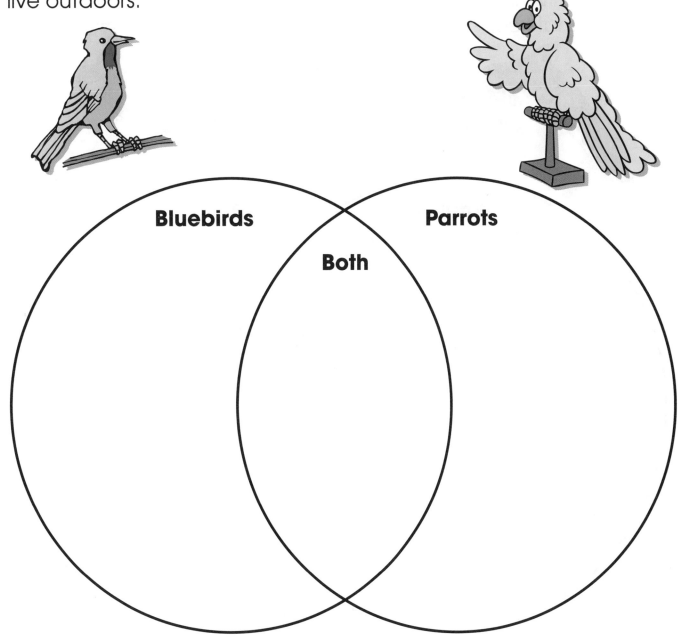

Bluebirds

Both

Parrots

Comprehensive Curriculum - **Grade 2**

Same/Different: Sleeping Whales

Directions: Read about whales. Then, complete the Venn diagram, telling how whales and people are the same and different.

Whales do not sleep like we do. They take many short naps. Like us, whales breathe air. Whales live in very cold water, but they have fat that keeps them warm.

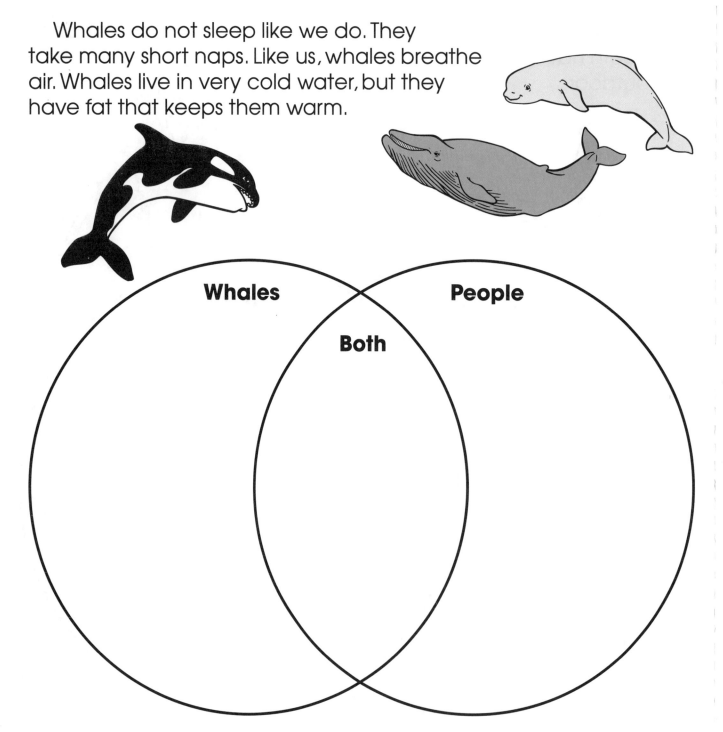

Whales

People

Both

Similes

A **simile** is a figure of speech that compares two different things. The words **like** and **as** are used in similes.

Directions: Draw a line to the picture that goes with each set of words.

as hard as a

as hungry as a

as quiet as a

as soft as a

as easy as

as light as a

as tiny as an

Classifying: A Rainy Day

Directions: Read the story. Then, circle the objects Jonathan needs to stay dry.

It is raining. Jonathan wants to play outdoors. What should he wear to stay dry? What should he carry to stay dry?

Classifying: Outdoor/Indoor Games

Classifying is putting things that are alike into groups.

Directions: Read about games. Draw an **X** on the games you can play indoors. Circle the objects used for outdoor games.

Some games are outdoor games. Some games are indoor games. Outdoor games are active. Indoor games are quiet.

Which do you like best? _____

Classifying: Art Tools

Directions: Read about art tools. Then, color only the art tools.

Andrea uses different art tools to help her design her masterpieces. To cut, she needs scissors. To draw, she needs a pencil. To color, she needs crayons. To paint, she needs a brush.

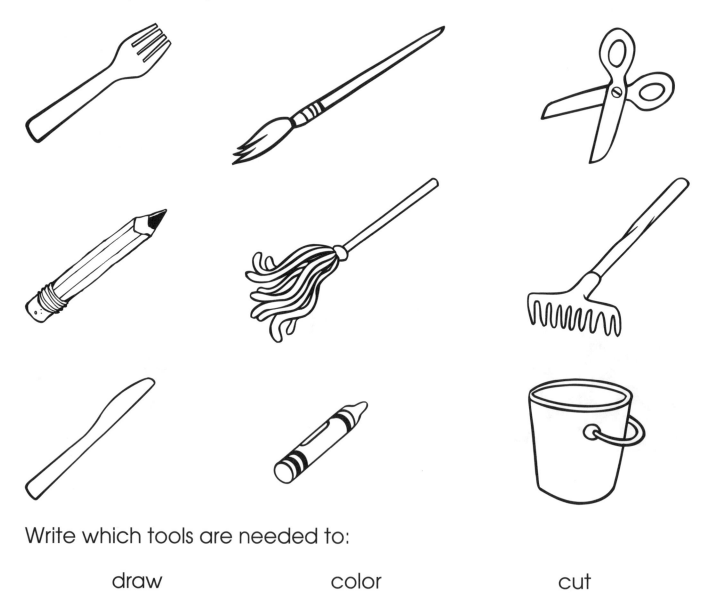

Write which tools are needed to:

draw	color	cut

_____   _____   _____

Classifying

Classifying is putting similar things into groups.

Directions: Write each word from the word box on the correct line.

baby	donkey	whale	family	fox
uncle	goose	grandfather	kangaroo	policeman

people   animals

 _____   _____

 _____   _____

 _____   _____

 _____    _____

 _____    _____

Classifying

Directions: Read the sentences. Write the words from the word box where they belong.

bush	rocket	strawberries	thunder	bicycle	Danger
airplane	wind	honey	rain	car	grass
Stop	truck	Poison	flower	apple juice	bird

1. These things taste sweet.

   _____   _____   _____

2. These things come when it storms.

   _____   _____   _____

3. These things have wheels.

   _____   _____   _____

4. These are words you see on signs.

   _____   _____   _____

5. These things can fly.

   _____   _____   _____

6. These things grow in the ground.

   _____   _____   _____

Classifying: Animals

Directions: Use a red crayon to circle the names of three animals that would make good pets. Use a blue crayon to circle the names of three wild animals. Use an orange crayon to circle the two animals that live on a farm.

BEAR   CAT   LION   SHEEP   BIRD   DOG   COW   TIGER

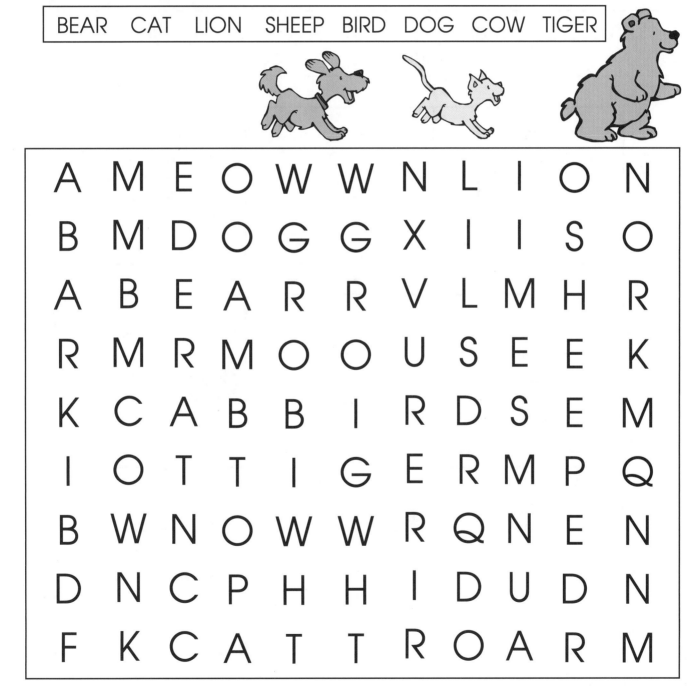

A M E O W W N L I O N

B M D O G G X I I S O

A B E A R R V L M H R

R M R M O O U S E E K

K C A B B I R D S E M

I O T T I G E R M P Q

B W N O W W R Q N E N

D N C P H H I D U D N

F K C A T T R O A R M

Classifying

Directions: The words in each box form a group. Choose the word from the word box that describes each group, and write it on the line.

clothes	family	noises	colors	flowers
fruits	animals	coins	toys	

rose
buttercup
tulip
daisy

_____

crash
bang
ring
pop

_____

mother
father
sister
brother

_____

puzzle
wagon
blocks
doll

_____

green
purple
blue
red

_____

grapes
orange
apple
plum

_____

shirt
socks
dress
coat

_____

 dime
penny
nickel
quarter

_____

dog
horse
elephant
moose

_____

Classifying

Living things need air, food, and water to live. **Non-living** things are not alive.

Directions: Cut out the words on the bottom. Glue each word in the correct column.

Living	Non-living

cut ✂ -

flower	book	boy	dog
chair	bread	tree	camera
car	horse	ant	shoe

Page is blank for cutting exercise on previous page.

Classifying: Foods

Darcy likes fruit and things made from fruit. She also likes bread.

Directions: Circle the things on the menu that Darcy will eat.

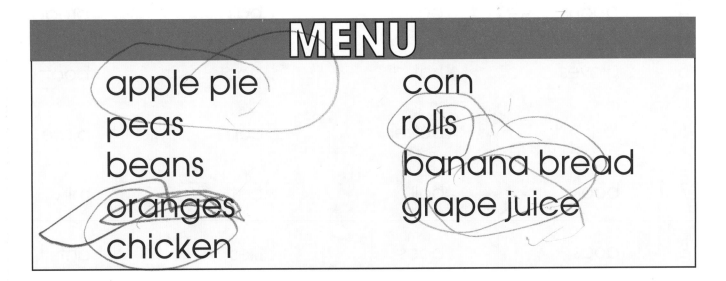

MENU

apple pie   corn

peas   rolls

beans   banana bread

oranges   grape juice

chicken

Classifying: Words

Dapper Dog is going camping.

Directions: Draw an **X** on the word in each row that does not belong in that group.

1.   flashlight   candle   radio   fire

2.   shirt   pants   coat   bat

3.   cow   car   bus   train

4.   beans   pasta   ball   bread

5.   gloves   hat   book   boots

6.   fork   butter   cup   plate

7.   book   ball   bat   milk

8.   dogs   bees   flies   ants

Classifying: Leaves

Directions: Look at each leaf, and read its name. Write the name of each leaf on the line. Then, color the leaves.

white oak   silver maple   poison ivy   ash

_____   _____

_____   _____

Classifying: Leaves

This tricky tree has four different kinds of leaves: ash, poison ivy, silver maple, and white oak.

Directions: Follow the instructions. Then, answer the questions.

1. Underline the white oak leaves. How many are there? _____

2. Circle the ash leaves. How many are there? _____

3. Draw an **X** on the poison ivy leaves. How many are there? _____

4. Draw a box around the silver maple leaves. How many are there? _____

Classifying: Watch Out for Poison Ivy!

Poison ivy is not safe. If you touch it, it can make your skin red and itchy. It can hurt. It grows on the ground. It has three leaves. It can be green or red. Watch out, Jay! There is poison ivy in these woods.

Directions: Color the poison ivy leaves red. Then, color the "safe" leaves other colors.

Comprehensive Curriculum - **Grade 2**

Classifying: Leaves

Directions: Gather some leaves. Put your leaves into groups by type. Then, answer the questions.

white oak   red oak   pine   ash

elm   silver maple   red maple

1. How many white oak leaves did you find?_____

2. How many red oak leaves did you find?_____

3. How many pine needles did you find?_____

4. How many ash leaves did you find? _____

5. How many elm leaves did you find? _____

6. How many silver maple leaves did you find?_____

7. How many red maple leaves did you find?_____

8. What other kinds of leaves did you find? Go online with an adult or use a book to help you name them. Write their names on the lines._____

_____

_____

Classifying: Animal Habitats

Directions: Read the story. Then, write each animal's name under **Water** or **Land** to tell where it lives.

Animals live in different habitats. A habitat is the place of an animal's natural home. Many animals live on land, and others live in water. Most animals that live in water breathe with gills. Animals that live on land breathe with lungs.

fish	shrimp	giraffe	dog
cat	eel	whale	horse
bear	deer	shark	jellyfish

WATER

1. _____   4. _____

2. _____   5. _____

3. _____   6. _____

LAND

1. _____   4. _____

2. _____   5. _____

3. _____   6. _____

Review

Directions: Compare the leaves on the left to the pictures of the other leaves. Write the missing names under the leaves.

_____

red oak

poison ivy

ash

_____

silver maple

elm

white oak

Directions: Color the pictures that are fruits.

apple   carrot   peach   corn

Directions: Draw an **X** on the word in each group that does not belong.

night   black   dark   sun

rose   ash   oak   elm

muffin   banana   rolls   bread

Comprehension: Ladybugs

Directions: Read about ladybugs. Then, answer the questions.

Have you ever seen a ladybug? Ladybugs are red. They have black spots. They have six legs. Ladybugs are pretty!

1. What color are ladybugs? _____

2. What color are their spots? _____

3. How many legs do ladybugs have? _____

Comprehension: Playful Cats

Directions: Read about cats. Then, follow the instructions.

Cats make good pets. They like to play. They like to jump. They like to run. Do you?

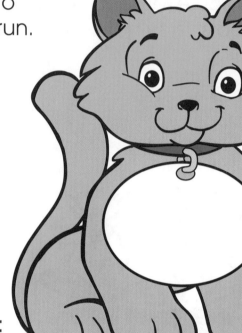

1. (Circle the correct answer.)
   Cats make good

   pets.

   friends.

2. Write three things cats like to do:

   a) _____

   b) _____

   c) _____

3. Think of a good name for a cat. Write it on the cat's tag.

Comprehension: Types of Tops

The **main idea** is the most important point or idea in a story.

Directions: Read about tops. Then, answer the questions.

Tops come in all sizes. Some tops are made of wood. Some tops are made of tin. All tops do the same thing. They spin! Do you have a top?

1. Circle the main idea:

   There are many kinds of tops.

   Some tops are made of wood.

2. What are some tops made of? _____

3. What do all tops do? _____

Comprehension: Playing Store

Directions: Read about playing store. Then, answer the questions.

Tyson and his friends like to play store. They use boxes and cans. They line them up. Then, they put them in bags.

1. Circle the main idea:

   Tyson and his friends use boxes, cans, and bags to play store.

   You need bags to play store.

2. (Circle your answer.) Who likes to play store?

   all kids   some kids

3. Do you like to play store?_____

Comprehension: Singing Whales

Directions: Read about singing whales. Then, follow the instructions.

Some whales can sing! We cannot understand the words. But, we can hear the tune of the humpback whale. Each season, humpback whales sing a different song.

1. Circle the main idea:

   All whales can sing.

   Some whales can sing.

2. Name one kind of whale that sings.

   _____

3. How many different songs does the humpback whale sing each year?

   1   2   3   4

Comprehension: Paper-Bag Puppets

Directions: Read about paper-bag puppets. Then, follow the instructions.

It is easy to make a hand puppet. You need a small paper bag. You need colored paper. You need glue. You need scissors. Are you ready?

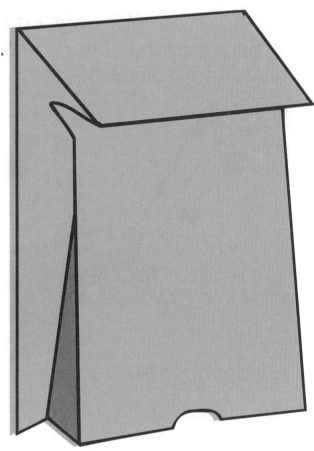

1. Circle the main idea:

   You need scissors.

   Making a hand puppet is easy.

2. Write the four objects you need to make a paper-bag puppet.

   a) _____

   b) _____

   c) _____

   d) _____

3. Draw a face on the paper-bag puppet.

Comprehension: Sea Horses Look Strange!

Directions: Read about sea horses. Then, answer the questions.

Sea horses are fish, not horses. A sea horse's head looks a little like a horse's head. It has a tail like a monkey's tail. A sea horse looks very strange!

1. (Circle the correct answer.)
   A sea horse is a kind of

   horse.

   monkey.

   fish.

2. What does a sea horse's head look like?

   _____

3. What makes a sea horse look strange?

   a.

   b.

Comprehension: Carla and Tony Jump Rope

Directions: Read about jumping rope. Then, follow the instructions.

Carla and Tony like to jump rope. Carla likes to jump rope alone. Tony likes to have two people turn the rope for him. Carla and Tony can jump slowly. They can also jump fast.

1. Name another way to jump rope.

   a. Have two people turn the rope.

   b. _____

   _____

2. Name two speeds for jumping rope.

   a)_____   b)_____

3. Do you like to jump rope? _____

   _____

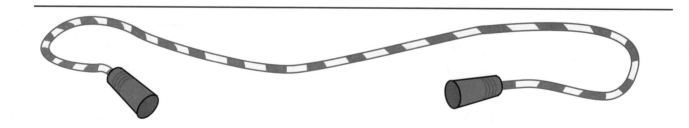

Comprehension: How to Stop a Dog Fight

Directions: Read about how to stop a dog fight. Then, answer the questions.

Sometimes, dogs fight. They bark loudly. They may bite. Do not try to pull apart fighting dogs. Turn on a hose, and spray them with water. This will stop the fight.

1. Name some things dogs may do if they are mad.

_____

_____

2. Why is it unwise to pull apart dogs that are fighting?

_____

_____

3. Do you think dogs like to get wet?

_____

Comprehension: Training a Dog

Directions: Read about how to train dogs. Then, answer the questions.

A dog has a ball in his mouth. You want the ball. What should you do? Do not pull on the ball. Hold out something else for the dog. The dog will drop the ball to take it!

1. Circle the main idea:

   Always get a ball away from a dog.

   Offer the dog something else to get him to drop the ball.

2. What should you **not** do if you want the dog's ball?

   _____

3. What could you hold out for the dog to take?

   _____

Comprehension: How to Meet a Dog

Directions: Read about how to meet a dog. Then, follow the instructions.

Do not try to pet a dog right away. First, let the dog sniff your hand. Do not move quickly. Do not talk loudly. Just let the dog sniff.

1. Predict what the dog will let you do if it likes you.

_____

_____

2. What should you let the dog do?_____

_____

3. Name three things you should not do when you meet a dog.

a)_____

b)_____

c)_____

Comprehension: Dirty Dogs

Directions: Read about dogs. Then, answer the questions.

Like people, dogs get dirty. Some dogs get a bath once a month. Baby soap is a good soap for cleaning dogs. Fill a tub with warm water. Get someone to hold the dog still in the tub. Then, wash the dog quickly.

1. How often do some dogs get a bath? _____

_____

2. What is a good soap to use on dogs? _____

3. Do you think most dogs like to take baths? _____

Comprehension: Pretty Parrots

Directions: Read about parrots. Then, follow the instructions.

Big parrots are pretty. Their feet have four toes each. Two toes are in front. Two toes are in back. Parrots use their feet to climb. They use them to hold food.

1. (Circle the correct answer.)
   A parrot's foot has

   four toes.

   two toes.

2. Name two things a parrot does with its feet.

   a) _____

   _____

   b) _____

   _____

3. Color the parrot.

Comprehension: A Winter Story

Directions: Read about parrots. Then, follow the instructions.

It is cold in winter. Snow falls in some parts of the country. Water freezes. Most kids like to play outdoors. Some kids make a snowman. Some kids skate. What do you do in winter?

1. Circle the main idea:

   Snow falls in winter.

   In winter, there are many things to do outside.

2. Write two things about winter weather.

   a) _____

   b) _____

3. Write what you like to do in winter.

Comprehension: The Puppet Play

Directions: Read the play out loud with a friend. Then, answer the questions.

Pip: Hey, Pep. What kind of turkey eats very fast?

Pep: Uh, I don't know.

Pip: A gobbler!

Pep: I have a good joke for you, Pip. What kind of burger does a polar bear eat?

Pip: Uh, a cold burger?

Pep: No, an iceberg-er!

Pip: Hey, that was a great joke!

1. Who are the characters in the play? _____

_____

2. Who are the jokes about? _____

_____

3. What are the characters in the play doing? _____

_____

Comprehension: Just Junk?

Directions: Read about saving things. Then, follow the instructions.

Do you save old crayons? Do you save old buttons or cards? Some people call these things junk. They throw them out. Leah saves these things. She likes to use them for art projects. She puts them in a box. What kinds of things do you save?

1. Circle the main idea:

   Everyone has junk.

   People have different ideas about what junk is.

2. Name two kinds of junk.

   a) _____

   b) _____

3. What are two things you can do with old things?

   a) _____

   b) _____

Comprehension: Snakes!

Directions: Read about snakes. Then, answer the questions.

There are many facts about snakes that might surprise someone. A snake's skin is dry. Most snakes are shy. They will hide from people. Snakes eat mice and rats. They do not chew them up. Snakes' jaws drop open so they can swallow their food whole.

1. How does a snake's skin feel? _____

2. Most snakes are _____.

3. What do snakes eat?

    a. _____

    b. _____

Comprehension: More About Snakes!

Directions: Read more about snakes. Then, follow the instructions.

Unlike people, snakes have cold blood. They like to be warm. They hunt for food when it is warm. They lie in the sun. When it is cold, snakes curl up into a ball.

1. What do snakes do when it is warm?

   a. _____

   b. _____

2. Why do you think snakes curl up when it is cold? _____

   _____

3. (Circle the correct answer.)
   People have:

   cold blood.   warm blood.

Comprehension: Sean's Basketball Game

Directions: Read about Sean's basketball game. Then, answer the questions.

Sean really likes to play basketball. One sunny day, he decided to ask his friends to play basketball at the park, but there were six people—Sean, Aki, Lance, Kate, Zac, and Oralia. A basketball team only allows five to play at a time. So, Sean decided to be the coach. Sean and his friends had fun.

1. How many kids wanted to play basketball?_____

2. Write their names in ABC order:

_____ _____ _____

_____ _____ _____

3. How many players can play on a basketball team

at a time? _____

4. Where did they play basketball?_____

5. Who decided to be the coach? _____

Comprehension: Outdoor/Indoor Games

Directions: Read the story. Then, answer the questions.

Derrick likes to play outdoor and indoor games. His favorite outdoor game is baseball because he likes to hit the ball with the bat and run around the bases. He plays this game in the park with the neighborhood kids.

When it rains, he plays checkers with Lorenzo on the dining-room table in his apartment. He likes the game, because he has to use his brain to think about his next move, and the rules are easy to follow.

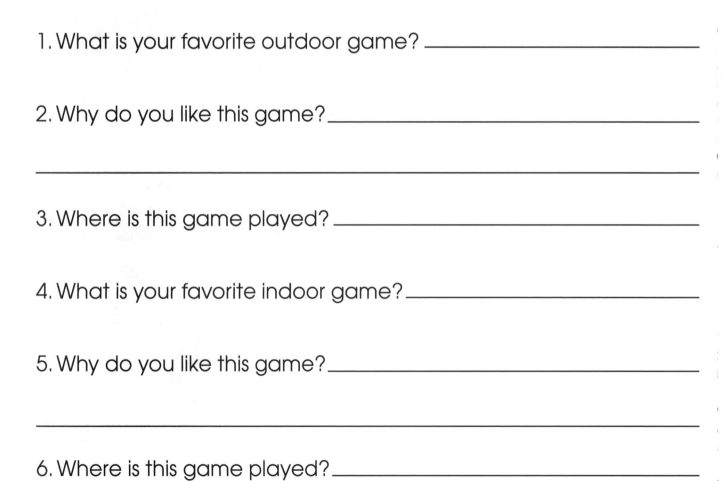

1. What is your favorite outdoor game? _____

2. Why do you like this game? _____

_____

3. Where is this game played? _____

4. What is your favorite indoor game? _____

5. Why do you like this game? _____

_____

6. Where is this game played? _____

Reading Comprehension

Directions: Read the story. Then, complete the sentences with words from the story.

Mike lives on a farm. There are many animals on the farm: birds, cows, pigs, goats, and chickens. But Mike likes his horse the best. His horse's name is Stormy. Stormy stays in a barn. For fun, Mike rides Stormy to the lake. Stormy helps Mike, too. Stormy pulls a cart to carry weeds from the garden. After a hard day, Mike feeds Stormy corn and hay. For a treat, Stormy gets a pear.

1. Mike lives on a _____.
2. His favorite animal is a _____.
3. The horse's name is _____.
4. Stormy stays in a _____.
5. It is fun to ride to the _____.
6. Stormy eats _____ and _____.
7. Stormy's treat is a _____.

Write 5 words from the story that have an **r-controlled vowel**.

_____   _____   _____

_____   _____

Now, write 5 words from the story that have a **long vowel sound**.

_____   _____   _____

_____   _____

Comprehensive Curriculum - **Grade 2**

Comprehension: Ant Farms

Directions: Read about ant farms. Then, answer the questions.

Ant farms are sold at toy stores and pet stores. Ant farms come in a flat frame. The frame has glass on each side. Inside the glass is sand. The ants live in the sand.

1. Where are ant farms sold? _____

2. The frame has _____ on each side.

Circle the correct answer.

3. The ants live in

    water.   sand.

4. The ant farm frame is

    flat.   round.

Comprehension: Amazing Ants

Directions: Read about ants. Then, answer the questions.

Ants are insects. Ants live in many parts of the world and make their homes in soil, sand, wood, and leaves. Most ants live for about 6 to 10 weeks. But the queen ant, who lays the eggs, can live for up to 15 years!

The largest ant is the bulldog ant. This ant can grow to be 5 inches long, and it eats meat! The bulldog ant can be found in Australia.

1. Where do ants make their homes? _____

_____

2. How long can a queen ant live? _____

_____

3. What is the largest ant? _____

4. What does it eat? _____

Comprehension: Sharks Are Fish, Too!

Directions: Read the story. Then, follow the instructions.

Angela learned a lot about sharks when her class visited the city aquarium. She learned that sharks are fish. Some sharks are as big as an elephant, and some can fit into a small paper bag. Sharks have no bones. They have hundreds of teeth, and when they lose them, they grow new ones. They eat animals of any kind. Whale sharks are the largest of all fish.

1. Circle the main idea:

   Angela learned a lot about sharks at the aquarium.

   Some sharks are as big as elephants.

2. When sharks lose teeth, they_____

   _____.

3. _____ are the largest of all fish.

4. Sharks have bones. (Circle the answer.)

   Yes   No

Comprehension: Fish

Directions: Read about fish. Then, follow the instructions.

Some fish live in warm water. Some live in cold water. Some fish live in lakes. Some fish live in oceans. There are almost 30,000 kinds of fish.

1. Name two types of water in which fish live.

   a. _____

   b. _____

2. Name another place fish live. _____

   Some fish live in lakes and some live in _____ .

3. There are almost _____ kinds of fish.

Comprehension: Fish Come in Many Colors

Directions: Read about the color of fish. Then, follow the instructions.

All fish live in water. Fish that live at the top are blue, green, or black. Fish that live down deep are silver or red. The colors make it hard to see the fish.

1. List the colors of fish at the top.

_____   _____   _____

2. List the two colors of fish that live down deep.

_____   _____

3. Color the top fish and the bottom fish the correct colors.

Comprehension: Fish Can Protect Themselves

Directions: Read about two fish. Then, follow the instructions.

Most fish have ways to protect themselves from danger. Two of these fish are the trigger fish and the porcupine fish. The trigger fish lives on the ocean reef. When it sees danger, it swims into its private hole and puts its top fin up and squeezes itself in tight. Then, it cannot be taken from its hiding place. The porcupine fish also lives on the ocean reef. When danger comes, it puffs up like a balloon by swallowing air or water. When it puffs up, poisonous spikes stand out on its body. When danger is past, it deflates its body.

1. Circle the main idea:

   Trigger fish and porcupine fish can be dangerous.

   Some fish have ways to protect themselves from danger.

2. Trigger fish and porcupine fish live on the _____ .

3. The porcupine fish puffs up by swallowing _____

   or _____ .

Comprehension: Ideas Come from Books

Directions: Read the story. Then, follow the instructions.

Zoe has many books. She gets different ideas from these books. Some of her books are about fish. Some are about cardboard and paper crafts. Some are about nature. Others are about reusing junk. Zoe wants to make a paper airplane. She reads about it in one of her books. Then, she asks an adult to help her.

1. Circle the main idea:

   Zoe learns about different ideas from books.

   Zoe likes crafts.

2. (Circle the correct answer.) Zoe is:

   a person who likes to read.

   a person who doesn't like books.

3. What does Zoe want to make from paper? _____

   _____

4. Write two ways to learn how to do something.

   a) _____

   b) _____

Predicting: A Rainy Game

Predicting is telling what is likely to happen based on the facts.

Directions: Read the story. Then, check each sentence below that tells how the story could end.

One cloudy day, Juan and his baseball team, the Bears, played the Crocodiles. In the last half of the fifth inning, it started to rain. The coaches and umpires had to decide what to do.

_____ They kept playing until nine innings were finished.

_____ They ran for cover and waited until the rain stopped.

_____ Each player grabbed an umbrella and returned to the field to finish the game.

_____ They canceled the game and played it another day.

_____ They acted like crocodiles and slid around the wet bases.

_____ The coaches played the game while the players sat in the dugout.

Comprehensive Curriculum - **Grade 2**

Predicting: Oops!

Directions: Look at the pictures on the left. On the right, draw and write what you predict will happen next.

Predicting: Dog Derby

Directions: Read the story. Then, answer the questions.

Maggie had a great idea for a game to play with her dogs, Marvin and Mugsy. The game was called "Dog Derby." Maggie would stand at one end of the driveway and hold on to the dogs by their collars. Her friend Mitch would stand at the other end of the driveway. When he said, "Go!" Maggie would let go of the dogs and they would race to Mitch. The first one there would get a dog biscuit. If there was a tie, both dogs would get a biscuit.

1. Who do you think will win the race?

_____

Why? _____

_____

2. What do you think will happen when they race again?

_____

_____

Predicting: What Will Bobby Do?

Directions: Read about Bobby the cat. Then, write what you think will happen.

One sunny spring day, Bobby was sleeping under her favorite tree. She was dreaming about her favorite food—tuna. Suddenly, she became hungry for a treat. Bobby woke up and listened when she heard someone call her name.

1. Why do you think Bobby was being called? _____

_____

2. What do you think will happen next? _____

_____

_____

Predicting: Dog-Gone!

Directions: Read the story. Then, follow the instructions.

Scotty and Simone were washing their dog, Willis. His fur was wet. Their hands were wet. Willis did NOT like to be wet. Scotty dropped the soap. Simone picked it up and let go of Willis. Uh-oh!

1. Write what happened next.

_____

_____

_____

2. Draw what happened next.

Comprehensive Curriculum - **Grade 2**

Name _____

Predicting Outcome

Directions: Read the story. Complete the story in the last box.

1. A cat is playing with a ball of yarn.

3. The mouse tiptoes past the playful cat.

2. A mouse peeks around the corner.

4. _____
_____
_____

Predicting Outcome

Directions: Read the story. Complete the story in the last box.

1. "Look at that elephant! He sure is big!"

3. "Stop, Amy! Look at that sign!"

2. "I'm hungry."
   "I bet that elephant is, too."

4. _____
   _____
   _____

Predicting Outcome

Directions: Read the story. In the last box, draw what you think will happen next. Then, write the words for the end of the story.

1. "Do you want to go to the library with me?"

   "Yes, I want a book about seashells."

3. "Excuse me. Where can I find a book about seashells?"

2. "Have you found your book?"
   "No. I can't find it."
   "Why don't you ask someone?"

4. _____

_____

Predicting Outcome

Directions: Complete the story. Then, draw pictures to match the four parts.

1. Grace and Jazmin are flying a kite.

Beginning

3. _____
_____

Middle

2. The kite gets stuck in a tree.

Middle

4. _____
_____

End

Predicting Outcome

Directions: Create your own story in the squares. Show the beginning in box 1, the middle in boxes 2 and 3, and the end in box 4.

Beginning (Setting)   Middle (Problem)

1.	3.
2.	4.

Middle (Problem)   End (Solution)

Predicting Outcome

Kelly and Gina always have fun at the fair.

Directions: Read the sentences. Write
what you think will happen next.

1. Kelly and Gina are riding the Ferris wheel. It stops when they are
   at the top.

   _____

   _____

   _____

2. As they walk into the animal barn, a little piglet runs toward them.

   _____

   _____

   _____

3. Snow cones are their favorite way to cool off. The ones they
   bought are made from real snow.

   _____

   _____

   _____

4. They play a "toss the ring over the bottle" game, but when the
   ring goes around the bottle, it disappears.

   _____

   _____

   _____

Predicting: Puff and Trigg

Directions: Read about Puff and Trigg. Then, write what happens next in the story.

It was a sunny, warm day in the Pacific Ocean. Puff, the happy porcupine fish, and Trigg, the jolly trigger fish, were having fun playing fish tag. They were good friends. Suddenly, they saw the shadow of a giant fish! It was coming right at them! They knew the giant fish might like eating smaller fish! What did they do?

What did Puff and Trigg do to get away from the giant fish?

_____

_____

_____

_____

Fact and Opinion: Games!

A **fact** is something that can be proven. An **opinion** is a feeling or belief about something and cannot be proven.

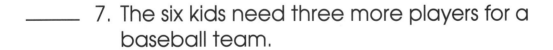

Directions: Read these sentences about different games. Then, write **F** next to each fact and **O** next to each opinion.

_____ 1. Tennis is cool!

_____ 2. There are red and black markers in a checkers game.

_____ 3. In football, a touchdown is worth six points.

_____ 4. Being a goalie in soccer is easy.

_____ 5. A yo-yo moves on a string.

_____ 6. June's sister looks like the queen on the card.

_____ 7. The six kids need three more players for a baseball team.

_____ 8. Table tennis is more fun than court tennis.

_____ 9. Hide-and-seek is a game that can be played outdoors or indoors.

_____ 10. Play money is used in many board games.

Comprehensive Curriculum - **Grade 2**

Fact and Opinion: Recycling

Directions: Read about recycling. Then, follow the instructions.

What do you throw away every day? What could you do with these things? You could change an old greeting card into a new card. You could make a puppet with an old paper bag. Old buttons make great refrigerator magnets. You can plant seeds in plastic cups. Cardboard tubes make perfect rockets. So, use your imagination!

1. Write **F** next to each fact and **O** next to each opinion.

_____ Cardboard tubes are ugly.

_____ Buttons can be made into refrigerator magnets.

_____ An old greeting card can be changed into a new card.

_____ Paper-bag puppets are cute.

_____ Seeds can be planted in plastic cups.

_____ Rockets can be made from cardboard tubes.

2. What could you do with a cardboard tube? _____

_____

Fact and Opinion: An Owl Story

Directions: Read the story. Then, follow the instructions.

My name is Owen Owl, and I am a bird. I go to Nocturnal School. Our teacher is Mr. Screech Owl. In his class, I learned that owls are birds that can sleep all day and hunt at night. Some of us live in nests in trees. In North America, it is against the law to harm owls. I like being an owl!

Write **F** next to each fact and **O** next to each opinion.

_____ 1. No one can harm owls in North America.

_____ 2. It would be great if owls could talk.

_____ 3. Owls sleep all day.

_____ 4. Some owls sleep in nests.

_____ 5. Mr. Screech Owl is a good teacher.

_____ 6. Owls are birds.

_____ 7. Owen Owl would be a good friend.

_____ 8. Owls hunt at night.

_____ 9. Nocturnal School is a good school for smart owls.

_____ 10. This story is for the birds.

Comprehensive Curriculum - **Grade 2**

Fact and Opinion: A Bounty of Birds

Directions: Read the story. Then, follow the instructions.

Tashi's family likes to go to the zoo. Her favorite animals are all the different kinds of birds. Tashi likes birds because they can fly, they have colorful feathers, and they make funny noises.

Write **F** next to each fact and **O** next to each opinion.

_____ 1. Birds have two feet.

_____ 2. All birds lay eggs.

_____ 3. Parrots are too noisy.

_____ 4. All birds have feathers and wings.

_____ 5. It would be great to be a bird and fly south for the winter.

_____ 6. Birds have hard beaks or bills instead of teeth.

_____ 7. Pigeons are fun to watch.

_____ 8. Some birds cannot fly.

_____ 9. Parakeets make good pets.

_____ 10. A penguin is a bird.

Fact and Opinion: Henrietta the Humpback

Directions: Read the story. Then, follow the instructions.

My name is Henrietta, and I am a humpback whale. I live in cold seas in the summer and warm seas in the winter. My long flippers are used to move forward and backward. I like to eat fish. Sometimes, I show off by leaping out of the water. Would you like to be a humpback whale?

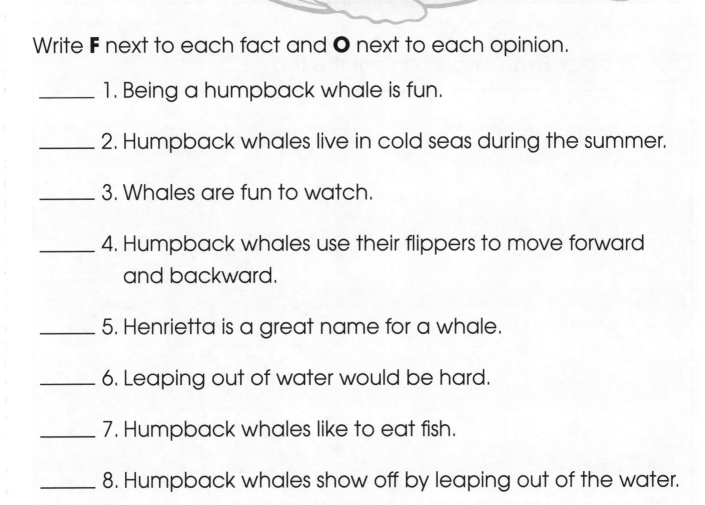

Write **F** next to each fact and **O** next to each opinion.

_____ 1. Being a humpback whale is fun.

_____ 2. Humpback whales live in cold seas during the summer.

_____ 3. Whales are fun to watch.

_____ 4. Humpback whales use their flippers to move forward
and backward.

_____ 5. Henrietta is a great name for a whale.

_____ 6. Leaping out of water would be hard.

_____ 7. Humpback whales like to eat fish.

_____ 8. Humpback whales show off by leaping out of the water.

Making Inferences: Ryan's Top

Directions: Read about Ryan's top. Then, follow the instructions.

Ryan got a new top. He wanted to place it where it would be safe. He asked his dad to put it up high. Where can his dad put the top?

1. Write where Ryan's dad can put the top. _____

_____

Draw a place Ryan's dad can put the top.

Making Inferences: Down on the Ant Farm

Directions: Read about ant farms. Then, answer the questions.

Ants are busy on the farm. They dig in the sand. They make roads in the sand. They look for food in the sand. When an ant dies, other ants bury it.

1. Where do you think ants are buried? _____

_____

2. Is it fair to say ants are lazy? _____

3. Write a word that tells about ants. _____

Comprehensive Curriculum - **Grade 2**

Making Inferences: Monty's Trip

Directions: Read Monty's answer. Then, circle the answer to each question. Color the pictures.

Monty says, "I want to learn more about big cats. Someday, I would like to be an animal trainer or a zoo director. Where can we learn about big cats?"

1. What cat does Monty want to learn about?

2. Where should he go?

Making Inferences

Directions: Read the story. Then, answer the questions.

Jeff is baking cookies. He wears special clothes when he bakes. He puts flour, sugar, eggs, and butter into a bowl. He mixes everything together. He puts the cookies in the oven at 11:15 A.M. It takes 15 minutes for the cookies to bake. Jeff wants something cold and white to drink when he eats his cookies.

1. Is Jeff baking a cake?   Yes   No

2. What are two things Jeff might wear when he bakes?
   hat   boots   apron   tie   raincoat   roller skates

3. What didn't Jeff put in the cookies?
   flour   eggs   milk   butter   sugar

4. What do you think Jeff does after he mixes the cookies but before he bakes them?_____

   _____

   _____

5. What time will the cookies be done? _____

6. What will Jeff drink with his cookies? _____

7. Why do you think Jeff wanted to bake cookies? _____

   _____

   _____

Making Inferences

Directions: Read the story. Then, answer the questions.

Shawn and his family are on a trip. It is very sunny. Shawn loves to swim. He also likes the waves. There is something else he likes even more. Shawn builds drip castles. He makes drips by using very wet sand. He lets it drip out of his hand into a tall pile. He makes the drip piles as high as he can.

1. Where is Shawn? _____

2. What does Shawn wear on his trip? _____

3. Is Shawn hot or cold? _____

4. What does Shawn like to do best? _____

5. What are drip castles made from? _____

6. What do you think happens when drip castles get too big?

_____

7. If Shawn gets too hot, what do you think he will do?

_____

Making Inferences

Directions: Read the story. Then, answer the questions.

   Mrs. Sweet looked forward to a visit from her niece, Candy. In the mor ning, she cleaned her house. She also baked some banana bread. An hour before Candy was to arrive, the phone rang. Mrs. Sweet said, "I understand." When she hung up the phone, she looked very sad.

1. Who do you think called Mrs. Sweet?

   _____

   _____

2. How do you know that?

   _____

   _____

3. Why is Mrs. Sweet sad?

   _____

   _____

Making Inferences: Sea Horses

Directions: Read more about sea horses. Then, answer the questions.

A father sea horse helps the mother. He has a small sack, or pouch, on the front of his body. The mother sea horse lays the eggs. She does not keep them. She gives the eggs to the father.

1. What does the mother sea horse do with her eggs?

_____

2. Where does the father sea horse put the eggs?

_____

3. Sea horses can change color. Color the sea horses.

Making Inferences: Using Pictures

Directions: Draw a picture for each idea. Then, write two sentences that tell about it.

You and a friend are playing your favorite game.

_____

_____

You and a friend are sharing your favorite food.

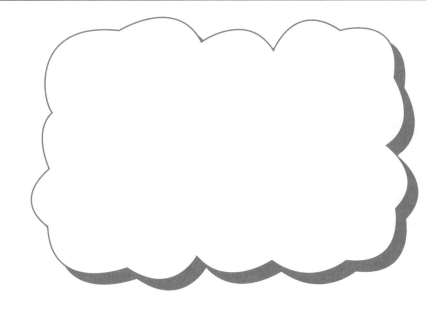

_____

_____

Making Inferences: Visualizing

Directions: Read this story about Ling and Bradley. Draw pictures for the beginning and middle to describe each part of the story.

Beginning: One sunny day, Ling and Bradley, wearing their empty backpacks, rode their bikes down the street to the park.

Middle: They stopped by an oak tree with many acorns under it. They picked up some and stuffed them into their backpacks.

Directions: Draw an ending for this story that tells what you think they did with the acorns.

End: With the heavy backpacks strapped on their backs, they pedaled home.

Making Inferences: Visualizing

Directions: Read the story about Melinda. Then, draw pictures that describe each part of the story.

Beginning: It was Halloween. Melinda's costume was a black cat with super-duper polka-dot sunglasses.

Middle: Her little brown dog, Marco, yelped and ran under a big red chair when he saw her come into the room.

End: Melinda took off her black cat mask and sunglasses. Then, she held out a dog biscuit. She picked Marco up and hugged him. Then, he was happy.

Making Inferences: Visualizing

Directions: Read the story about Chad and Leon. Then, draw pictures that describe each part of the story.

Beginning: One chilly morning, Chad and Leon rolled two big snowballs to make a snowman in Chad's front yard.

Middle: Chad put his big snowball on top of the bigger one. Leon added a carrot nose, two charcoal eyes, a stick mouth, and a cowboy hat. Then, they went into the house.

End: Later, when they looked out the window, they saw the snowman dancing around. "Thank you!" he shouted to the boys.

Making Inferences: Point of View

Juniper has three problems to solve. She needs your help.

Directions: Read each problem. Write what you think she should do.

1. Juniper is watching her favorite TV show when the power goes out.

_____

_____

_____

_____

2. Juniper is riding her bike to school when the front tire goes flat.

_____

_____

_____

_____

3. Juniper loses her father while shopping in the supermarket.

_____

_____

_____

_____

Making Inferences: Point of View

Toran also has three problems. Now that you have helped Juniper, he would like you to help him, too.

Directions: Read each problem. Write what you think he should do.

1. The class is having a picnic, and Toran left his lunch at home.

_____

_____

_____

2. Toran wants to buy a special video game, but he needs three more dollars.

_____

_____

_____

3. Toran's best friend, Felix, made the third out, and their team lost the kickball game.

_____

_____

_____

Making Inferences: Sequencing

Directions: Draw three pictures to tell a story about each topic.

1. Feeding a pet

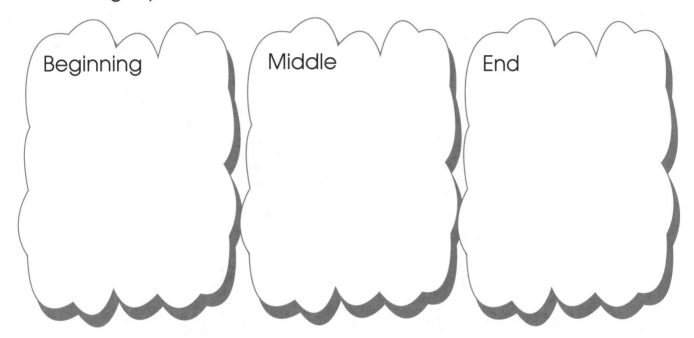

Beginning

Middle

End

2. Playing with a friend

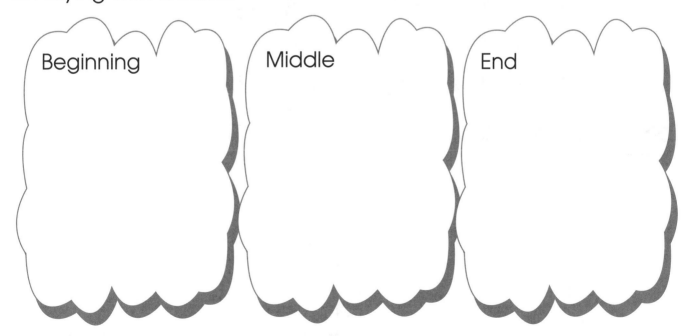

Beginning

Middle

End

Making Inferences: Sequencing

Help make a doggie pizza for Spotty Dog. The steps to follow are all mixed up. Three of the steps are not needed.

Directions: Number the steps in order from 1 to 7. Draw a dog bone by the 3 steps that are not needed.

_____ Place the dough on a round pan.

_____ Cover the top with cheese.

_____ Take a nap.

_____ Make the pizza dough.

_____ Run out the door.

_____ Bake it in a hot oven.

_____ Roll the dough out flat.

_____ Play ball with Spotty.

_____ Spread the sauce on the dough.

_____ Sprinkle bits of dog biscuits on top.

Directions: Draw Spotty Dog's pizza in the box.

Making Deductions: Find the Books

Directions: Use the clues to help the children find their books. Draw a line from each child's name to the correct book.

Brett   Aki   Lorenzo   Kate   Zac   Oralia

CHILDREN	BOOKS
Brett	jokes
Aki	cakes
Lorenzo	monsters
Kate	games
Zac	flags
Oralia	space

Clues

1. Lorenzo likes jokes.

2. Kate likes to bake.

3. Oralia likes far away places.

4. Aki does not like monsters or flags.

5. Zac does not like space or monsters.

6. Brett does not like games, jokes, or cakes.

Making Deductions: Travel

Six children from the same neighborhood each travel to school in a different way. Can you find out how each one gets to school?

Directions: Read the clues. Draw a dot to show how each child travels to school. Draw **X**'s on the remaining boxes.

	Brian	Gina	Lawrence	Luna	Taylor	Marianna
car						
bus						
walk						
bicycle						
truck						
van						

Clues:

1. Lawrence likes to walk to school.
2. Taylor hates to walk, so his mother takes him in the car.
3. Luna lives next door to Lawrence and waves to Gina as Gina goes by in a pickup truck.
4. Brian joins his pals on the bus.
5. Gina's friend, who lives next door to Lawrence, rides a bike to school.
6. Marianna likes to sit in the middle seat while riding to school.

Making Deductions: Sports

Children all over the world like to play sports. They like many different kinds of sports: football, soccer, basketball, softball, in-line skating, swimming, and more.

Directions: Read the clues. Draw dots and **X**'s on the chart to match the children with their sports.

	swimming	football	soccer	basketball	baseball	in-line skating
J.J.						
Zoe						
Andy						
Amber						
Raul						
Sierra						

Clues
1. Zoe hates football.
2. Andy likes basketball.
3. Raul likes to pitch in his favorite sport.
4. J.J. likes to play what Zoe hates.
5. Amber is good at kicking the ball to her teammates.
6. Sierra needs a pool for her favorite sport.

Making Deductions: What Day Is It?

Dad is cooking dinner tonight. Find out what day of the week it is.

Directions: Read the clues. Complete the menu. Answer the question.

Menu

Monday _____

Tuesday _____

Wednesday _____

Thursday _____

Friday _____

Saturday _____

Sunday _____

1. Mom fixed pizza on Monday.
2. Dad fixed a salad the day before that.
3. Tess made soup three days after Mom fixed pizza.
4. Tom fixed tacos the day before Tess made soup.
5. Mom fixed pasta the day after Tess made soup.
6. Tess cooked fish the day before Dad fixed a salad.
7. Dad is making chicken today. What day is it? _____

Review

Directions: Read the story. Then, answer the questions.

Randa, Emily, Ali, Dave, Liesl, and Deana all love to read. Every Tuesday, they all go to the library together and pick out their favorite books. Randa likes books about fish. Emily likes books about sports and athletes. Ali likes books about art. Dave likes books about wild animals. Liesl likes books with riddles and puzzles. Deanna likes books about cats and dogs.

1. Circle the main idea:

   Randa, Emily, Ali, Dave, Liesl, and Deana are good friends.

   Randa, Emily, Ali, Dave, Liesl, and Deana all like books.

2. Who do you think might grow up to be an artist?

   _____

3. Who do you think might grow up to be an oceanographer (someone who studies the ocean)?

   _____

4. Who do you think might grow up to be a veterinarian (an animal doctor)?

   _____

5. Who do you think might grow up to be a zookeeper (someone who cares for zoo animals)?

   _____

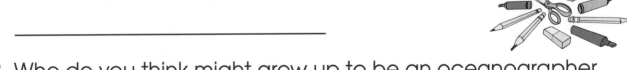

Comprehensive Curriculum - **Grade 2**

Fiction/Nonfiction: Heavy Hitters

Stories that are **fiction** are make-believe.
Stories that are **nonfiction** are true stories.

Directions: Read the stories about two famous baseball players. Then, write **fiction** or **nonfiction** in the baseball bats.

    Even if you are not a baseball fan, you might know who Jackie Robinson was. African American players were not allowed to play in the major leagues. Then, in 1947, Jackie joined the Brooklyn Dodgers. He was the first African American player in the major leagues. People said hateful things to him. But Jackie was strong and did not fight back. He made history and became one of the best major league players ever!

    The Mighty Casey played baseball for the Mudville Nine and was the greatest of all baseball players. He could hit the cover off the ball with the power of a hurricane. But, when the Mudville Nine was behind 4 to 2 in the championship game, Mighty Casey struck out with the bases loaded. There was no joy in Mudville that day, because the Mudville Nine had lost the game.

Nonfiction: Tornado Tips

Directions: Read about tornadoes. Then, follow the instructions.

A tornado begins over land with strong winds and thunderstorms. The spinning air becomes a funnel. It can cause damage. If you are inside, go to the lowest floor of the building. A basement is a safe place. A bathroom or closet in the middle of a building can be a safe place, too. If you are outside, lie in a ditch. Remember, tornadoes are dangerous.

Write five facts about tornadoes.

1. _____

_____

2. _____

_____

3. _____

_____

4. _____

_____

5. _____

_____

Fiction: Hercules

The **setting** is where a story takes place. The characters are the people in a story or play.

Directions: Read about Hercules. Then, answer the questions.

Hercules was born in the warm Atlantic Ocean. He was a very small and weak baby. He wanted to be the strongest hurricane in the world. But he had one problem. He couldn't blow 75-mile-per-hour winds. Hercules blew and blew in the ocean, until one day, his sister, Hola, told him it would be more fun to be a breeze than a hurricane. Hercules agreed. It was a breeze to be a breeze!

1. What is the setting of the story? _____

2. Who are the characters? _____

3. What is the problem? _____

4. How does Hercules solve his problem? _____

_____

Fiction/Nonfiction: The Fourth of July

Directions: Read each story. Then, write whether it is fiction or nonfiction.

One sunny day in July, a dog named Stan ran away from home. He went up one street and down the other looking for fun, but all the yards were empty. Where was everybody? Stan kept walking until he heard the sound of band music and happy people. Stan walked faster until he got to Central Street. There he saw men, women, children, and dogs getting ready to walk in a parade. It was the Fourth of July!

Fiction or nonfiction? _____

Americans celebrate the Fourth of July every year because it is the birthday of the United States of America. On July 4, 1776, the United States won its independence from Great Britain. Today, Americans celebrate this holiday with parades, picnics, and fireworks as they proudly wave the red, white, and blue American flag.

Fiction or nonfiction? _____

Fiction and Nonfiction: Which Is It?

Directions: Read about fiction and nonfiction books. Then, follow the instructions.

    There are many kinds of books. Some books have make-believe stories about princesses and dragons. Some books contain poetry and rhymes, like Mother Goose. These are fiction.

    Some books contain facts about space and plants. And still other books have stories about famous people in history, like Abraham Lincoln. These are nonfiction.

Write **F** for fiction and **NF** for nonfiction.

_____ 1. nursery rhyme

_____ 2. fairy tale

_____ 3. true life story of a famous athlete

_____ 4. Aesop's fables

_____ 5. dictionary entry about foxes

_____ 6. weather report

_____ 7. story about a talking tree

_____ 8. text about how a tadpole becomes a frog

_____ 9. text about animal habitats

_____ 10. riddles and jokes

Writing: My Snake Story

Directions: Write a fictional (make-believe) story about a snake. Make sure to include details and a title.

_____
title

_____

_____

_____

_____

_____

_____

_____

_____

Review: All About You!

Directions: What are some of your interests? Write a story telling what you like to do. Then, on another sheet of paper, draw a picture to go with your story.

_____

_____

_____

_____

_____

_____

_____

_____

_____

_____

_____

Name _____

ABC Order

Directions: Put the words in ABC order on the bags.

grapes _____

bread _____

soup _____

apples _____

napkins _____

rolls _____

lettuce _____

pizza _____

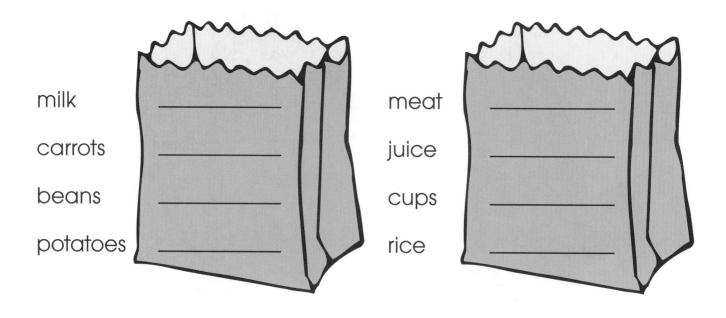

milk _____

carrots _____

beans _____

potatoes _____

meat _____

juice _____

cups _____

rice _____

Alphabetical Order

Directions: Cut out the scoops of ice cream on the bottom. Place them on the correct cone in alphabetical order.

cut ✂ -

lemon

dog

truck

frost

apple

house

ring

Page is blank for cutting exercise on previous page.

ABC Order

Directions: Write each group of words in alphabetical order. If two words start with the same letter, look at the second letter in each word.

Example: **lamb**   **Lamb** comes first because **a** comes before **i**
              light   in the alphabet.

tree   _____

branch   _____

leaf   _____

dish   _____

dog   _____

bone   _____

rain   _____

umbrella   _____

cloud   _____

mail   _____

stamp   _____

slot   _____

Name _____

Sequencing: ABC Order

Directions: Write 1, 2, 3, or 4 on the lines in each row to put the words in ABC order.

Example:

1. __1__ bell   __4__ well   __2__ smell   __3__ tell

2. _____ bite   _____ kite   _____ write   _____ might

3. _____ tar   _____ car   _____ far   _____ bar

4. _____ sand   _____ land   _____ band   _____ fanned

5. _____ sweet   _____ meat   _____ eat   _____ treat

6. _____ hair   _____ pear   _____ tear   _____ wear

7. _____ lake   _____ bake   _____ rake   _____ take

8. _____ round   _____ sound   _____ pound   _____ found

Sequencing: ABC Order

If the first letters of two words are the same, look at the second letters in both words. If the second letters are the same, look at the third letters.

Directions: Write 1, 2, 3, or 4 on the lines in each row to put the words in ABC order.

Example:

1. __1__ candle   __2__ carrot   __4__ duck   __3__ dance

2. _____ cold   _____ hot   _____ carry   _____ hit

3. _____ flash   _____ fan   _____ fun   _____ garden

4. _____ seat   _____ sun   _____ saw   _____ sit

5. _____ row   _____ ring   _____ rock   _____ run

6. _____ truck   _____ turn   _____ twin   _____ talk

7. _____ seven   _____ shoe   _____ soup   _____ smell

Name _____

Sequencing: ABC Order

Directions: Write the following names in ABC order: Oscar, Ali, Lance, Kim, Zane, and Bonita.

_____

_____

_____

_____

_____

_____

Directions: Write the names of six friends or family members in ABC order.

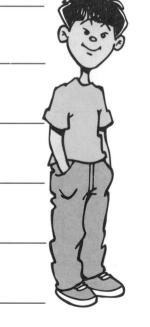

_____

_____

_____

_____

_____

_____

Sequencing: ABC Order

Kwan likes to make rhymes. Help Kwan think of rhyming words.

Directions: Write three words in ABC order that rhyme with each word Kwan wrote.

cap   bet   bill

_____   _____   _____

_____   _____   _____

_____   _____   _____

dog   man   hat

_____   _____   _____

_____   _____   _____

_____   _____   _____

Directions: Write a short poem using some of the rhyming words you wrote.

_____

_____

_____

_____

Synonyms

Words that mean the same or nearly the same are called **synonyms**.

Directions: Read the sentence that tells about the picture. Draw a circle around the word that means the same as the **bold** word.

The child is **unhappy**.

sad   hungry

The flowers are **lovely**.

pretty   green

The baby was very **tired**.

sleepy   hurt

The **funny** clown made us laugh.

silly   glad

The ladybug is so **tiny**.

small   red

We saw a **scary** tiger.

frightening   ugly

Synonyms

Synonyms are words that have almost the same meaning.

Directions: Read the story. Then, fill in the blanks with the synonyms.

| funny | unhappy |
| windy | little |

A New Balloon

It was a breezy day. The wind blew the small child's balloon away. The child was sad. A silly clown gave him a new balloon.

1. It was a _____ day.

2. The wind blew the _____ child's balloon away.

3. The child was _____ .

4. A _____ clown gave him a new balloon.

Name _____

Synonyms

Directions: Read each sentence. Fill in the blanks with the synonyms.

friend	tired	story
presents	little	

I want to go to bed because I am very <u>sleepy</u>. _____

On my birthday, I like to open my <u>gifts</u>. _____

My <u>pal</u> and I like to play together. _____

My favorite <u>tale</u> is *Cinderella*. _____

The mouse was so <u>tiny</u> that it was hard to catch him. _____

Antonyms

Antonyms are words that mean the opposite of another word.

Examples:
 hot and **cold**
 short and **tall**

Directions: Draw a line from each word on the left to its antonym on the right.

sad	white
bottom	stop
black	fat
tall	top
thin	hard
little	found
cold	short
lost	hot
go	big
soft	happy

Antonyms

Antonyms are words that are opposites.

Directions: Read the words next to the pictures. Draw a line to the antonyms.

dark   empty

hairy   dry

closed   happy

dirty   bald

sad   clean

full   light

wet   open

Antonyms: Words

Directions: Read the sentences. Complete each sentence with the correct antonym. Use the clues in the picture and below each sentence. Then, color the picture.

1. Spotty's suitcase is _____ . _____
   (antonym for **closed**)

2. Spotty has a ___ on his face. _____
   (antonym for **frown**)

3. His pillow is _____ . _____
   (antonym for **hard**)

4. His coat is _____ . _____
   (antonym for **little**)

5. Spotty packs his stuffed animal _____ . _____
   (antonym for **first**)

Antonyms: Words and Pictures

Anna and Luke often like to do opposite things. Help them design their new white T-shirts—using opposites, of course.

Directions: Think of a pair of antonyms. Write one on each shirt. Draw pictures on their shirts to match the antonyms.

Antonyms

Words that mean the opposite are called **antonyms**.

Directions: Read the sentence. Write the word from the word box that means the opposite of the **bold** word.

bottom	outside	black	summer	after
light	sister	clean	last	evening

1. Lena has a new baby **brother**. _____

2. The class went **inside** for recess. _____

3. There is a **white** car in the driveway. _____

4. We went to the park **before** dinner. _____

5. Joe's puppy is **dirty**. _____

6. My name is at the **top** of the list. _____

7. I like to play outside in the **winter**. _____

8. I like to take walks in the **morning**. _____

9. The sky was **dark** after the storm. _____

10. Our team is in **first** place. _____

Name _____

Antonyms

Directions: Look at each picture, and read the sentence. Cross out the incorrect word, and write its antonym in the blank.

When it is light, we go
to bed.   _____

When I broke the vase,
it made my mom smile.   _____

The hot chocolate is
very cold, so be careful!   _____

My pants were tight, so
I needed to wear a belt.   _____

The balloons float down
in the sky.   _____

Homophones

Homophones are words that sound alike but are spelled differently and have different meanings. Sometimes, homophones can be more than two words.

Examples:

Pear and **pair** are homophones.
To, **too**, and **two** are three homophones.

Directions: Draw a line from each word on the left to its homophone on the right.

blue	knight
night	too
beet	blew
write	see
hi	meet
two	son
meat	bee
sea	high
be	right
sun	beat

Name _____

Homophones

Directions: Look at each picture. Circle the correct homophone.

deer   dear

blue   blew

two   to

hi   high

by   bye

new   knew

ate   eight

red   read

Homophones

Directions: Write the homophone from the box next to each picture.

| so | see | blew | pear |

sew _____

pair _____

sea _____

blue _____

Homophones

Directions: Read each word. Circle the picture that goes with the word.

1. sun

2. ate

3. buy

4. hi

5. four

6. hear

Homophones

Directions: Match each word with its homophone.

eight	blew
buy	whole
pail	ate
red	pale
hole	read
blue	hour
our	by

Directions: Choose 3 homophone pairs, and write sentences using them.

1. _____

2. _____

3. _____

Homophones: Doggy Birthday Cake

Homophones are words that sound alike but have different spellings and meanings.

Directions: Read the sentences. The bold words are homophones. Then, follow the directions for a doggy birthday cake.

1. The baker **read** a recipe to bake a doggy cake. Color the plate he put it on **red**.

2. Draw a **hole** in the middle of the doggy cake. Then, color the **whole** cake yellow.

3. Look **for** the top of the doggy cake. Draw **four** candles there.

4. In the hole, draw what you think the doggy would really like.

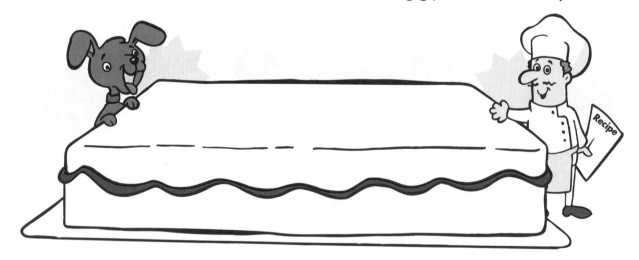

5. Write a sentence using the words **hole** and **whole**.

_____

6. Write a sentence using the words **read** and **red**.

_____

Nouns

A **noun** is the name of a person, place, or thing.

Directions: Read the story, and circle all the nouns. Then, write the nouns next to the pictures below.

Our family likes to go to the park.

_____

_____

We play on the swings.

_____

We eat sandwiches.

_____

We drink lemonade.

_____

We throw the ball to our dog. _____

_____

Then, we go home. _____

Nouns

Directions: Look through a magazine. Cut out pictures of nouns, and glue them below. Write the name of the noun next to the picture.

Proper Nouns

Proper nouns are the names of specific people, places, and things. Proper nouns begin with a capital letter.

Directions: Write the proper nouns on the lines below. Use capital letters at the beginning of each word.

logan, utah

mike smith

_____

lynn cramer

buster

_____

fluffy

chicago, illinois

_____

Proper Nouns

The days of the week and the months of the year are always capitalized.

Directions: Circle the words that are written correctly. Write the words that need capital letters on the lines below.

sunday	July	Wednesday	may	december
friday	tuesday	june	august	Monday
january	February	March	Thursday	April
September	saturday	October		

Days of the Week   **Months of the Year**

1. _____   1. _____

2. _____   2. _____

3. _____   3. _____

4. _____   4. _____

5. _____

Capitalization

The first word and all of the important words in a title begin with a capital letter.

Directions: Write the book titles on the lines below. Use capital letters.

1. _____

2. _____

3. _____

4. _____

5. _____

6. _____

Name _____

Review

Directions: Write capital letters where they should appear in the sentences below.

Example: joe can play in january.

Joe can play in January.

1. we celebrate thanksgiving on the fourth thursday in november.

_____

_____

2. in june, michelle and mark will go camping every friday.

_____

_____

3. on mondays in october, i will take piano lessons.

_____

_____

Plural Nouns

Plural nouns name more than one person, place, or thing.

Directions: Read the words in the box. Write the words in the correct column.

hats	girl	cows	kittens	melon
spoons	glass	book	horse	trees

_____   _____

_____   _____

_____   _____

_____   _____

_____   _____

Plurals

Plurals are words that mean more than one. To make a word plural, add **s** or **es** to it. In some words ending in **y**, the **y** changes to an **i** before adding **es**. For example, **baby** changes to **babies**.

Directions: Look at the following lists of plural words. Next to each, write the word that means one. The first one has been done for you.

foxes   **fox** _____

bushes _____

dresses _____

chairs _____

shoes _____

stories _____

puppies _____

matches _____

cars _____

glasses _____

balls _____

candies _____

wishes _____

boxes _____

ladies _____

bunnies _____

desks _____

dishes _____

pencils _____

trucks _____

Pronouns

Pronouns are words that can be used instead of nouns. **She**, **he**, **it**, and **they** are pronouns.

Directions: Read the sentence. Then, write the sentence again, using **she**, **he**, **it**, or **they** in the blank.

1. Dan likes funny jokes. _____ likes funny jokes.

2. Mei and Sam went to the zoo. _____ went to the zoo.

3. My dog likes to dig in the yard. _____ likes to dig in the yard.

4. Sara is a very good dancer. _____ is a very good dancer.

5. Levi and Leo are twins. _____ are twins.

Comprehensive Curriculum - **Grade 2**

Subjects

The **subject** of a sentence is the person, place, or thing the sentence is about.

Directions: Underline the subject in each sentence.

Example: Mom read a book.

   (Think: Who is the sentence about? <u>Mom</u>)

1. The bird flew away.

2. The kite was high in the air.

3. The children played a game.

4. The books fell down.

5. The monkey climbed a tree.

Compound Subjects

Two similar sentences can be joined into one sentence if the predicate is the same. A **compound subject** is made of two subjects joined together by a conjunction, such as **and**.

Example: Jamie can sing.
Sofia can sing.

Jamie **and** Sofia can sing.

Directions: Combine the sentences. Write the new sentence on the line.

1. The cats are my pets.
   The dogs are my pets.

_____

2. Chairs are in the store.
   Tables are in the store.

_____

3. Myles can ride a bike.
   Jack can ride a bike.

_____

Verbs

A **verb** is the action word in a sentence. Verbs tell what something does.

Example: Run, **sleep**, and **jump** are verbs.

Directions: Circle the verbs in the sentences below.

1. We play baseball every day.

2. Maddy pitches the ball very well.

3. Marco swings the bat harder than anyone.

4. Chris slides into home base.

5. Laura hit a home run.

Verbs

Verbs tell when something happens. Add **ed** to verbs to tell that something has already happened.

Example: Today, we will **play**. Yesterday, we **played**.

Directions: Write the correct verb in the blank.

1. Today, I will _____ my dog, Fritz.
   wash   washed

2. Last week, Fritz _____ when we said, "Bath time, Fritz."
   cry   cried

3. My sister likes to _____ wash Fritz.
   help   helped

4. One time she _____ Fritz by herself.
   clean   cleaned

5. Fritz will _____ a lot better after his bath.
   look   looked

Name _____

Verbs

Directions: Write each verb in the correct column.

| rake | talked | look | hopped | skip |
| cooked | fished | call | clean | sewed |

Yesterday   ## Today

_____   _____

_____   _____

_____   _____

_____   _____

_____   _____

Predicates

The **predicate** is the part of the sentence that tells about the action.

Directions: Circle the predicate in each sentence.

Example: The boys ran on the playground.

(Think: The boys did what? (Ran))

1. The woman painted a picture.

2. The puppy chases his ball.

3. The students went to school.

4. Butterflies fly in the air.

5. The baby wants a drink.

Compound Predicates

A **compound predicate** is made by joining two sentences that have the same subject. The predicates are usually joined together by the word **and**.

Example: Evan can jump.
Evan can run.

Evan can <u>run</u> **and** <u>jump</u>.

Directions: Combine the sentences. Write the new sentence on the line.

1. The dog can roll over.
   The dog can bark.

_____

2. My mom plays with me.
   My mom reads with me.

_____

3. Tara is tall.
   Tara is smart.

_____

Subjects and Predicates

The **subject** of the sentence is the person, place, or thing the sentence is about. The **predicate** is the part of the sentence that describes the subject or tells what the subject does.

Directions: Draw a line between the subject and the predicate. Underline the noun in the subject, and circle the verb in the predicate.

Example: The furry <u>cat</u> | (ate) food.

1. Hannah walks to school.

2. The bus driver drove the children.

3. The school bell rang very loudly.

4. The teacher spoke to the students.

5. The girls opened their books.

Compound Subjects and Predicates

The following sentences have either a compound subject or a compound predicate.

Directions: If the sentence has a compound subject (more than one thing doing the action), **underline** the subject. If it has a compound predicate (more than one action), **circle** the predicate.

Examples: <u>Bats and owls</u> like the night.

The fox (slinks and spies.)

1. Raccoons and mice steal food.

2. Monkeys and birds sleep in trees.

3. Elephants wash and play in the river.

4. Bears eat honey and scratch trees.

5. Owls hoot and hunt.

Compound Subjects and Predicates

Directions: Write one new sentence using a compound subject or predicate.

Example: The boy will jump. The girl will jump.

The <u>boy and girl</u> will jump.

1. The clowns run. The clowns play.

_____

2. The dogs dance. The bears dance.

_____

3. Seals bark. Seals clap.

_____

4. The girls play. The girls laugh.

_____

Name _____

Parts of a Sentence

Directions: Draw a circle around the noun, the naming part of the sentence. Draw a line under the verb, the action part of the sentence.

Example: (John) <u>drinks</u> juice every morning.

1. Our class skates at the roller-skating rink.

2. Mason and Sadie go very fast.

3. Carson eats hot dogs.

4. Maya dances to the music.

5. Everyone likes the skating rink.

Parts of a Sentence

Directions: Look at the pictures. Draw a line from the naming part of the sentence to the action part to complete the sentence.

The boy   delivered the mail.

A small dog   threw a football.

The mailman   fell down.

The goalie   chased the ball.

Comprehensive Curriculum - **Grade 2**

Name _____

Adjectives

Adjectives are words that tell more about a person, place, or thing.

Examples: cold, fuzzy, dark

Directions: Circle the adjectives in the sentences.

1. The juicy apple is on the plate.

2. The furry dog is eating a bone.

3. It was a sunny day.

4. The kitten drinks warm milk.

5. The baby has a loud cry.

Adjectives

Directions: Choose an adjective from the box to fill in the blanks.

hungry	sunny	busy	funny
fresh	deep	pretty	cloudy

1. It is a _____ day on the Browns' farm.

2. Mr. Brown is a very _____ man.

3. Mrs. Brown likes to feed the _____ chickens.

4. Every day she collects the _____ eggs.

5. The ducks swim in the _____ pond.

Name _____

Adjectives

Directions: Think of your own adjectives. Write a story about Fluffy the cat.

1. Fluffy is a _____ cat.

2. The color of his fur is _____ .

3. He likes to chew on my _____ shoes.

4. He likes to eat _____ cat food.

5. I like Fluffy because he is so _____.

Articles

Articles are small words that help us to better understand nouns. **A** and **an** are articles. We use **an** before a word that begins with a vowel. We use **a** before a word that begins with a consonant.

Example: We looked in **a** nest. It had **an** eagle in it.

Directions: Read the sentences. Write **a** or **an** in the blank.

1. I found _____ book.

2. It had a story about _____ ant in it.

3. In the story, _____ lion gave three wishes to _____ ant.

4. The ant's first wish was to ride _____ elephant.

5. The second wish was to ride _____ alligator.

6. The last wish was _____ wish for three more wishes.

Name _____

Sentences and Non-Sentences

A **sentence** tells a complete idea. It has a noun and a verb. It begins with a capital letter and has punctuation at the end.

Directions: Circle the group of words if it is a sentence.

1. Grass is a green plant.

2. Mowing the lawn.

3. Grass grows in fields and lawns.

4. Tickle the feet.

5. Sheep, cows, and horses eat grass.

6. We like to play in.

7. My sister likes to mow the lawn.

8. A picnic on the grass.

9. My dog likes to roll in the grass.

10. Plant flowers around.

Sentences and Non-Sentences

Directions: Circle the group of words if it tells a complete idea.

1. A secret is something you know.

2. My mom's birthday gift is a secret.

3. No one else.

4. If you promise not to.

5. I'll tell you a secret.

6. Something nobody knows.

Statements

Statements are sentences that tell us something. They begin with a capital letter and end with a period.

Directions: Write the sentences on the lines below. Begin each sentence with a capital letter, and end it with a period.

1. we like to ride our bikes

_____

2. we go down the hill very fast

_____

3. we keep our bikes shiny and clean

_____

4. we know how to change the tires

_____

Name _____

Surprising Sentences

Surprising sentences tell a strong feeling and end with an exclamation point. A surprising sentence may be only one or two words showing fear, surprise, or pain. **Example: Oh, no!**

Directions: Put a period at the end of the sentences that tell something. Put an exclamation point at the end of the sentences that tell a strong feeling. Put a question mark at the end of the sentences that ask a question.

1. The cheetah can run very fast

2. Wow

3. Look at that cheetah go

4. Can you run fast

5. Oh, my

6. You're faster than I am

7. Let's run together

8. We can run as fast as a cheetah

9. What fun

10. Do you think cheetahs get tired

Commands

Commands tell someone to do something. **Example: Be careful.** It can also be written as "Be careful!" if it tells a strong feeling.

Directions: Put a period at the end of the command sentences. Use an exclamation point if the sentence tells a strong feeling. Write your own commands on the lines below.

1. Clean your room

2. Now

3. Be careful with your goldfish

4. Watch out

5. Be a little more careful

_____

_____

Questions

Questions are sentences that ask something. They begin with a capital letter and end with a question mark.

Directions: Write the questions on the lines below. Begin each sentence with a capital letter, and end it with a question mark.

1. will you be my friend

_____

2. what is your name

_____

3. are you eight years old

_____

4. do you like rainbows

_____

Making Inferences: Writing Questions

Tommy likes to answer questions. He knows the answers, but you need to write the questions.

Directions: Write two questions for each answer.

Answer: It has four legs.

1. _____?

_____?

Answer: It lives on a farm.

2. _____?

_____?

Answer: It is soft.

3. _____?

_____?

Making Inferences: Writing Questions

Toban and Sean use many colors when they paint.

Directions: Write two questions for each answer.

Answer: It is red.

1. _____ ?

_____ ?

Answer: It is purple.

2. _____ ?

_____ ?

Answer: It is green.

3. _____ ?

_____ ?

Name _____

Making Inferences: Writing Questions

Tomas likes sports. He enjoys meeting athletes. He would like to be a sports reporter someday.

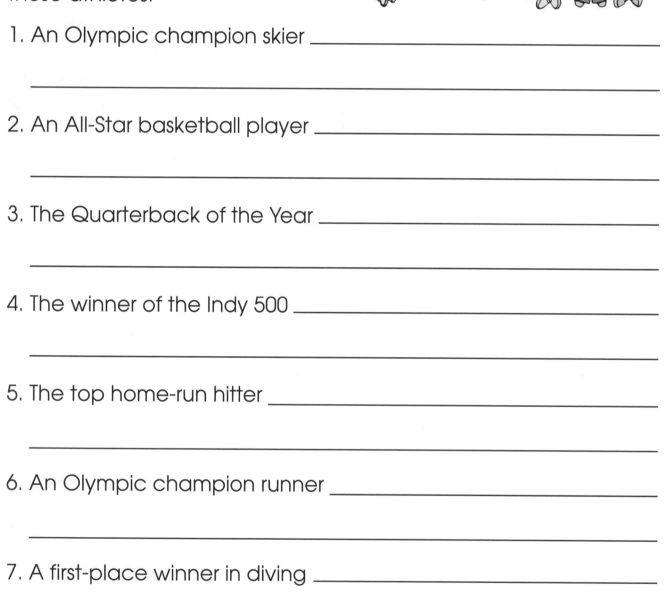

Directions: Write a question Tomas could ask each of these athletes.

1. An Olympic champion skier _____

_____

2. An All-Star basketball player _____

_____

3. The Quarterback of the Year _____

_____

4. The winner of the Indy 500 _____

_____

5. The top home-run hitter _____

_____

6. An Olympic champion runner _____

_____

7. A first-place winner in diving _____

_____

Making Inferences: Writing Questions

Erin found many solid shapes in her house.

Directions: Write two questions for each answer.

Answer: It is a cube.

1. _____?

_____?

Answer: It is a cylinder.

2. _____?

_____?

Answer: It is a sphere.

3. _____?

_____?

Making Inferences: Point of View

Chelsea likes to pretend she will meet famous people someday. She would like to ask them many questions.

Directions: Write a question you think Chelsea would ask if she met these people.

1. an actor in a popular, new film _____

   _____?

2. an Olympic gold medal winner _____

   _____?

3. an alien from outer space _____

   _____?

Directions: Now, write the answers these people might have given to Chelsea's questions.

4. an actor in a popular, new film _____

   _____

5. an Olympic gold medal winner _____

   _____

6. an alien from outer space _____

   _____

Making Inferences: Point of View

Ellen likes animals. Someday, she might want to be a veterinarian.

Directions: Write one question you think Ellen would ask each of these animals if she could speak their language.

1. a giraffe _____?

2. a mouse _____?

3. a shark _____?

4. a hippopotamus _____?

5. a penguin _____?

6. a gorilla _____?

7. an eagle _____?

Directions: Now, write the answers you think these animals might have given Ellen.

8. a giraffe _____

9. a mouse _____

10. a shark _____

11. a hippopotamus _____

12. a penguin _____

13. a gorilla _____

14. an eagle _____

Creative Writing

Directions: Look at the picture below. Write a story about the picture.

_____

_____

_____

_____

_____

Ownership

Add **'s** to nouns (people, places, or things) to tell who or what owns something.

Directions: Read the sentences. Fill in the blanks to show ownership.

Example: The doll belongs to **Sara**.

It is **Sara's** doll.

1. Sparky has a red collar.

 collar is red.

2. Jimmy has a blue coat.

 coat is blue.

3. The tail of the cat is short.

The _____ tail is short.

4. The name of my mother is Karen.

My _____ name is Karen.

Ownership

Directions: Read the sentences. Choose the correct word, and write it in each sentence below.

1. The _____ lunchbox is broken.   boys   boy's

2. The _____ played in the cage.   gerbil's   gerbils

3. _____ hair is brown.   Anns   Ann's

4. The _____ ran in the field.   horse's   horses

5. My _____ coat is torn.   sister's   sisters

6. The _____ fur is brown.   cats   cat's

7. Three _____ flew past our window.   birds   bird's

8. The _____ paws are muddy.   dogs   dog's

9. The _____ neck is long.   giraffes   giraffe's

10. The _____ are big and powerful.   lion's   lions

Is, *Are*, and *Am*

Is, **are**, and **am** are special action words that tell us something is happening now.

Use **am** with **I**. **Example: I am.**
Use **is** to tell about one person or thing. **Example: He is.**
Use **are** to tell about more than one. **Example: We are.**
Use **are** with **you**. **Example: You are.**

Directions: Write **is**, **are**, or **am** in the sentences below.

1. My friends _____ helping me build a tree house.

2. It _____ in my backyard.

3. We _____ using hammers, wood, and nails.

4. It _____ a very hard job.

5. I _____ lucky to have good friends.

Was and Were

Was and **were** tell about something that already happened.

Use **was** to tell about one person or thing. **Example: I was**, he **was**. Use **were** to tell about more than one person or thing or when using the word **you**. **Example:** We **were**, you **were**.

Directions: Write **was** or **were** in each sentence.

1. Lily _____ eight years old on her birthday.

2. Colin and Charley _____ happy to be at the party.

3. Megan _____ too shy to sing "Happy Birthday."

4. Ben _____ sorry he dropped his cake.

5. All of the children _____ happy to be invited.

Go, Going, and Went

Use **go** or **going** to tell about now or later. Sometimes, **going** is used with the words **am** or **are**. Use **went** to tell about something that already happened.

Directions: Write **go**, **going**, or **went** in the sentences below.

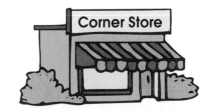

1. Today, I will _____ to the store.

2. Yesterday, we _____ shopping.

3. I am _____ to take Muffy to the vet.

4. Colin and Charley _____ to the party.

5. They are _____ to have a good day.

Have, Has, and Had

Use **have** and **has** to tell about now. Use **had** to tell about something that already happened.

Directions: Write **has**, **have**, or **had** in the sentences below.

1. We _____ three cats at home.

2. Ginger _____ brown fur.

3. Bucky and Charlie _____ gray fur.

4. My friend Antonio _____ one cat, but it ran away.

5. Antonio _____ a new cat now.

See, Saw, and Sees

Use **see** or **sees** to tell about now. Use **saw** to tell about something that already happened.

Directions: Write **see**, **sees**, or **saw** in the sentences below.

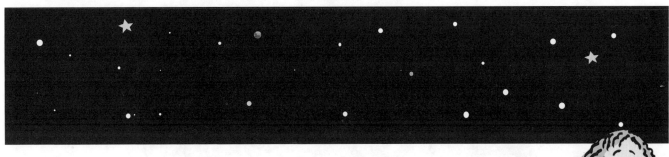

1. Last night, we _____ the stars.

2. John can _____ the stars from his window.

3. He _____ them every night.

4. Last week, he _____ the Big Dipper.

5. Can you _____ it in the night sky, too?

6. If you _____ it, you would remember it!

7. John _____ it often now.

8. How often do you _____ it?

Eat, Eats, and Ate

Use **eat** or **eats** to tell about now. Use **ate** to tell about what already happened.

Directions: Write **eat**, **eats**, or **ate** in the sentences below.

1. We like to _____ in the lunchroom.

2. Today, my teacher will _____ in a different room.

3. She _____ with the other teachers.

4. Yesterday, we _____ pizza, pears, and peas.

5. Today, we will _____ turkey and potatoes.

Leave, Leaves, and Left

Use **leave** and **leaves** to tell about now. Use **left** to tell about what already happened.

Directions: Write **leave**, **leaves**, or **left** in the sentences below.

1. Last winter, we _____ seeds in the bird feeder every day.

2. My mother likes to _____ food out for the squirrels.

3. When it rains, she _____ bread for the birds.

4. Yesterday, she _____ popcorn for the birds.

Comprehensive Curriculum - **Grade 2**

Learning Dictionary Skills

A **dictionary** is a book that gives the meaning of words. It also tells how words sound. Words in a dictionary are in ABC order. That makes them easier to find. A picture dictionary lists a word, a picture of the word, and its meaning.

Directions: Look at this page from a picture dictionary. Then, answer the questions.

baby

A very young child

band

A group of people who play music

bank

A place where money is kept

bark

The sound a dog makes

berry

A small, juicy fruit

board

A flat piece of wood

1. What is a small, juicy fruit? _____

2. What is a group of people who play music? _____

3. What is the name for a very young child? _____

4. What is a flat piece of wood called? _____

Learning Dictionary Skills

Directions: Look at this page from a picture dictionary. Then, answer the questions.

safe

A metal box

sea

A body of water

seed

The beginning of a plant

sheep

An animal that has wool

skate

A shoe with wheels or a blade on it

store

A place where items are sold

snowstorm

A time when much snow falls

squirrel

A small animal with a bushy tail

stone

A rock

1. What kind of animal has wool? _____

2. What do you call a shoe with wheels on it? _____

3. When a lot of snow falls, what is it called? _____

4. What is a small animal with a bushy tail? _____

5. What is a place where items are sold? _____

6. When a plant starts, what is it called? _____

Name _____

Learning Dictionary Skills

Directions: Look at this page from a picture dictionary. Then, answer the questions.

table

Furniture with legs and a flat top

tail

A slender part that is on the back of an animal

teacher

A person who teaches lessons

telephone

A machine that sends and receives sounds

ticket

A paper slip or card that allows someone to enter an event

tiger

An animal with stripes

1. Who is a person who teaches lessons? _____

2. What is the name of an animal with stripes? _____

3. What is a piece of furniture with legs and a flat top? _____

4. What is the definition of a ticket?

_____

5. What is a machine that sends and receives sounds?

_____

Learning Dictionary Skills

The **guide words** at the top of a page in a dictionary tell you what the first and last words on the page will be. Only words that come in ABC order between those two words will be on that page. **Guide words** help you find the page you need to look up a word.

Directions: Write each word from the box in ABC order between each pair of guide words.

faint	far	fence	feed	farmer
fan	feet	farm	family	face

face   **fence**

_____   _____

_____   _____

_____   _____

_____   _____

Learning Dictionary Skills

Directions: Write each word from the box in ABC order between each pair of guide words.

fierce	fix	fight	first	few
fish	fill	flush	flat	finish

few

flush

_____

_____

_____

_____

_____

_____

_____

_____

_____

_____

Learning Dictionary Skills

Directions: Create your own dictionary page. Include guide words at the top. Write the words with their meanings in ABC order.

_____
guide word

_____
guide word

1. _____
word

4. _____
word

_____

_____

_____

_____

2. _____
word

5. _____
word

_____

_____

_____

_____

3. _____
word

6. _____
word

_____

_____

_____

_____

Learning Dictionary Skills

When words have more than one meaning, the meanings are numbered in a dictionary.

Directions: Read the meanings of **tag**. Write the number of the correct definition after each sentence.

tag

1. A small strip or tab attached to something else

2. To label

3. To follow closely and constantly

4. A game of chase

1. We will play a game of tag after we study. _____

2. I will tag this coat with its price. _____

3. My little brother will tag along with us. _____

4. My mother already took off the price tag. _____

5. The tag on the toy said, "For Sale." _____

6. Do not tag that tree. _____

Silly Sentences!

Directions: Cut out the binoculars. Cut out the beginning and ending sentence strips on the next page. Thread the strips through the lenses to make sentences. Write each sentence on a piece of paper. Draw a picture to illustrate your silly sentences. Staple your sentences and illustrations into a book to share.

cut ✂ -

cut _____
cut _____

cut _____
cut _____

Page is blank for cutting exercise on previous page.

Cats

Boats

Flowers

Birds

Horses

Garbage cans

Some trees

Children

Snakes

live in nests.

read books.

have apples.

smell pretty.

can slither.

are playful.

smell stinky.

float in water.

eat hay.

Page is blank for cutting exercise on previous page.

SPELLING

Number Words

Directions: Write each number word beside the correct picture. Then, write it again.

Example:

<u>six six</u> _____

| one | two | three | four | five | six | seven | eight | nine | ten |

_____

_____

_____

_____

_____

_____

_____

_____

Number Words

Directions: Write the correct number words in the blanks.

one two three four five six seven eight nine ten

Add a letter to each of these words to make a number word.

Example:

even   on   tree

seven   _____   _____

Change a letter to make these words into number words.

Example:

live   fix   line

five   _____   _____

Write the number words that sound the same as these.

Example:

ate   to   for

eight   _____   _____

Write the number word you did not use: _____

Name _____

Number Words: Asking Sentences

Directions: Write an asking sentence about each picture. Begin each sentence with **How many**. Then, answer your question. Begin each sentence with a capital letter, and end it with a period or a question mark.

one two three four five six seven eight nine ten

Example:

How many cookies does the boy have? He has six cookies.

_____

_____

_____

_____

_____

Number Words: Sentences

Directions: Change the telling sentences into asking sentences. Change the asking sentences into telling sentences. Begin each one with a capital letter, and end it with a period or a question mark.

Examples:

Is she eating the grapes?

She is eating the grapes.

He is bringing one truck.

Is he bringing one truck?

1. Is he painting two blue birds?

_____

2. Did she find four apples?

_____

3. She will be six on her birthday.

_____

Short *A* Words: Rhyming Words

Short a is the sound you hear in the word **math**.

Directions: Use the **short a** words in the box to write rhyming words.

lamp	fat	bat	van
path	can	cat	Dan
math	stamp	fan	sat

1. Write four words that rhyme with **mat**.

_____   _____

_____   _____

2. Write two words that rhyme with **bath**.

_____   _____

3. Write two words that rhyme with **damp**.

_____   _____

4. Write four words that rhyme with **pan**.

_____   _____

_____   _____

Short *A* Words: Sentences

Directions: Use a word from the box to complete each sentence.

fat	path	lamp	can
van	stamp	Dan	math
sat	cat	fan	bat

Example:

1. The _____ lamp _____ had a pink shade.

2. The bike _____ led us to the park.

3. I like to add in _____ class.

4. The cat is very _____.

5. The _____ of beans was hard to open.

6. The envelope needed a _____.

7. He swung the _____ and hit the ball.

8. The _____ blew air around.

9. My mom drives a blue _____.

10. I _____ in the backseat.

Name _____

Long A Words

Long a is a vowel sound that says its own name. **Long a** can be spelled **ai**, as in the word **mail**, **ay**, as in the word **say**, and **a** with a **silent e** at the end of a word, as in the word **same**.

Directions: Say each word, and listen for the **long a** sound. Then, write each word, and underline the letters that make the **long a** vowel sound.

mail	bake	train
game	day	sale
paint	play	name
made	gray	tray

1. _____

2. _____

3. _____

4. _____

5. _____

6. _____

7. _____

8. _____

9. _____

10. _____

11. _____

12. _____

Long *A* Words: Rhyming Words

Long a is the vowel sound you hear in the word **cake**.

Directions: Use the **long a** words in the box to write rhyming words.

paint	gray	train	tray
mail	day	sale	play
game	made	name	bake

1. Write the word that rhymes with **make**.

_____

2. Write the words that rhyme with **hail**.

_____   _____

3. Write the words that rhyme with **say**.

_____   _____

_____   _____

4. Write the word that rhymes with **shade**.

_____

5. Write the words that rhyme with **same**.

_____   _____

Name _____

Long *A* Words: Sentence Order

Directions: Write the words in order so that each sentence tells a complete idea. Begin each sentence with a capital letter, and end it with a period or a question mark.

1. plate was on the cake a

_____

2. like you would to play a game

_____

3. gray around the a corner train came

_____

4. was on mail Bob's name the

_____

5. sail for on day we went a nice a

_____

Short *O* Words

Short o is the vowel sound you hear in the word **pot**.

Directions: Say each word, and listen for the **short o** sound. Then, write each word, and underline the letter that makes the **short o** sound.

hot	box	sock	mop
stop	not	fox	cot
Bob	rock	clock	lock

1. _____

2. _____

3. _____

4. _____

5. _____

6. _____

7. _____

8. _____

9. _____

10. _____

11. _____

12. _____

Comprehensive Curriculum - **Grade 2**

Name _____

Short *O* Words: Rhyming Words

Short o is the vowel sound you hear in the word **got**.

Directions: Use the **short o** words in the box to write rhyming words.

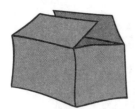

hot	rock	lock	cot
stop	sock	fox	mop
box	mob	clock	Bob

1. Write the words that rhyme with **dot**.

_____   _____

2. Write the words that rhyme with **socks**.

_____   _____

3. Write the words that rhyme with **hop**.

_____   _____

4. Write the words that rhyme with **dock**.

_____   _____

_____   _____

5. Write the words that rhyme with **cob**.

_____   _____

Long *O* Words

Long o is a vowel sound that says its own name. **Long o** can be spelled **oa**, as in the word **float**, or **o** with a **silent e** at the end, as in **cone**.

Directions: Say each word, and listen for the **long o** sound. Then, write each word, and underline the letters that make the **long o** sound.

rope	coat	soap	wrote
note	hope	boat	cone
bone	pole	phone	hole

1. _____

2. _____

3. _____

4. _____

5. _____

6. _____

7. _____

8. _____

9. _____

10. _____

11. _____

12. _____

Name _____

Long *O* Words: Rhyming Words

Long o is the vowel sound you hear in the word **home**.

Directions: Use the **long o** words in the box to write rhyming words.

rope	soap	coat	wrote
note	boat	hope	cone
bone	phone	pole	hole

1. Write the words that rhyme with **mope**.

_____ _____ _____

2. Write the words that rhyme with **tote**.

_____ _____

_____ _____

3. Write the words that rhyme with **lone**.

_____ _____ _____

4. Write the words that rhyme with **goal**.

_____ _____

Long *O* Words: Sentences

Directions: Draw a line from the first part of the sentence to the part that completes the sentence.

1. Do you know

in the water.

2. The dog

was in the tree.

3. The boat floats

who wrote the note?

4. I hope the phone

has a bone.

5. Ebony's ice-cream cone

rings soon for me!

6. The rope swing

a coat in the cold.

7. I had to wear

was melting.

Name ______________________

Animal Words

Directions: Write the animal names twice beside each picture.

fox	rabbit	bear	squirrel	mouse	deer

Example:

squirrel squirrel

rabbit

bear

mouse

fox

deer

Animal Words

Directions: Circle the word in each sentence that is not spelled correctly. Then, write it correctly.

| squirrel | bears | rabbit | deer | fox | mouse |

Example:

Animals like to live in (threes.)   _trees_

1. Bares do not eat people.

2. The squirel found a nut.

3. Sometimes, a little moose might get into your house.

4. Dear eat leaves and grass.

5. A focks has a bushy tail.

6. One day, a rabitt came into our yard.

Animal Words: More Than One

To show more than one of something, add **s** to most words.

Example: one dog – **two dogs**   one book – **two books**

But some words are different. For words that end with **x**, use **es** to show two.

Example: one fox – **two foxes**   one box – **two boxes**

The spelling of some words changes a lot when there are two.

Example: one mouse – **two mice**

Some words stay the same, even when you mean two of something.

Example: one deer – **two deer**   one fish – **two fish**

Directions: Complete the sentences below with the correct word.

1. The  run fast.   _____

2. The  are eating.   _____

3. Have you seen any  today?   _____

4. Where do the  live?   _____

5. Did you ever have  for pets? _____

Animal Words: More Than One

Directions: Write the two sentences below as one sentence. Remember the special spelling of **fox**, **mouse**, and **deer** when there are more than one.

Example:

I saw a mouse. You saw a mouse.

We saw two mice.

1. Julie petted a deer.
   Matt petted a deer.

_____

_____

2. Avi colored a fox.
   Nora colored a fox.

_____

_____

Animal Words: Kinds of Sentences

Another name for an asking sentence is a **question**.

Directions: Use the words in the box to write a telling sentence. Then, use the words to write a question.

Example:

a	mouse	I	see
the	bed	under	do

Telling sentence:

I see a mouse under the bed.

Question:

Do I see a mouse under the bed?

in	live
these	woods
bears	do

Telling sentence:

_____

Question:

_____

Animal Words: Sentences

Directions: Read the sentences on each line, and draw a line between them. Then, write each sentence again on the lines below. Begin each one with a capital letter, and put a period or question mark at the end.

Example:

why do squirrels hide nuts | they eat them in the winter

Why do squirrels hide nuts?
They eat them in the winter.

1. bears sleep in the winter they don't need food then

_____

_____

2. he said he saw a fox do you think he did

_____

_____

Name _____

Review

Directions: Complete each line of the poem below with a word from the box. Make sure each line rhymes.

deer	fox	house	here	mouse	box

A little gray _____

Once ran through my _____ .

Then, a bushy-tailed _____

Ran into a _____ .

Last came a _____ .

What was he doing _____ ?

Now, make your own poem using the words **bear** and **there**.

_____

_____

Family Words

Directions: This is Andy's **family tree**. It shows all the people in his family. Use the words in the box to finish writing the names in Andy's family tree.

grandmother	mother
grandfather	father
aunt	uncle
brother	sister

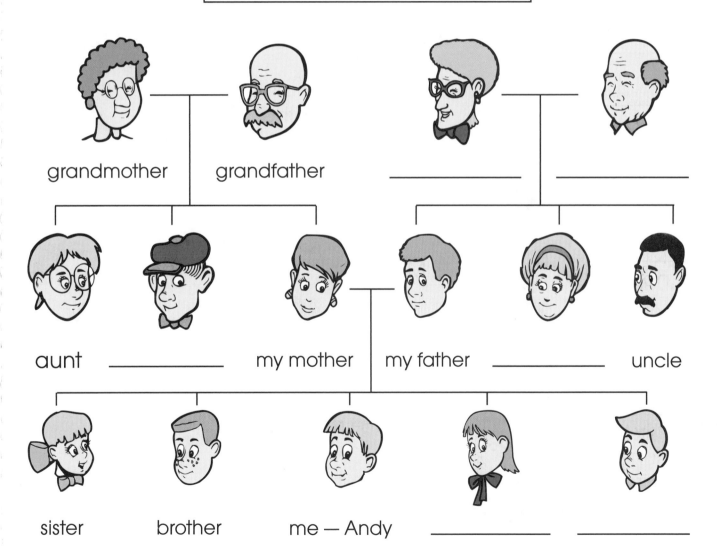

grandmother   grandfather   _____   _____

aunt   _____   my mother   my father   _____   uncle

sister   brother   me — Andy   _____   _____

Family Words

Some words tell how a person looks or feels. These are called **describing** words, or **adjectives**.

Directions: Help Andy write about the people in his family. In each box, cross out the word that does not tell about the picture next to it. Finish the sentence using the other two describing words.

Example:

| ~~asleep~~ |
| funny |
| tall |

My aunt

is tall and funny.

| fast |
| happy |
| smiling |

1. My grandmother

_____

| hot |
| broken |
| tired |

2. My uncle

_____

| thirsty |
| hungry |
| hard |

3. My little brother

_____

Family Words: Joining Words

Joining words often join two sentences to make one long sentence. Three words help do this:

and — if both sentences are much the same.
Example: I took my dog for a walk, **and** I played with my cat.

but — if the second sentence says something different from the first sentence. Sometimes, the second sentence tells why you can't do the first sentence.
Example: I want to play outside, **but** it is raining.

or — if each sentence names a different choice.
Example: You could eat your cookie, **or** you could give it to me.

Directions: Use the word given to join the two short sentences into one longer sentence.

Example: (but)
My aunt lives far away. She calls me often.

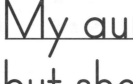

My aunt lives far away but she calls me often.

1. **(and)**
My sister had a birthday. She got a new bike.

_____

_____

2. **(or)**
We can play outside. We can play inside.

_____

_____

Family Words: Joining Words

Directions: Read each pair of sentences. Then, join them with **and**, **but**, or **or**.

1. My uncle likes popcorn.
   He does not like peanuts.

   _____

   _____

2. He could read a book.
   He could tell me his own story.

   _____

   _____

3. My little brother is sleepy.
   He wants to go to bed.

   _____

   _____

Family Words: Completing a Story

Directions: Write family words in the blanks to complete the story.

One day, my family had a picnic. My _____

baked chicken. _____ baked some rolls.

My _____ Jack brought corn. My

_____ made something green and white in a big dish.

I ate the chicken my _____ brought. I had two

rolls made by my _____. My

_____ gave me some corn. I liked it all! Then my

_____ and I looked in the dish my

_____ had brought. "Did you try it?" I asked him.

"You're my big _____," he said. "You try it!" I put a

tiny bit in my mouth. It tasted good! But the dish was almost empty.

"It's terrible!" I said. "I'll eat the rest of it so you won't have to. That's

what a big _____ is for!" My _____

watched me eat it all. I tried not to look too happy!

Name _____

Short *E* Words

Short e is the vowel sound you hear in the word **pet**.

Directions: Say each word, and listen for the **short e** sound. Then, write each word, and underline the letter that makes the **short e** sound.

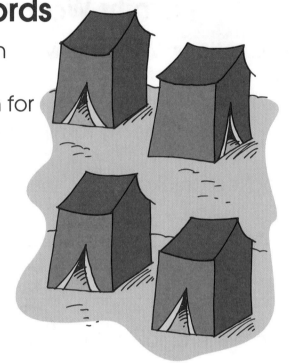

get	Meg	rest	tent
red	spent	test	help
bed	pet	when	best

1. _____

2. _____

3. _____

4. _____

5. _____

6. _____

7. _____

8. _____

9. _____

10. _____

11. _____

12. _____

Short *E* Words: Rhyming Words

Short e is the vowel sound you hear in the word **egg**.

Directions: Use the **short e** words in the box to write rhyming words.

get	test	pet	help
let	head	spent	red
best	tent	rest	bed

1. Write the words that rhyme with **fed**.

_____   _____   _____

2. Write the words that rhyme with **bent**.

_____   _____

3. Write the words that rhyme with **west**.

_____   _____   _____

4. Write the words that rhyme with **bet**.

_____   _____   _____

Short *E* Words: Sentences

Directions: Write the correct **short e** word in each sentence.

get	Meg	rest	bed	spent	best
test	help	head	pet	red	tent

1. Of all my crayons, I like the color _____

the _____ !

2. I always make my _____ when I _____ up.

3. My new hat keeps my _____ warm.

4. _____ wanted a dog for a _____ .

5. When we go camping, my job is to _____ put up

the _____ .

6. I have a _____ in math tomorrow, so I want to get

a good night's _____ .

Long *E* Words

Long e is the vowel sound that says its own name. **Long e** can be spelled **ee**, as in the word **teeth, ea**, as in the word **meat**, or **e**, as in the word **me**.

Directions: Say each word, and listen for the **long e** sound. Then, write the words, and underline the letters that make the **long e** sound.

street	neat	treat	feet
sleep	keep	deal	meal
mean	clean	beast	feast

1. _____

2. _____

3. _____

4. _____

5. _____

6. _____

7. _____

8. _____

9. _____

10. _____

11. _____

12. _____

Name _____

Long *E* Words: Rhyming Words

Long e is the vowel sound you hear in the word **meet**.

Directions: Use the **long e** words in the box to write rhyming words.

street	feet	neat	treat
keep	deal	sleep	meal
mean	beast	clean	feast

1. Write the words that rhyme with **beat**.

_____ _____

_____ _____

2. Write the words that rhyme with **deep**.

_____ _____

3. Write the words that rhyme with **feel**.

_____ _____

4. Write the words that rhyme with **bean**.

_____ _____

5. Write the words that rhyme with **least**.

_____ _____

Long *E* Words: Sentences

Directions: Write a word from the box to complete each sentence.

street	feet	neat	treat
keep	deal	sleep	meal
mean	beast	clean	feast

1. I went to _____ late last night.

2. One of my favorite stories is "Beauty and

the _____ ."

3. Look both ways when you cross the _____ .

4. It would be _____ to kick someone.

5. I wear socks and shoes on my _____ .

6. The most important _____ of the day

is breakfast.

Name _____

Verbs

Verbs are words that tell the action in the sentence.

Directions: Draw a line from each sentence to its picture. Then, finish the sentence with the verb or action word that is under each picture.

Example:
    He will ___help___ the baby.

1. I can _____ my book.

2. It is time to _____ up.

3. That chair might _____ .

4. They _____ houses.

5. I _____ this out myself.

6. Is that too heavy to _____ ?

carry

help

cut

build

clean

fix

break

Verbs: Sentences

Directions: Read the two sentences in each story below. Then, write one more sentence to tell what happened next. Use the verbs from the box.

break	build	fix	clean	cut	carry

 Today is Nate's birthday.

Nate asked four friends to come.

 _____

 Audrey's dog walked in the mud.

He got mud in the house.

 _____

Name _____

Verbs: Sentences

Directions: Join each pair of sentences to make one longer sentence. Use one of the **joining** words: **and**, **but**, or **or**. In the second part of the sentence, use **he**, **she**, or **they** in place of the person's name.

Example: I asked Tim to help me. Tim wanted to play.

I asked Tim to help me, but he wanted to play.

1. Kelly dropped a glass.
   Kelly cut her finger.

_____

_____

2. Linda and Allen got a new dog.
   Linda and Allen named it Baby.

_____

_____

Verbs: Word Endings

Most **verbs** end with **s** when the sentence tells about one thing. The **s** is taken away when the sentence tells about more than one thing.

Example:

One dog walks.
Two dogs **walk**.

One boy runs.
Three boys **run**.

The spelling of some **verbs** changes when the sentence tells about only one thing.

Example:

One girl carries her lunch.
Two girls **carry** their lunches.

The boy fixes his car.
Two boys **fix** their cars.

Directions: Write the missing verbs in the sentences.

Example:

Alma works hard. She and Peter ___work___ all day.

1. The father bird builds a nest.

   The mother and father _____ it together.

2. The girls clean their room. Jenny _____ under her bed.

3. The children cut out their pictures. Henry _____ his slowly.

4. These workers fix things. This man _____ televisions.

5. Two trucks carry horses. One truck _____ pigs.

Name _____

Verbs: Completing a Story

Directions: Write a sentence that tells what happens in each picture. Use the **verb** under the picture.

Example:

fall

break

clean

A glass falls off the table.

_____

_____

fix

cut

carry

_____

_____

_____

Name _____

Verbs

Directions: Circle the words in each sentence that are not spelled correctly. Then, write the sentence correctly.

Example:

I need to (klean) the cage my (mouses) live in.

I need to clean the cage my mice live in.

2. The chair will brake if tree of us sit on it.

_____

_____

3. A muther bare carries her baby in hir mouth.

_____

_____

Name _____

Short *I* Words

Short i is the vowel sound you hear in the word **pig**.

Directions: Say each word, and listen for the **short i** sound. Then, write each word, and underline the letter that makes the **short i** sound.

pin	fin	dip	dish
kick	rich	ship	wish
win	fish	sick	pitch

1. _____

2. _____

3. _____

4. _____

5. _____

6. _____

7. _____

8. _____

9. _____

10. _____

11. _____

12. _____

Short *I* Words: Rhyming Words

Short i is the sound you hear in the word **pin**.

Directions: Use the **short i** words in the box to write rhyming words.

pin	fin	win	fish
pitch	wish	rich	kick
ship	dip	dish	sick

1. Write the words that rhyme with **spin**.

_____ _____ _____

2. Write the words that rhyme with **ditch**.

_____ _____

3. Write the words that rhyme with **rip**.

_____ _____

4. Write the words that rhyme with **squish**.

_____ _____ _____

5. Write the words that rhyme with **lick**.

_____ _____

Name _____

Short *I* Words: Sentences

Directions: Complete the sentences by matching the words to the correct sentence.

1. I made a _____ on a star.   fin

2. All we could see was the shark's _____ above the water.   fish

3. I like to eat vegetables with _____ .   kick

4. We saw lots of _____ in the water.   win

5. The soccer player will _____ the ball and score a goal.   dish

6. If you feel _____ , see a doctor.   dip

7. Did Kenji _____ the race?   wish

8. The _____ was full of candy.   sick

Long *I* Words

Long i is the vowel sound that says its own name. **Long i** can be spelled **igh**, as in **sight**, **i** with a **silent e** at the end, as in **mine**, and **y** at the end, as in **fly**.

Directions: Say each word, and listen for the **long i** sound. Then, write each word, and underline the letters that make the **long i** sound.

bike	fry	ride	line
glide	ripe	nine	pipe
fight	high	light	sigh

1. _____

2. _____

3. _____

4. _____

5. _____

6. _____

7. _____

8. _____

9. _____

10. _____

11. _____

12. _____

Name _____

Long *I* Words: Rhyming Words

Long i is the sound you hear in the word **fight**.

Directions: Use the **long i** words in the box to write rhyming words.

hide	ride	line	my
by	nine	high	light
sight	fly		

1. Write the words that rhyme with **sigh**.

_____ _____ _____ _____

2. Write the words that rhyme with **side**.

_____ _____

3. Write the words that rhyme with **fine**.

_____ _____

4. Write the words that rhyme with **fight**.

_____ _____

Review

Directions: Write **igh** in each blank below. Then, read the words.

Example:

sight   f____t   t____t

m____t   l____t   br____t

n____t   r____t   fl____t

Choose two of the **igh** words above. Draw, label, and color a picture for each word.

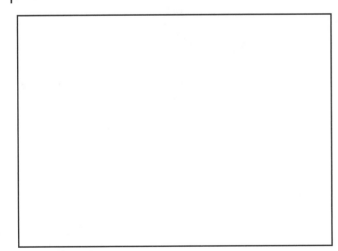 

_____   _____

Name _____

Location Words

Directions: Use one of the location words from the box to complete each sentence.

between	around	inside	outside	beside	across

Example:

She will hide ___under___ the basket.

1. In the summer, we like to play _____.

2. She can swim _____ the lake.

3. Put the bird _____ its cage so it won't fly away.

4. Sit _____ Bill and me so we can all work together.

5. Your picture is right _____ mine on the wall.

6. The fence goes _____ the house.

Location Words

Directions: Draw a line from each sentence to its picture. Then, complete each sentence with the word under the picture.

Example:

He is walking **behind** the tree.

outside

1. We stay _____ when it rains.

behind

between

2. She drew a dog _____ his house.

3. She stands _____ her friends.

across

4. They walked _____ the bridge.

around

5. Let the cat go _____ .

beside

inside

6. Draw a circle _____ the fish.

Location Words

Directions: Write the location words that answer the questions.

| between | around | inside | outside | beside | across |

1. Write all the smaller words you find in the location words.

_____

_____

2. Which two words begin with the same sound as ?

_____   _____

3. Put these clues together to write a location word.

a + ◯   _____

a + ✝   _____

4. Write three words that rhyme with **hide**.

_____   _____   _____

Location Words: Sentences

Directions: Use a location word from the first box and other words from the second box to complete each sentence.

between	around	inside	outside	beside	across

the yard	the house	the table	the school	the box
the hill	the picture	the field	the puddle	the park

Example:

Our garden grows <u>outside in the yard.</u>

1. We like to play _____

2. The street goes _____

3. Can you run _____

4. Let's ride bikes _____

Name _____

Location Words: Sentences

Directions: Join each pair of sentences to make a longer sentence. Use one of the **joining** words **and**, **but**, or **or**.

Example: We play outside when it is sunny.
Today it is raining.

We play outside when it is sunny, but today it is raining.

1. We could walk between the buildings. We could walk around them.

_____

_____

2. I drew a tree beside the house. I drew flowers beside the house.

_____

_____

Location Words: Sentences

Directions: Use a location word to tell where the cat is in each sentence.

 The cat is behind the box.

 _____

_____

 _____

_____

 _____

_____

 _____

Short *U* Words

Short u is the sound you hear in the word **bug**.

Directions: Say each word, and listen for the **short u** sound. Then, write each word, and underline the letter that makes the **short u** sound.

dust	must	nut	bug
bump	pump	tub	jump
cut	hug	rug	cub

1. _____

2. _____

3. _____

4. _____

5. _____

6. _____

7. _____

8. _____

9. _____

10. _____

11. _____

12. _____

Short *U* Words: Sentences

Directions: Circle the words in each sentence that are not correct.
Then, write the correct **short u** words from the box on the lines.

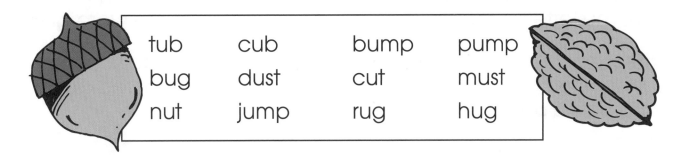

tub	cub	bump	pump
bug	dust	cut	must
nut	jump	rug	hug

1. The crust made me sneeze. _____

2. I need to take a bath in the cub. _____

3. The mug bite left a big pump on my arm.

_____   _____

4. It is time to get my hair hut. _____

5. The mother bear took care of her shrub. _____

6. We need to jump more gas into the car. _____

Name _____

Long *U* Words

Long u is a vowel sound that says its own name. **Long u** is spelled **u** with a silent **e** at the end, as in **cute**. The letters **oo** make a sound very much like **long u**. They make the sound you hear in the word **zoo**. The letters **ew** also make the **oo** sound, as in the word **grew**.

Directions: Say the words, and listen for the **u** and **oo** sounds. Then, write each word, and underline the letters that make the **long u** and **oo** sounds.

choose	blew	moon	fuse
cube	Ruth	tooth	use
flew	loose	goose	noon

1. _____

2. _____

3. _____

4. _____

5. _____

6. _____

7. _____

8. _____

9. _____

10. _____

11. _____

12. _____

Long *U* Words: Rhyming Words

Long u is the vowel sound you hear in the word **cube**. Another vowel sound that is very much like the **long u** sound is the **oo** sound you hear in the word **boot**.

Directions: Use the **long u** and **oo** words in the box to write rhyming words.

moon	tooth	use	blew
flew	loose	Ruth	choose
fuse	noon	goose	

1. Write the words that rhyme with **soon**.

_____   _____

2. Write the words that rhyme with **lose**.

_____   _____   _____

3. Write the words that rhyme with **grew**.

_____   _____

4. Write the words that rhyme with **moose**.

_____   _____

5. Write the words that rhyme with **booth**.

_____   _____

Comprehensive Curriculum - **Grade 2**

Name _____

Long *U* Words: Sentences

Directions: Write the words in the sentences below in the correct order. Begin each sentence with a capital letter, and end it with a period or a question mark.

1. the pulled dentist tooth my loose

_____

2. ice cubes I choose in my drink to put

_____

3. a Ruth fuse blew yesterday

_____

4. loose the got in garden goose the

_____

5. flew the goose winter for the south

_____

6. is full there a moon tonight

_____

Spelling Concentration Game

Play this game with a friend. Cut out each word card below and on pages 353 and 355. Lay the cards facedown on a flat surface. Take turns turning over two cards at a time. If the cards match, give the pair to your friend. Then, spell the word from memory. If you spelled it correctly, you can keep the pair. If not, put the cards back facedown. When all of the word cards have been matched and spelled correctly, the players count their pairs. The winner is whoever has the most pairs.

You can also play this by yourself—or with more than one friend!

		dust
light	clean	bump
dust	sleep	clean
bump	light	sleep

Page is blank for cutting exercise on previous page.

note	head	write
soap	made	nine
stop	play	grew
clock	stamp	cute
tent	math	choose

Page is blank for cutting exercise on previous page.

note	head	write
soap	made	nine
stop	play	grew
clock	stamp	cute
tent	math	choose

Page is blank for cutting exercise on previous page.

Opposite Words

Directions: Opposites are words that are different in every way.
Use the opposite words from the box to complete these sentences.

hard	hot	bottom	quickly	happy
sad	slowly	cold	soft	top

Example:

My new coat is blue on __top__ and

red on the __bottom__ .

1. Snow is _____ , but fire is _____ .

2. A rabbit runs _____ , but a turtle

   moves _____ .

3. A bed is _____ , but a floor is _____ .

4. I feel _____ when my friends come

   and _____ when they leave.

Name _____

Opposite Words

Directions: Draw a line from each sentence to its picture. Then, complete each sentence with the word under the picture.

Example:

She bought a __new__ bat.

hard

new

1. I like my _____ pillow.

2. Birthdays make me _____.

top

3. Put that book on _____.

 **sad**

4. Sydney runs _____.

slowly

5. A rock makes a _____ seat.

 quickly

6. I feel _____ when it rains.

happy

7. He eats _____.

 **soft**

Opposite Words: Sentences

Directions: Cross out the word in each box that does not tell about the picture. Write a sentence about the picture using the other two words.

Example:

| ~~teeth~~ | garden | digs |

<u>She digs in her garden.</u>

| swims | quickly | five |

_____

_____

| soft | fly | happy |

_____

_____

| popcorn | bottom | sad |

_____

_____

Opposite Words: Sentences

Directions: Look at each picture. Then, write a sentence that uses the word under the picture and tells how something is the same as the picture.

Example:

cold

My hands are as cold as ice.

hard

_____

_____

slow

_____

_____

soft

_____

_____

happy

_____

_____

Opposite Words: Completing a Story

Directions: Write opposite words in the blanks to complete the story.

hot	smiled	long	cold
huge	quickly	happy	sad

On Saturday, Dad and I went to the dog park. It was a cold day, but I actually felt _____ by the time we walked all the way there. The park was filled with all kinds of dogs! There were tiny dogs with short fur and _____ dogs with _____ fur. They were running and jumping all around. I have never seen a group of dogs look so _____! I knew I would feel _____ when it was time to leave.

A small mutt came up to me and licked my hands. At first, I frowned because his nose was _____ and clammy. He was so friendly, though, that I did not really mind. I threw a ball for him, and he _____ ran to fetch it.

I slowly looked at all the joyful dogs around us. "Dad," I said, "I think we're ready to get a dog of our own." Dad _____. "That's just what I was thinking," he agreed.

Name _____

Review

Directions: Tell a story about the picture by following the directions. Write one or two sentences for each answer.

1. Write about something that is happening **quickly** or **slowly** in the picture.

_____

_____

2. Use **top** or **bottom** in a sentence about the picture.

_____

_____

3. Tell about something **hard** and something **soft** in the picture. Use the word **but** in your sentence.

_____

_____

Learning Words

Directions: Write a learning word to complete each sentence. Use each word only once.

| start | watch | listen | teach | finish | write |

1. You see with your eyes, but you _____ with your ears.

2. After you think of an idea, _____ it on your paper.

3. She will _____ you how to write your name.

4. To see what to do, you have to _____ the teacher.

5. Show me your picture after you _____ drawing it.

6. When you have everything you need, you can _____ working.

Name _____

Learning Words

Directions: Circle the words in each sentence that are not spelled correctly. Then, write each word correctly on the line.

| start | watch | listen | teach | finish | write |

1. Do you like to wach television? _____

2. Right your name at the bottom. _____

3. I will teech you to ride a bike. _____

4. You have to lisen to me. _____

5. Did you finnish reading your book? _____

6. Everyone will strat running at the same time. _____

Change one letter in each word below to make one of the learning words. Write the new word on the line.

reach   white   match

_____   _____   _____

Learning Words: Verb Endings

Remember: Verbs end with **s** when the sentence tells about only one thing.

Example: One girl **reads**.   Two girls **read**.

But when an action word ends with **ch** or **sh**, add **es**.

Example: We **watch** the baby.   She **watches** the baby.
       Jane and Omar **finish** their work. Peter **finishes** his work.

start	watch	listen	teach	finish	write

Directions: Write the verb from the box that completes each sentence. Add **s** or **es** to the end of the verb if needed.

Example:
   Carrie reads the book. She and Chris _**read**_ it together.

1. Todd listens to the teacher. We all _____ to her.

2. Joy finishes the race first. We _____ after her.

3. They write letters to our class. Tony _____ back to them.

4. We watch the puppet show.

   She _____ with us.

5. He starts at the top of the page. We _____ in the middle.

Learning Words: Completing a Story

Directions: Write learning words to complete this story.

"How can I _____ you anything if you don't _____ ?" James asked his little sister, Wendy. He was trying to show her how to _____ her name. Wendy smiled up at James. "I'll _____ now," she said. "Okay. Let's _____ again. _____ what I do," he said. "First, you make a big **W**." "Up and down," Wendy said. She tried to _____ a **W** like James, but it looked like a row of upside-down mountains. "That's better," James said. "But you have to know when to stop." He showed her how to _____ the **e**, **n**, and **d**. "Now, I'll _____ you how to _____ your name," he said. He wrote a **y** for her. Wendy made the tail on her **y** go down to the bottom of the page. "I can do it!" she said. "I can _____ my name from _____ to _____ !" She smiled at her brother again. "Would you _____ me how to read now, James?" He smiled back at her. "Maybe later, okay?"

Time Words

The time between breakfast and lunch is **morning**.

The time between lunch and dinner is **afternoon**.

The time between dinner and bedtime is **evening**.

Directions: Write a time word from the box to complete each sentence. Use each word only once.

| evening | morning | today | tomorrow | afternoon |

1. What did you eat for breakfast

   this _____?

2. We came home from school in the _____ .

3. I help wash the dinner dishes in

   the _____ .

4. I feel a little tired _____ .

5. If I rest tonight, I will feel better _____ .

Name _____

Time Words: Sentences

Directions: Make each pair of short sentences into one long sentence. Use the joining words **and**, **or**, **but**, or **because**.

Example:

This morning, I am sleepy. I stayed up late last night.

This morning I am sleepy because I stayed up late last night.

1. Do you want to go in the morning?
   Do you want to go in the afternoon?

_____

_____

2. Mom asked me to clean my room today. I forgot.

_____

_____

Time Words: Sentences

Directions: Write a sentence for these time words. Tell something you do at that time.

Example:

day

Every day, I walk to school.

morning

_____

_____

afternoon

_____

_____

evening

_____

_____

Review

Directions: Write the story below again, and correct all the mistakes. Watch for words that are not spelled correctly, missing periods and question marks, question marks at the end of telling sentences, and sentences with the wrong joining words.

One mourning, my granmother said I could have a pet mouse. That evenening, we got my mouse at the pet store, or the next afernoon my mouse had babies! Now, I had nyne mouses! I really liked to wach them? I wanted to pick the babies up, and they were too little. When they get bigger, I have to give too mouses to my sisster.

_____

_____

_____

_____

_____

_____

_____

MATH

Name _____

Less Than, Greater Than

Directions: The open mouth points to the larger number. The small point goes to the smaller number. Draw the symbol **<** or **>** to the correct number.

Example: 5 $\left(\,>\,\right)$ 3   This means that 5 is greater than 3, and 3 is less than 5.

12 $\bigcirc$ 2   16 $\left(\,>\,\right)$ 6

16 $\left(\,>\,\right)$ 15   1 $\bigcirc$ 2

7 $\left(\,>\,\right)$ 1   19 $\left(\,>\,\right)$ 5

9 $\left(\,>\,\right)$ 6   11 $\left(\,<\,\right)$ 13

Counting

Directions: Write the numbers that are:

next in order	one less	one greater
22, 23, _24_ , _25_	_15_ , 16	6, _7_
674, _675_ , _676_	_24_ ,247	125, _126_
227, _228_ , _229_	_549_ ,550	499, _500_
199, _200_ , _201_	_332_ , 333	750, _76_
329, _330_ , _331_	_861_ , 862	933, _934_

Directions: Write the missing numbers.

13 14 15 16 17 18

163 164 165 166 167 168

821 822 823 824 825 826

Counting by Twos

Directions: Each basket the players make is worth 2 points. Help your team win by counting by twos to beat the other team's score.

2

4

6

8

10

12

16

18

20

22

24

26

28

30

32

34

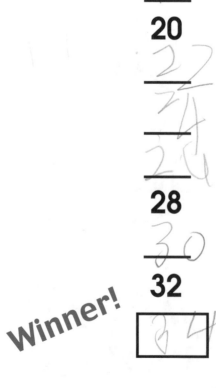

Winner!

Final Score	
Home	Visitor
	30

Counting: Twos, Fives, Tens

Directions: Write the missing numbers.

Count by twos:

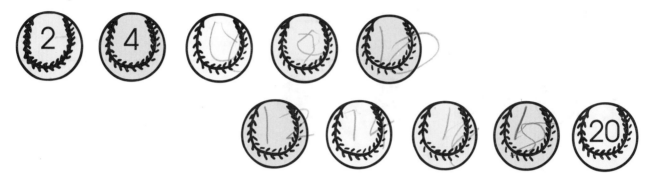

Count by fives:

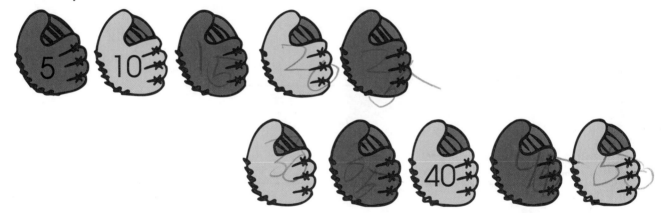

Count by tens:

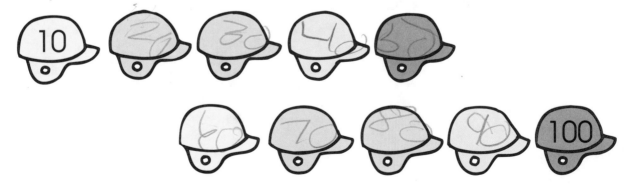

Name _____

Patterns

Directions: Write or draw what comes next in the pattern.

Example: 1, 2, 3, 4, __5__

1.    _____

2. A, 1, B, 2, C, _____

3. 2, 4, 6, 8, _____

4. A, C, E, G, _____

5. 5, 10, 15, 20, _____

Finding Patterns: Numbers

Mia likes to count by twos, threes, fours, fives, tens, and hundreds.

Directions: Complete the number patterns.

1. 5, ____, ____, 20, ____, ____, 35, ____, ____, 50

2. 100, ____, ____, 400, ____, ____, ____, 800, ____

3. ____, 4, 6, ____, ____, 12, ____, 16, ____, ____

4. 10, ____, ____, 40, ____, ____, 70, ____, 90

5. 4, ____, 12, ____, ____, 24, ____, 32, ____, 40

6. ____, 6, 9, ____, ____, 18, ____, 24, ____, 30

Directions: Make up two of your own number patterns.

____, ____, ____, ____, ____, ____, ____, ____

____, ____, ____, ____, ____, ____, ____, ____

Finding Patterns: Shapes

Directions: Complete each row by drawing the correct shape.

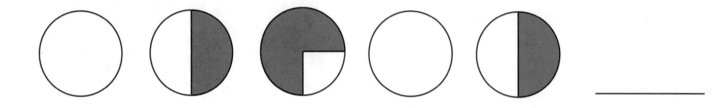

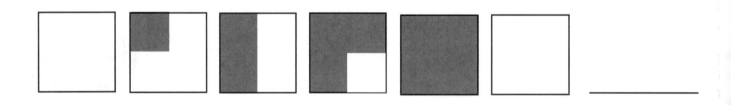

Ordinal Numbers

Ordinal numbers indicate order in a series, such as **first**, **second**, or **third**.

Directions: Follow the instructions to color the train cars. The first car is the engine.

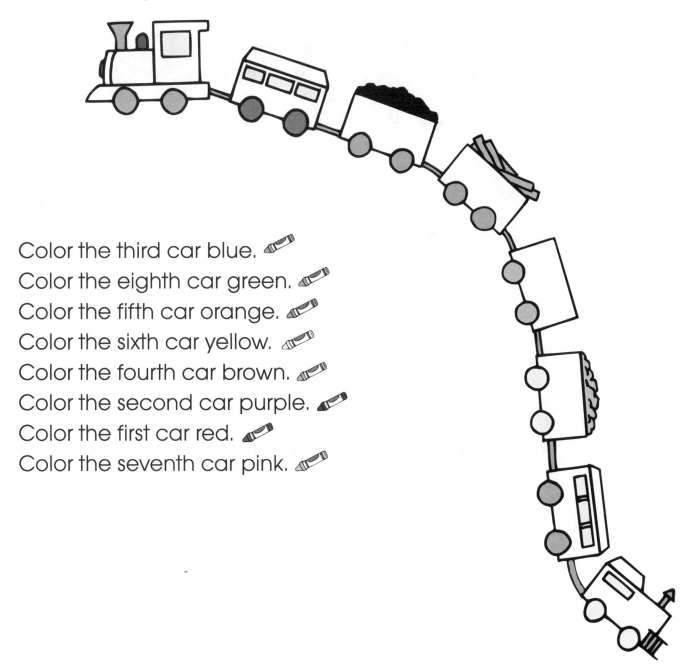

Color the third car blue.
Color the eighth car green.
Color the fifth car orange.
Color the sixth car yellow.
Color the fourth car brown.
Color the second car purple.
Color the first car red.
Color the seventh car pink.

Ordinal Numbers

Directions: Follow the instructions.

Draw glasses on the second child.

Put a hat on the fourth child.

Color blonde hair on the third child.

Draw a tie on the first child.

Draw ears on the fifth child.

Draw black hair on the seventh child.

Put a bow on the head of the sixth child.

Addition

Addition is "putting together" or adding two or more numbers to find the sum.

Directions: Add.

Example:

```
  2
+5
  7
```

```
  3        6        7        8        5        3
+4       +2       +1       +2       +4       +1
```

```
  8        9       10        6        4        7
+2       +5       +3       +6       +9       +7
```

```
  9        8        6        7        7        9
+3       +7       +5       +9       +6       +9
```

Name _____

Addition: Commutative Property

The **commutative property** of addition states that even if the order of the numbers is changed in an addition sentence, the sum will stay the same.

Example: 2 + 3 = 5
              3 + 2 = 5

Directions: Look at the addition sentences below. Complete the addition sentences by writing the missing numerals.

5 + 4 = 9   3 + 1 = 4   2 + 6 = 8
4 + __ = 9   1 + __ = 4   6 + __ = 8

6 + 1 = 7   4 + 3 = 7   1 + 9 = 10
1 + __ = 7   3 + __ = 7   9 + __ = 10

Now, try these:

6 + 3 = 9   10 + 2 = 12   8 + 3 = 11
__ + __ = 9   __ + __ = 12   __ + __ = 11

Look at these sums. Can you think of two number sentences that would show the commutative property of addition?

__ + __ = 7   __ + __ = 11   __ + __ = 9

__ + __ = 7   __ + __ = 11   __ + __ = 9

Adding 3 or More Numbers

Directions: Add all the numbers to find the sum. Draw pictures to break up the problem into two smaller problems.

Example:

$$\begin{array}{r} 1 \\ 2 \\ +3 \\ \hline 6 \end{array}$$ ○ ○○ ○○○

$$\begin{array}{r} +\,{2 \atop 5} \end{array} \bigg\rangle \; 7$$

$$\begin{array}{r} +\,{2 \atop 4} \end{array} \bigg\rangle \; \begin{array}{r} +6 \\ \hline 13 \end{array}$$

$$\begin{array}{r} 3 \\ 6 \\ +2 \\ \hline \end{array} \qquad \begin{array}{r} 8 \\ 5 \\ +4 \\ \hline \end{array} \qquad \begin{array}{r} 3 \\ 1 \\ +5 \\ \hline \end{array} \qquad \begin{array}{r} 8 \\ 2 \\ +9 \\ \hline \end{array}$$

$$\begin{array}{r} 2 \\ 8 \\ 4 \\ +3 \\ \hline \end{array} \qquad \begin{array}{r} 3 \\ 6 \\ 5 \\ +2 \\ \hline \end{array} \qquad \begin{array}{r} 4 \\ 1 \\ 2 \\ +5 \\ \hline \end{array} \qquad \begin{array}{r} 6 \\ 7 \\ 3 \\ +1 \\ \hline \end{array}$$

Subtraction

Subtraction is "taking away" or subtracting one number from another to find the difference.

Directions: Subtract.

Example:

$$\begin{array}{r} 4 \\ -3 \\ \hline 1 \end{array}$$

$$\begin{array}{r} 5 \\ -3 \\ \hline 2 \end{array} \qquad \begin{array}{r} 6 \\ -1 \\ \hline 5 \end{array} \qquad \begin{array}{r} 4 \\ -3 \\ \hline 1 \end{array} \qquad \begin{array}{r} 3 \\ -1 \\ \hline 2 \end{array} \qquad \begin{array}{r} 2 \\ -0 \\ \hline 2 \end{array} \qquad \begin{array}{r} 1 \\ -1 \\ \hline 0 \end{array}$$

$$\begin{array}{r} 9 \\ -2 \\ \hline 7 \end{array} \qquad \begin{array}{r} 7 \\ -4 \\ \hline 3 \end{array} \qquad \begin{array}{r} 10 \\ -\ 5 \\ \hline 5 \end{array} \qquad \begin{array}{r} 14 \\ -\ 6 \\ \hline 8 \end{array} \qquad \begin{array}{r} 15 \\ -\ 9 \\ \hline 4 \end{array} \qquad \begin{array}{r} 12 \\ -\ 3 \\ \hline 9 \end{array}$$

$$\begin{array}{r} 18 \\ -\ 8 \\ \hline 10 \end{array} \qquad \begin{array}{r} 13 \\ -\ 5 \\ \hline 8 \end{array} \qquad \begin{array}{r} 14 \\ -\ 7 \\ \hline 7 \end{array} \qquad \begin{array}{r} 11 \\ -\ 4 \\ \hline 8 \end{array} \qquad \begin{array}{r} 17 \\ -\ 9 \\ \hline 8 \end{array} \qquad \begin{array}{r} 16 \\ -\ 8 \\ \hline 8 \end{array}$$

Addition and Subtraction

Addition is "putting together" or adding two or more numbers to find the sum. Subtraction is "taking away" or subtracting one number from another to find the difference.

Directions: Add or subtract. Circle the answers that are less than 10.

Examples:

$$
\begin{array}{r}
3 \\
+1 \\
\hline
4
\end{array}
$$

$$
\begin{array}{r}
3 \\
-1 \\
\hline
2
\end{array}
$$

$$
\begin{array}{r}
9 \\
+3 \\
\hline
12
\end{array}
\qquad
\begin{array}{r}
6 \\
-2 \\
\hline
4
\end{array}
\qquad
\begin{array}{r}
12 \\
-1 \\
\hline
11
\end{array}
\qquad
\begin{array}{r}
18 \\
+1 \\
\hline
19
\end{array}
\qquad
\begin{array}{r}
15 \\
-6 \\
\hline
9
\end{array}
$$

$$
\begin{array}{r}
7 \\
+6 \\
\hline
130
\end{array}
\qquad
\begin{array}{r}
16 \\
-9 \\
\hline
7
\end{array}
\qquad
\begin{array}{r}
10 \\
-3 \\
\hline
7
\end{array}
\qquad
\begin{array}{r}
14 \\
+5 \\
\hline
19
\end{array}
\qquad
\begin{array}{r}
16 \\
-8 \\
\hline
8
\end{array}
$$

$$
\begin{array}{r}
8 \\
+7 \\
\hline
15
\end{array}
\qquad
\begin{array}{r}
12 \\
+2 \\
\hline
14
\end{array}
\qquad
\begin{array}{r}
13 \\
-4 \\
\hline
9
\end{array}
\qquad
\begin{array}{r}
17 \\
+2 \\
\hline
19
\end{array}
\qquad
\begin{array}{r}
9 \\
+9 \\
\hline
18
\end{array}
$$

Name _____

Place Value: Ones, Tens

The **place value** of a digit or numeral is shown by where it is in the number. For example, in the number **23**, **2** has the place value of **tens**, and **3** is **ones**.

Directions: Add the tens and ones, and write your answers in the blanks.

Example:

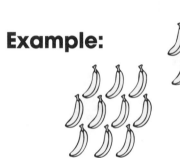 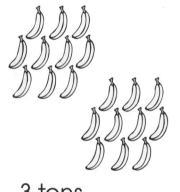 + = 33

3 tens   +   3 ones   =   33

	tens ones			tens ones
7 tens + 5 ones =	_____	4 tens + 0 ones =	_____
2 tens + 3 ones =	_____	8 tens + 1 one =	_____
5 tens + 2 ones =	_____	1 ten + 1 one =	_____
5 tens + 4 ones =	_____	6 tens + 3 ones =	_____
9 tens + 5 ones =	_____		

Directions: Draw a line to the correct number.

6 tens + 7 ones	73
4 tens + 2 ones	67
8 tens + 0 ones	51
7 tens + 3 ones	80
5 tens + 1 one	42

Place Value: Ones, Tens

Directions: Write the numbers for the tens and ones. Then, add.

Example:

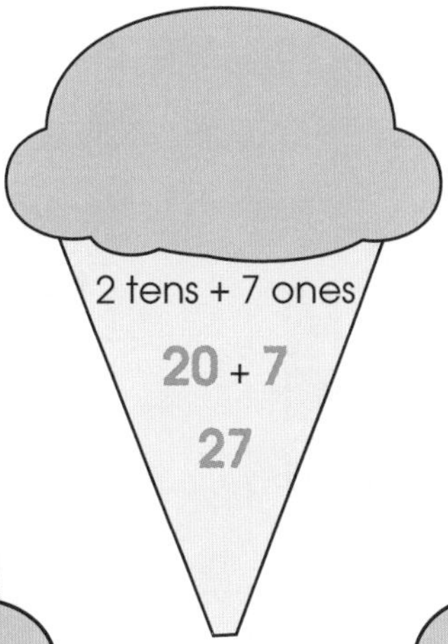

2 tens + 7 ones

20 + 7

27

6 tens + 2 ones

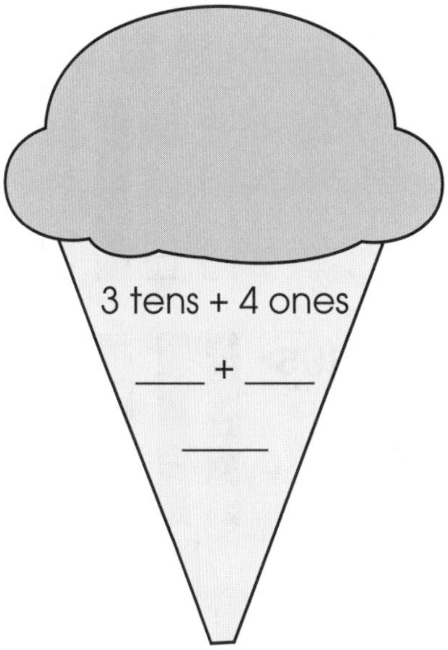

___ + ___

___

3 tens + 4 ones

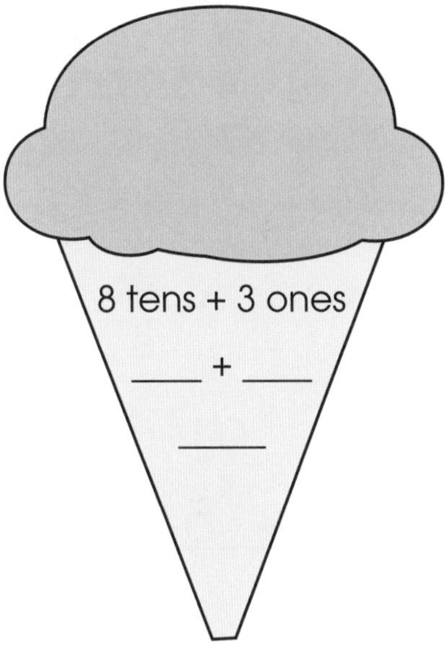

___ + ___

___

8 tens + 3 ones

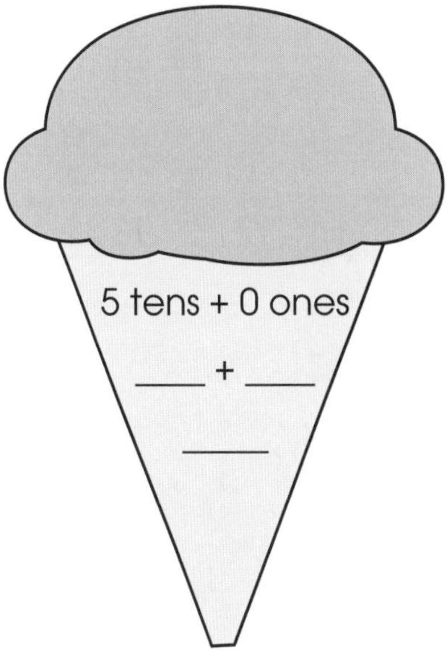

___ + ___

___

5 tens + 0 ones

___ + ___

___

2-Digit Addition

Directions: Study the example. Follow the steps to add.

Example:

$$\begin{array}{r} 33 \\ +41 \\ \hline \end{array}$$

Step 1: Add the ones.

tens	ones
3	3
+4	1
	4

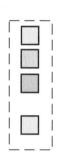

Step 2: Add the tens.

tens	ones
3	3
+4	1
7	4

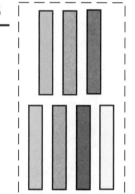

tens	ones
4	2
+2	4
6	6

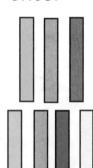
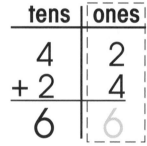
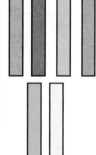

tens	ones
5	0
+4	7
9	7

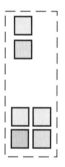
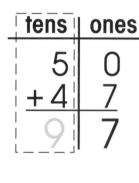
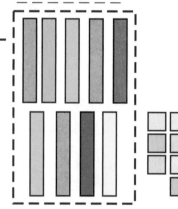

24	15	38	11	37	72	33	10
+62	+23	+61	+26	+42	+11	+51	+30

25	62	32	25	82	91	16	55
+42	+14	+44	+13	+ 6	+ 5	+71	+ 3

2-Digit Addition

Directions: Add the total points scored in each game. Remember to add **ones** first and **tens** second.

Example:

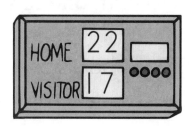

Total __39__

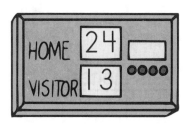

Total _____

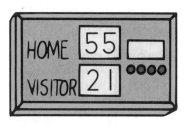

Total _____

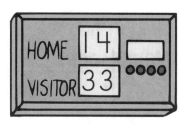

Total _____

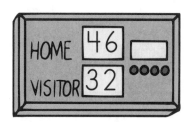

Total _____

Total _____

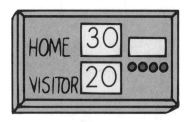

Total _____

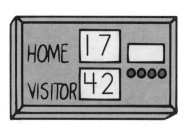

Total _____

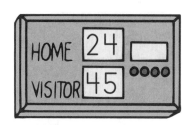

Total _____

2-Digit Addition: Regrouping

Addition is "putting together" or adding two or more numbers to find the sum. Regrouping is using **ten ones** to form **one ten**, **ten tens** to form **one 100**, **fifteen ones** to form **one ten** and **five ones**, and so on.

Directions: Study the examples. Follow the steps to add.

Example:
$$\begin{array}{r} 14 \\ +\ 8 \\ \hline \end{array}$$

Step 1: Add the ones.

tens	ones
1	4
+	8
1	2

Step 2: Regroup the tens.

tens	ones
1	4
+	8
	2

Step 3: Add the tens.

tens	ones
1	4
+	8
2	2

tens	ones
1	6
+3	7
5	3

tens	ones
3	8
+5	3
9	1

tens	ones
2	4
+4	7
7	1

$$\begin{array}{r} 28 \\ +17 \\ \hline \end{array} \qquad \begin{array}{r} 32 \\ +38 \\ \hline \end{array} \qquad \begin{array}{r} 54 \\ +25 \\ \hline \end{array} \qquad \begin{array}{r} 19 \\ +55 \\ \hline \end{array} \qquad \begin{array}{r} 44 \\ +48 \\ \hline \end{array} \qquad \begin{array}{r} 25 \\ +64 \\ \hline \end{array} \qquad \begin{array}{r} 29 \\ +33 \\ \hline \end{array} \qquad \begin{array}{r} 79 \\ +15 \\ \hline \end{array}$$

2-Digit Addition: Regrouping

Directions: Add the total points scored in each game. Remember to add the ones, regroup, and then add the tens.

Example:

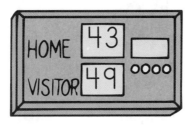

HOME 47
VISITOR 38

Total __85__

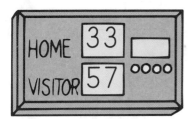

HOME 33
VISITOR 57

Total _____

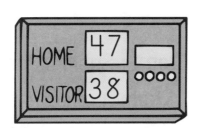

HOME 43
VISITOR 49

Total _____

HOME 57
VISITOR 34

Total _____

HOME 29
VISITOR 22

Total _____

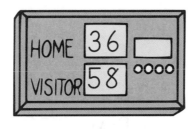

HOME 36
VISITOR 58

Total _____

HOME 45
VISITOR 39

Total _____

HOME 66
VISITOR 26

Total _____

HOME 72
VISITOR 19

Total _____

HOME 54
VISITOR 26

Total _____

2-Digit Subtraction

Directions: Study the example. Follow the steps to subtract.

Example:

$$\begin{array}{r} 28 \\ -14 \\ \hline \end{array}$$

Step 1: Subtract the ones.

tens	ones
2	8
-1	4
	4

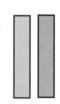

Step 2: Subtract the tens.

tens	ones
2	8
-1	4
1	4

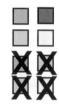

tens	ones
2	4
-1	2
1	2

tens	ones
3	8
-1	5
2	3

 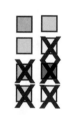

$$\begin{array}{r} 24 \\ -12 \\ \hline \end{array} \qquad \begin{array}{r} 61 \\ -30 \\ \hline \end{array} \qquad \begin{array}{r} 77 \\ -44 \\ \hline \end{array} \qquad \begin{array}{r} 85 \\ -24 \\ \hline \end{array} \qquad \begin{array}{r} 57 \\ -23 \\ \hline \end{array} \qquad \begin{array}{r} 87 \\ -33 \\ \hline \end{array} \qquad \begin{array}{r} 59 \\ -34 \\ \hline \end{array} \qquad \begin{array}{r} 96 \\ -16 \\ \hline \end{array}$$

$$\begin{array}{r} 29 \\ -15 \\ \hline \end{array} \qquad \begin{array}{r} 74 \\ -51 \\ \hline \end{array} \qquad \begin{array}{r} 46 \\ -32 \\ \hline \end{array} \qquad \begin{array}{r} 69 \\ -35 \\ \hline \end{array} \qquad \begin{array}{r} 95 \\ -32 \\ \hline \end{array} \qquad \begin{array}{r} 33 \\ -33 \\ \hline \end{array} \qquad \begin{array}{r} 78 \\ -26 \\ \hline \end{array} \qquad \begin{array}{r} 22 \\ -11 \\ \hline \end{array}$$

2-Digit Subtraction: Regrouping

Subtraction is "taking away" or subtracting one number from another to find the difference. Regrouping is using **one ten to form ten ones**, **one 100 to form ten tens**, and so on.

Directions: Study the examples. Follow the steps to subtract.

Example:
$$37$$
$$-19$$

Step 1: Regroup.

tens	ones
2	17
3̸	7̸
-1	9

Step 2: Subtract the ones.

tens	ones
2	17
3̸	7̸
-1	9
	8

Step 3: Subtract the tens.

tens	ones
2	17
3̸	7̸
-1	9
1	8

tens	ones
0	12
1̸	2̸
-	9
3	

tens	ones
2	14
3̸	4̸
-1	6
1	8

tens	ones
3	15
4̸	5̸
-2	9
1	6

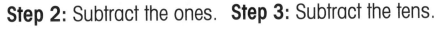

28	46	12	30	52	47	21	45
− 19	− 18	− 8	− 12	− 25	− 35	− 13	− 25

2-Digit Subtraction: Regrouping

Directions: Study the steps for subtracting. Solve the problems using the steps.

STEPS FOR SUBTRACTING

1. DO YOU REGROUP?
   YES, WHEN BOTTOM NUMBER IS BIGGER THAN THE TOP.

2. SUBTRACT THE ONES.

3. SUBTRACT THE TENS.

TENS	ONES		TENS	ONES
3 4̸	12	REGROUP? YES	3	7
-2	4		-1	4	REGROUP? NO
1	8		2	3

tens	ones
4	17
- 2	8

tens	ones
6	4
- 3	4

tens	ones
5	3
- 3	9

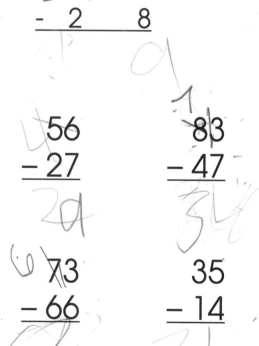

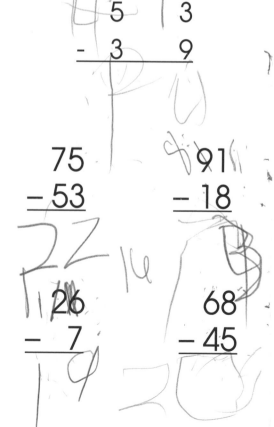

```
  56        83        43        75        91
- 27      - 47      - 39      - 53      - 18
```

```
  73        35        67        26        68
- 66      - 14      - 58      -  7      - 45
```

Review

Directions: Add or subtract. Use regrouping when needed.
Always do ones first and tens last.

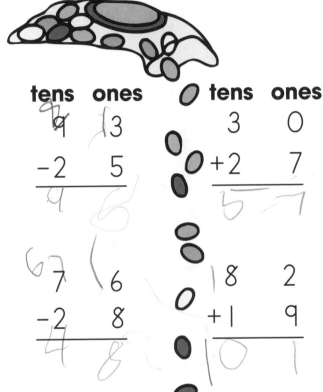

tens	ones		tens	ones		tens	ones		tens	ones
9	3		3	0		6	5		7	1
−2	5		+2	7		+1	7		−3	6

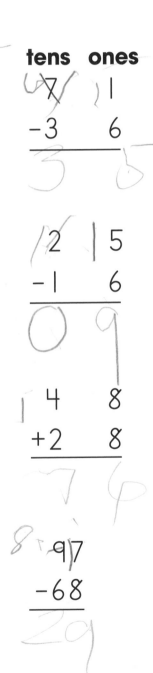

First row answers (student): 8, 5 7, 8 2, 3 5

tens	ones		tens	ones		tens	ones		tens	ones
7	6		8	2		5	6		2	5
−2	8		+1	9		−2	8		−1	6

tens	ones		tens	ones		tens	ones		tens	ones
4	3		5	3		2	4		4	8
−1	4		−1	5		+5	7		+2	8

```
  33          52          46          97
+47         +29         −37         −68
```

Name _____

2-Digit Addition and Subtraction

Addition is "putting together" or adding two or more numbers to find the sum. Subtraction is "taking away" or subtracting one number from another to find the difference. Regrouping is using **one ten** to form **ten ones**, **one 100** to form **ten tens**, and so on.

Directions: Add or subtract using regrouping.

Example:

```
 tens  ones
  2    15
  3     5
 -2     7
        8
```

```
  56     40     35     42     53     97     44     93
 -27    -16    +27    -14    +38    -48    +27    -39
```

```
  56     44     68     73     33     49     77     27
 -17    +28    -49    -24    +18    +32    -68    +19
```

2-Digit Addition and Subtraction

Directions: Add or subtract using regrouping.

```
  23        84        69        41
 +48       -56       +29       -17
____      ____      ____      ____
```

```
  52        73        84        57
 -28       +18       -27       -39
____      ____      ____      ____
```

```
  33        64        37        36
 -15       +17       +58       -19
____      ____      ____      ____
```

```
  65        48        33        25
 -28       -30       +18       +35
____      ____      ____      ____
```

Place Value: Hundreds

The place value of a digit or numeral is shown by where it is in the number. For example, in the number **123**, **1** has the place value of **hundreds**, **2** is **tens**, and **3** is **ones**.

Directions: Study the examples. Then, write the missing numbers in the blanks.

Examples:

2 hundreds + 3 tens + 6 ones =   1 hundred + 4 tens + 9 ones =

hundreds	tens	ones
2	3	6	= _236_

hundreds	tens	ones
1	4	9	= _149_

	hundreds	tens	ones	total
3 hundreds + 4 tens + 8 ones =	3	4	8	= _____
_ hundreds + _ ten + _ ones =	2	1	7	= _____
_ hundreds + _ tens + _ ones =	6	3	5	= _____
_ hundreds + _ tens + _ ones =	4	7	9	= _____
_ hundreds + _ tens + _ ones =	2	9	4	= _____
_ hundreds + 5 tens + 6 ones =	4			= _____
3 hundreds + 1 ten + 3 ones =				= _____
3 hundreds + _ tens + 7 ones =		5		= _____
6 hundreds + 2 tens + _ ones =			8	= _____

Place Value: Hundreds

Directions: Write the numbers for hundreds, tens, and ones. Then, add.

Example:

1 hundred + 4 tens + 6 ones
100 + 40 + 6
146

7 hundreds + 3 tens + 5 ones

_____ + _____ + _____

_____

3 hundreds + 1 ten + 9 ones

_____ + _____ + _____

_____

5 hundreds + 8 tens + 0 ones

_____ + _____ + _____

_____

9 hundreds + 0 tens + 7 ones

_____ + _____ + _____

_____

Comprehensive Curriculum - Grade 2

Name _____

3-Digit Addition: Regrouping

Directions: Study the examples. Follow the steps to add.

Example:

Step 1: Add the ones. | **Step 2:** Add the tens. | **Step 3:** Add the hundreds.

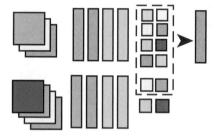 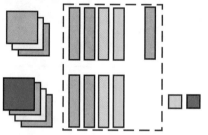 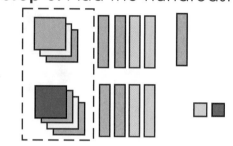

Do you regroup? Yes   Do you regroup? No

hundreds	tens	ones	hundreds	tens	ones	hundreds	tens	ones
	1			1			1	
3	4	8	3	4	8	3	4	8
+4	4	4	+4	4	4	+4	4	4
7	8	2	7	9	2	7	9	2

hundreds	tens	ones	hundreds	tens	ones	hundreds	tens	ones
	1						1	
2	1	4	3	6	8	1	1	9
+2	3	8	+2	1	3	+5	6	5
4	5	2		8	1			4

$$418 \quad 471 \quad 334 \quad 659 \quad 736 \quad 426 \quad 567 \quad 327$$
$$+323 \quad +319 \quad +528 \quad +127 \quad +145 \quad +165 \quad +228 \quad +354$$

Place Value: Thousands

$$6 \,,\, 4 \; 3 \; 1$$

thousands | hundreds | tens | ones

Directions: Tell which number is in each place.

 Thousands place:

2,456   4,621   3,456

_____   _____   _____

 Tens place:

4,286   1,234   5,678

_____   _____   _____

 Hundreds place:

6,321   3,210   7,871

_____   _____   _____

 Ones place:

5,432   6,531   9,980

_____   _____   _____

Name _____

Place Value: Thousands

Directions: Use the code to color the fan.

If the answer has:

9 thousands, color it pink.

6 thousands, color it green.

5 hundreds, color it orange.

8 tens, color it red.

3 ones, color it blue.

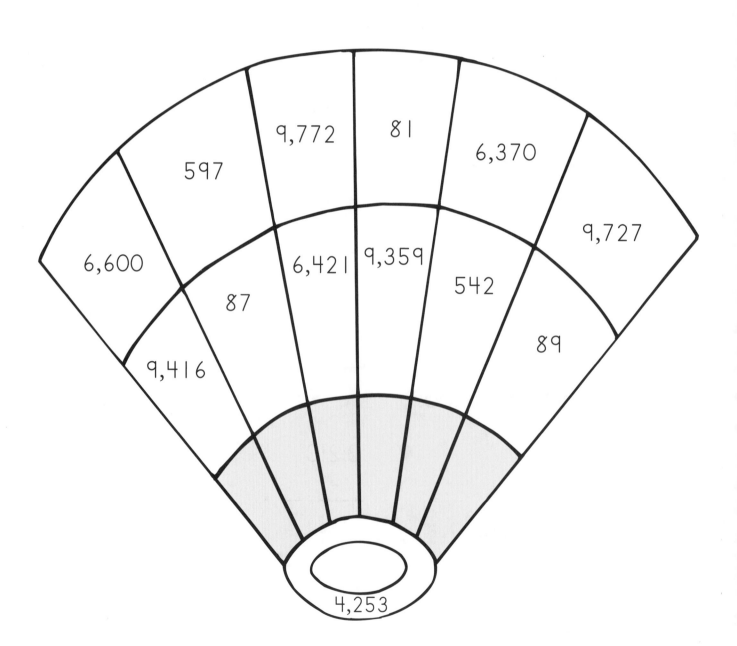

Graphs

A **graph** is a drawing that shows information about numbers.

Directions: Count the apples in each row. Color the boxes to show how many apples have bites taken out of them.

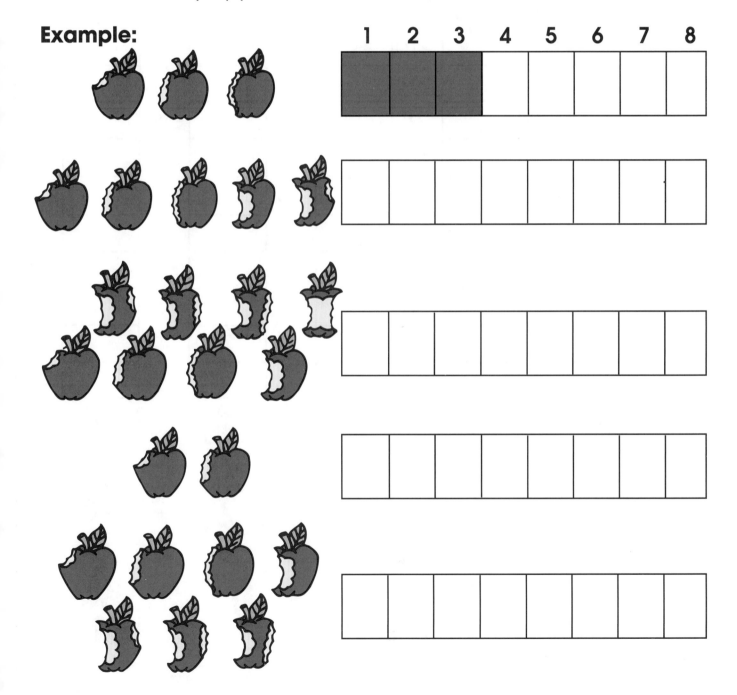

Comprehensive Curriculum - **Grade 2**

Name _____

Graphs

Directions: Count the bananas in each row. Color the boxes to show how many have been eaten by the monkeys.

Graphs

Directions: Count the fish. Color the bowls to make a graph that shows the number of fish.

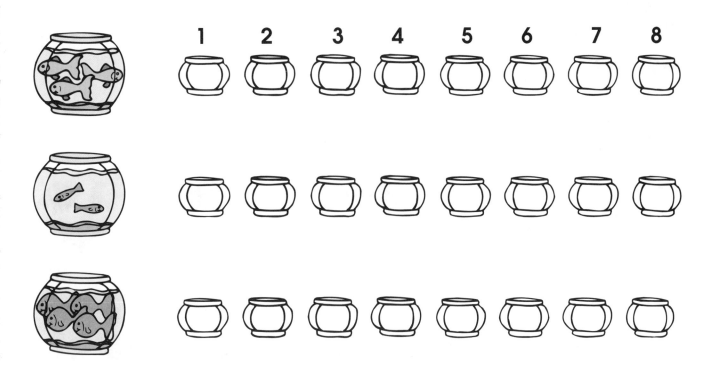

	1	2	3	4	5	6	7	8

Directions: Use your fishbowl graphs to find the answers to the following questions. Draw a line to the correct bowl.

The most fish

The fewest fish

Multiplication

Multiplication is a short way to find the sum of adding the same number a certain amount of times. For example, **4 x 7 = 28** instead of **7 + 7 + 7 + 7 = 28**.

Directions: Study the example. Solve the problems.

Example:

3 + 3 + 3 = 9
3 threes = 9
3 x 3 = 9

7 + 7 = _14_
2 sevens = _14_
2 x 7 = _14_

4 + 4 + 4 + 4 = ____
4 fours = ____
4 x ____ = ____

5 + 5 = ____
2 fives = ____
2 x ____ = ____

2 + 2 + 2 + 2 = ____
4 twos = ____
4 x ____ = ____

6 + 6 = ____
2 sixes = ____
2 x ____ = ____

Multiplication

Multiplication is repeated addition.

Directions: Draw a picture for each problem. Then, write the missing numbers.

Example:

Draw 2 groups of 3 apples.

$3 + 3 = 6$

or $2 \times 3 = 6$

Draw 3 groups of 4 hearts.	Draw 2 groups of 5 boxes.
 $4 + 4 + 4 =$ ____ or $3 \times$ ____ $=$ ____	$5 +$ ____ $=$ ____ or $2 \times$ ____ $=$ ____

Draw 6 groups of 2 circles.

$2 +$ ____ $+$ ____ $+$ ____ $+$ ____ $+$ ____ $=$ ____

or $6 \times$ ____ $=$ ____

Draw 7 groups of 3 triangles.

$3 +$ ____ $+$ ____ $+$ ____ $+$ ____ $+$ ____ $+$ ____ $=$ ____

or ____ $\times$ ____ $=$ ____

Multiplication

Directions: Study the example. Draw the groups, and write the total.

Example:

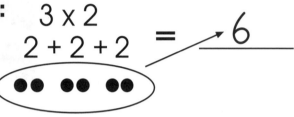

3×2
$2 + 2 + 2 = 6$

3×4

___ + ___ + ___ = _____

2×5

____ + ____ = _____

5×3

___ + ___ + ___ + ___ + ___ = _____

Multiplication

Directions: Solve the problems.

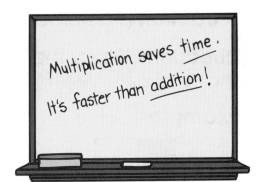

Multiplication saves time.
It's faster than addition!

9 + 9 = __18__

2 nines = ____

2 x 9 = ____

7 + 7 = ____

2 sevens = ____

2 x __7__ = ____

4 + 4 + 4 + 4 = ____

__4__ fours = ____

____ x 4 = ____

8 + 8 + 8 + 8 + 8 = ____

____ eights = ____

____ x 8 = ____

5 + 5 + 5 = ____

____ fives = ____

____ x 5 = ____

9 + 9 = ____

____ nines = ____

____ x 9 = ____

6 + 6 + 6 = ____

____ sixes = ____

____ x 6 = ____

3 + 3 = ____

____ threes = ____

____ x 3 = ____

7 + 7 + 7 + 7 = ____

____ sevens = ____

____ x 7 = ____

2 + 2 = ____

____ twos = ____

____ x 2 = ____

Name _____

Fractions: Half, Third, Fourth

A **fraction** is a number that names part of a whole, such as $\frac{1}{2}$ or $\frac{1}{3}$.

Directions: Study the examples. Color the correct fraction of each shape.

Examples:

shaded part   1
equal parts   2
$\frac{1}{2}$ (one-half) shaded

shaded part   1
equal parts   3
$\frac{1}{3}$ (one-third) shaded

shaded part   1
equal parts   4
$\frac{1}{4}$ (one-fourth) shaded

Color: $\frac{1}{3}$ red	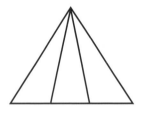 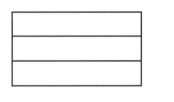 
Color: $\frac{1}{4}$ blue	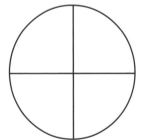 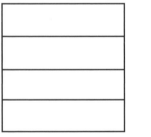 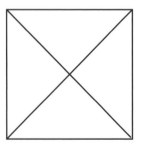
Color: $\frac{1}{2}$ orange	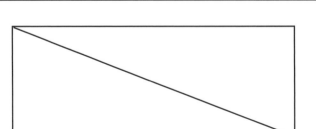 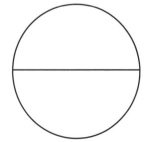

Fractions: Half, Third, Fourth

Directions: Study the examples. Circle the fraction that shows the shaded part. Then, circle the fraction that shows the white part.

Examples:

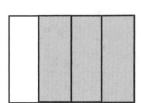

shaded   **white**   **shaded**   **white**   **shaded**   **white**

$\dfrac{1}{4}$ $\dfrac{1}{3}$ $\boxed{\dfrac{1}{2}}$ $\dfrac{1}{3}$ $\boxed{\dfrac{1}{2}}$ $\dfrac{1}{4}$ $\dfrac{1}{2}$ $\boxed{\dfrac{2}{3}}$ $\dfrac{3}{4}$ $\dfrac{2}{3}$ $\dfrac{1}{2}$ $\boxed{\dfrac{1}{3}}$ $\dfrac{1}{4}$ $\dfrac{1}{2}$ $\boxed{\dfrac{3}{4}}$ $\boxed{\dfrac{1}{4}}$ $\dfrac{2}{3}$ $\dfrac{1}{2}$

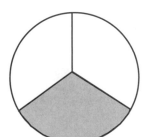

shaded   **white**

$\dfrac{1}{4}$ $\dfrac{1}{3}$ $\dfrac{1}{2}$ $\dfrac{2}{4}$ $\dfrac{2}{3}$ $\dfrac{2}{2}$

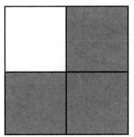

shaded   **white**

$\dfrac{3}{4}$ $\dfrac{1}{3}$ $\dfrac{3}{2}$ $\dfrac{1}{2}$ $\dfrac{1}{4}$ $\dfrac{1}{3}$

shaded   **white**

$\dfrac{2}{3}$ $\dfrac{2}{4}$ $\dfrac{2}{2}$ $\dfrac{1}{3}$ $\dfrac{2}{4}$ $\dfrac{2}{2}$

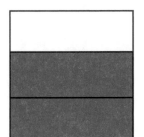

shaded   **white**

$\dfrac{2}{4}$ $\dfrac{2}{3}$ $\dfrac{2}{2}$ $\dfrac{1}{2}$ $\dfrac{1}{4}$ $\dfrac{1}{3}$

Fractions: Half, Third, Fourth

Directions: Draw a line from the fraction to the correct shape.

$\frac{1}{4}$ shaded

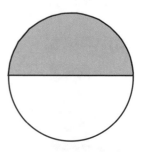

$\frac{2}{4}$ shaded

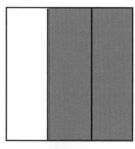

$\frac{1}{2}$ shaded

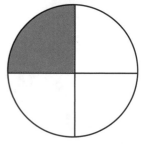

$\frac{1}{3}$ shaded

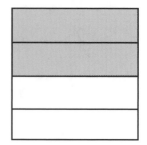

$\frac{2}{3}$ shaded

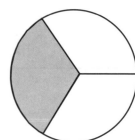

Geometry

Geometry is mathematics that has to do with lines and shapes.

Directions: Color the shapes.

Color the triangles blue.
Color the circles red.
Color the squares green.
Color the rectangles pink.

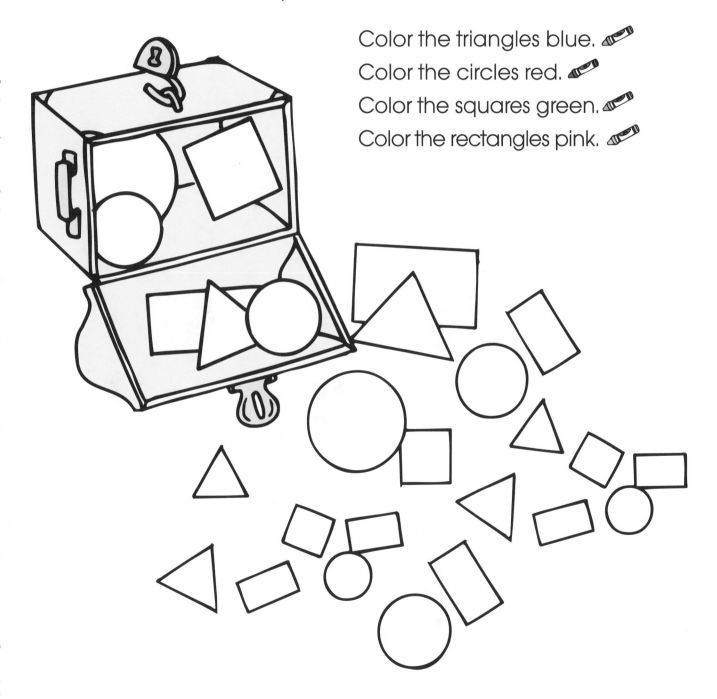

Name _____

Geometry

Directions: Draw a line from the word to the shape.

Use a red line for circles. Use a yellow line for rectangles.
Use a blue line for squares. Use a green line for triangles.

Circle　　　**Square**　　　**Triangle**　　　**Rectangle**

Geometry

Directions: Cut out the tangram below. Mix up the pieces. Try to put it back together into a square.

Page is blank for cutting exercise on previous page.

Measurement: Inches

Directions: Cut out the ruler. Measure each object to the nearest inch.

_____ inches

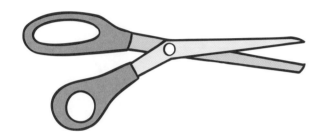

_____ inches

_____ inches

Measurement

Directions: Measure objects around your house. Write the measurement to the nearest inch.

can of soup   _____ inches

pen   _____ inches

toothbrush   _____ inches

paper clip   _____ inches

small toy   _____ inches

cut out

8 7 6 5 4 3 2 1

Page is blank for cutting exercise on previous page.

Measurement: Inches

An **inch** is a unit of length in the standard measurement system.

Directions: Use a ruler to measure each object to the nearest inch.

1 inch

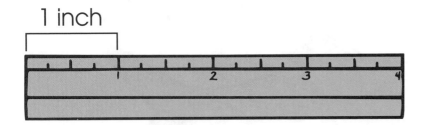

about ___1___ inches

about _____ inches

about _____ inches

about _____ inches

about _____ inches

about _____ inches

about _____ inches

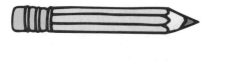

Measurement: Inches

Directions: Use the ruler to measure the fish to the nearest inch.

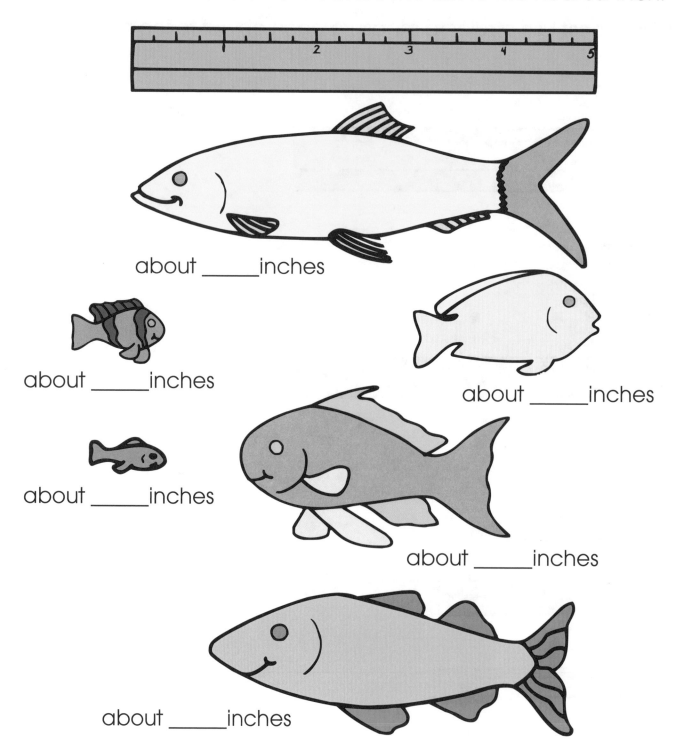

about _____ inches

about _____ inches

about _____ inches

about _____ inches

about _____ inches

about _____ inches

Measurement: Centimeters

A **centimeter** is a unit of length in the metric system. There are 2.54 centimeters in an inch.

Directions: Use a centimeter ruler to measure the crayons to the nearest centimeter.

Example: The first crayon is about 7 centimeters long.

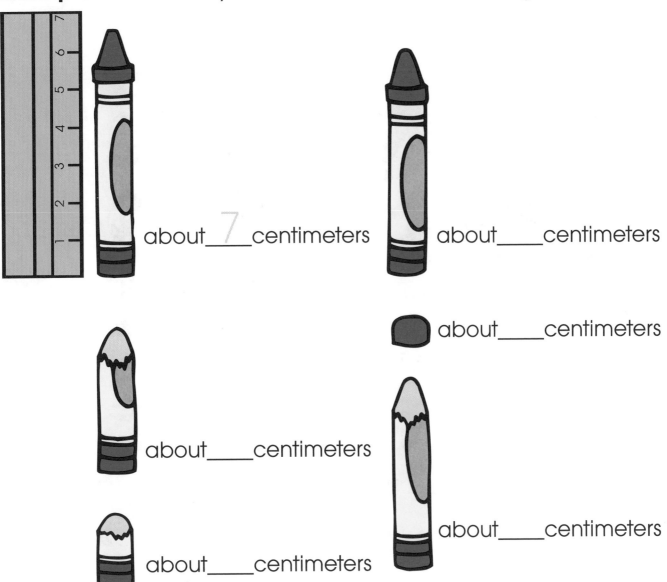

about __7__ centimeters

about ____ centimeters

about ____ centimeters

about ____ centimeters

about ____ centimeters

about ____ centimeters

Name _____

Measurement: Centimeters

Directions: The giraffe is about 8 centimeters high. How many centimeters (cm) high are the trees? Write your answers in the blanks.

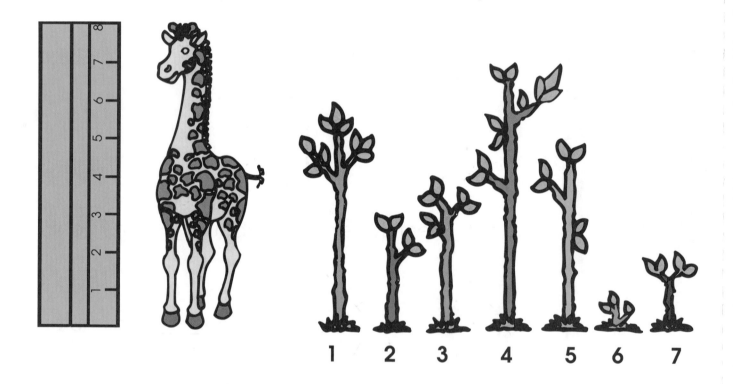

1   2   3   4   5   6   7

1)_____cm   2)_____cm   3)_____cm

4)_____cm   5)_____cm   6)_____cm   7)_____cm

Time: Hour, Half-Hour

An hour is sixty minutes. The short hand of a clock tells the hour. It is written **0:00**, such as **5:00**. A half-hour is thirty minutes. When the long hand of the clock is pointing to the six, the time is on the half-hour. It is written **:30**, such as **5:30**.

Directions: Study the examples. Tell what time it is on each clock.

Examples:

 **9:00**

The minute hand is on the 12.
The hour hand is on the 9.
It is 9 o'clock.

 **4:30**

The minute hand is on the 6.
The hour hand is *between* the 4 and 5.
It is 4:30.

2:00   3:30   1:00   5:30   8:00

10:30   12:00   9:30   2:30   3:00

Name _____

Time: Hour, Half-Hour

Directions: Draw lines between the clocks that show the same time.

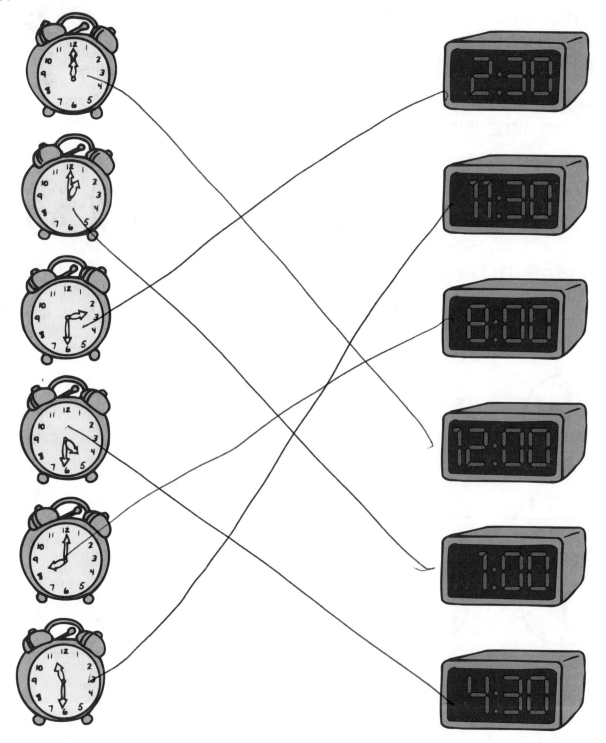

Time: Counting by Fives

The minute hand of a clock takes 5 minutes to move from one number to the next. Start at the 12, and count by fives to tell how many minutes it is past the hour.

Directions: Study the examples. Tell what time is on each clock.

Examples:

 9:10

 8:25

_____

_____

_____

Name _____

Time: Quarter-Hours

Time can also be shown as fractions. 30 minutes = $\frac{1}{2}$ hour

Directions: Shade the fraction of each clock, and tell how many minutes you have shaded.

Example:

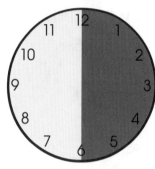

$\frac{1}{2}$ hour

<u>30</u> minutes

$\frac{1}{4}$ hour

____ minutes

$\frac{2}{4}$ hour

____ minutes

$\frac{3}{4}$ hour

____ minutes

$\frac{1}{2}$ hour

____ minutes

Review
Counting

Directions: Write the number that is

next.	one less.	one greater.
68, 69, ____	____ , 57	12, ____
786, 787, ____	____ , 650	843, ____

Place Value: Tens & Ones

Directions: Draw a line to the correct number.

4 tens + 7 ones	20
2 tens + 0 ones	51
7 tens + 3 ones	47
5 tens + 1 one	73

Addition and Subtraction

Directions: Add or subtract.

$$\begin{array}{r} 15 \\ + 5 \\ \hline \end{array} \qquad \begin{array}{r} 14 \\ - 4 \\ \hline \end{array} \qquad \begin{array}{r} 7 \\ + 3 \\ \hline \end{array} \qquad \begin{array}{r} 8 \\ - 6 \\ \hline \end{array} \qquad \begin{array}{r} 10 \\ + 7 \\ \hline \end{array} \qquad \begin{array}{r} 14 \\ - 5 \\ \hline \end{array}$$

Review

2-Digit Addition and Subtraction

Directions: Add or subtract using regrouping, if needed.

$$\begin{array}{r} 66 \\ -\ 37 \\ \hline \end{array} \qquad \begin{array}{r} 38 \\ +\ 18 \\ \hline \end{array} \qquad \begin{array}{r} 87 \\ -\ 69 \\ \hline \end{array} \qquad \begin{array}{r} 52 \\ -\ 15 \\ \hline \end{array} \qquad \begin{array}{r} 40 \\ +\ 17 \\ \hline \end{array}$$

$$\begin{array}{r} 84 \\ +\ 17 \\ \hline \end{array} \qquad \begin{array}{r} 65 \\ +\ 14 \\ \hline \end{array} \qquad \begin{array}{r} 99 \\ -\ 48 \\ \hline \end{array} \qquad \begin{array}{r} 61 \\ -\ 36 \\ \hline \end{array} \qquad \begin{array}{r} 56 \\ +\ 46 \\ \hline \end{array}$$

Place Value: Hundreds and Thousands

Directions: Draw a line to the correct number.

4 hundreds + 3 tens + 2 ones	7,201
6 hundreds + 7 tens + 6 ones	290
5 thousands + 3 hundreds + 7 tens + 2 ones	432
2 hundreds + 9 tens + 0 ones	676
7 thousands + 2 hundreds + 0 tens + 1 one	5,372

3-Digit Addition and Subtraction

Directions: Add or subtract, remembering to regroup, if needed.

$$\begin{array}{r} 458 \\ -\ 248 \\ \hline \end{array} \quad \begin{array}{r} 793 \\ -\ 414 \\ \hline \end{array} \quad \begin{array}{r} 822 \\ -\ 460 \\ \hline \end{array} \quad \begin{array}{r} 528 \\ +\ 319 \\ \hline \end{array} \quad \begin{array}{r} 697 \\ +\ 108 \\ \hline \end{array} \quad \begin{array}{r} 569 \\ +\ 288 \\ \hline \end{array}$$

Review

Multiplication

Directions: Solve the problems. Draw groups if necessary.

2	6	3	8	5	2
x 8	x 4	x 2	x 4	x 3	x 2

Fractions

Directions: Circle the correct fraction of each shape's white part.

$$\frac{1}{2} \quad \frac{1}{3} \quad \frac{1}{4}$$

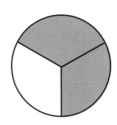

$$\frac{1}{4} \quad \frac{1}{3} \quad \frac{1}{2}$$

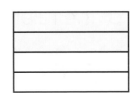

$$\frac{2}{3} \quad \frac{2}{4} \quad \frac{1}{3}$$

$$\frac{1}{4} \quad \frac{1}{2} \quad \frac{3}{4}$$

Graphs

Directions: Count the flowers. Color the pots to make a graph that shows the number of flowers.

1   2   3   4   5   6   7   8

Review

Geometry

Directions: Match the shapes.

rectangle

square

circle

triangle

Measurement

Directions: Look at the ruler. Measure the objects to the nearest inch.

   _____ inches

   _____ inches

CRAYON   _____ inches

Time

Directions: Tell what time is on each clock.

_____   _____   _____   _____

Money: Penny, Nickel

Penny **1¢**   Nickel **5¢**

Directions: Count the coins, and write the amount.

Example:

 _____8_____ ¢

5¢   1¢   1¢   1¢

 _____ ¢

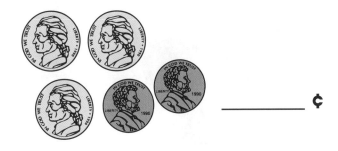 _____ ¢

 _____ ¢

 _____ ¢

Comprehensive Curriculum - **Grade 2**

Name _____

Money: Penny, Nickel, Dime

Penny **1¢**   Nickel **5¢**   Dime **10¢**

Directions: Count the coins, and write the amount.

   _16_ ¢

   _____ ¢

   _____ ¢

   _____ ¢

   _____ ¢

Money: Penny, Nickel, Dime

Directions: Draw a line from the toy to the amount of money it costs.

Money: Penny, Nickel, Dime

Directions: Draw a line to match the amounts of money.

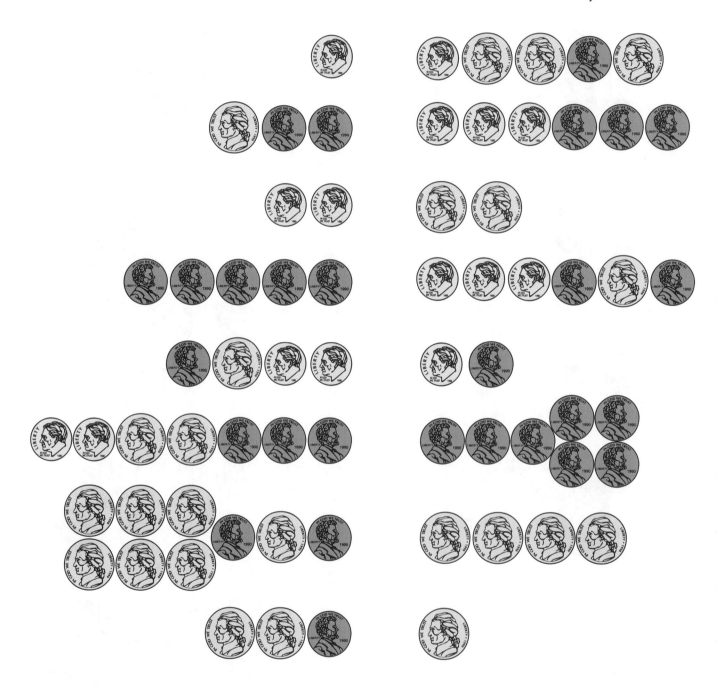

Money: Quarter

A quarter is worth 25¢.

Directions: Count the coins, and write the amounts.

  _____ ¢

 _____ ¢

   _____ ¢

 _____ ¢

    _____ ¢

 _____ ¢

    _____ ¢

   _____ ¢

Money: Decimals

A **decimal** is a number with one or more places to the right of a decimal point, such as 6.5 or 2.25. Money amounts are written with two places to the right of the decimal point.

| 25¢ | 10¢ | 5¢ | 1¢ |
| $.25 | $.10 | $.05 | $.01 |

Directions: Count the coins, and circle the amount shown.

Example:

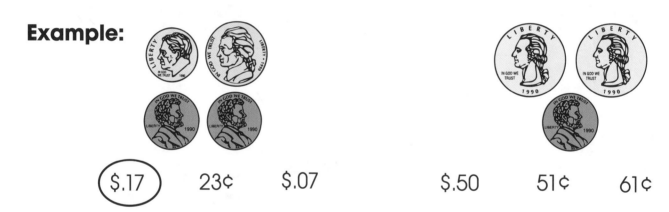

($.17)   23¢ $.07 $.50   51¢   61¢

$.28   36¢   42¢   37¢   43¢ $.47

Money: Decimals

Directions: Draw a line from the coins to the correct amount in each column.

3¢ $.55

55¢ $.41

31¢ $.37

37¢ $.31

41¢ $.03

Money: Dollar

One dollar equals 100 cents. It is written $1.00.

Directions: Count the money, and write the amounts.

 $ ___._____

 $ ___._____

 $ ___._____

 $ ___._____

  $ ___._____

 $ ___._____

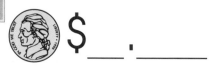  $ ___._____

 $ ___._____

Adding Money

Directions: Write the amount of money using decimals. Then, add to find the total amount.

Example:

$$\begin{aligned} \$1&.00 \\ &.05 \\ +\ &.02 \\ \hline \$1&.07 \end{aligned}$$

$ ___ . ___
$ ___ . ___
$ ___ . ___
+$ ___ . ___

___ . ___

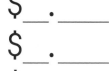

$ ___ . ___
$ ___ . ___
$ ___ . ___
+$ ___ . ___

___ . ___

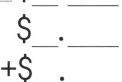

$ ___ . ___
$ ___ . ___
+$ ___ . ___

___ . ___

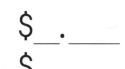

$ ___ . ___
$ ___ . ___
$ ___ . ___
+$ ___ . ___

___ . ___

Review

Directions: Add the money, and write the total.

_____ ¢   _____ ¢

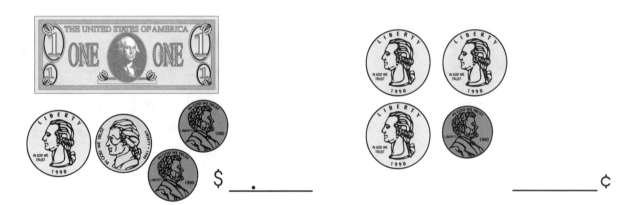

$ _____ . _____   _____ ¢

$ _____ . _____

Problem Solving

Directions: Tell whether you should add or subtract. **In all** is a clue to add. **Left** is a clue to subtract. Draw pictures to help you.

Example:

Jane's dog has 5 bones. He ate 3 bones. How many bones are left?

subtract

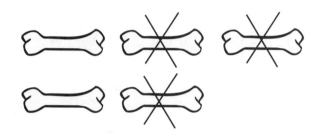

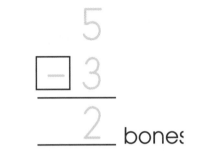

_____ bones

Lucky the cat had 5 mice. She got 4 more for her birthday. How many mice did she have in all?

_____

_____ mice

Sam bought 6 fish. She gave 2 fish to a friend. How many fish does she have left?

_____

_____ fish

Comprehensive Curriculum - **Grade 2**

Problem Solving: Addition, Subtraction, Multiplication

Directions: Tell if you add, subtract, or multiply. Then, write the answer.

Example:
There were 12 frogs sitting on a log by a pond, but 3 frogs hopped away. How many frogs are left?

__subtract_____ __9__ frogs

There are 9 flowers growing by the pond.
Each flower has 2 leaves.
How many leaves are there?

_____ _____ leaves

A tree had 7 squirrels playing in it.
Then, 8 more came along.
How many squirrels are there in all?

_____ _____ squirrels

There were 27 birds living in the trees around the pond, but 9 flew away.
How many birds are left?

_____ _____ birds

Problem Solving: Fractions

A fraction is a number that names part of a whole, such as $\frac{1}{2}$ or $\frac{1}{3}$.

Directions: Read each problem. Use the pictures to help you solve the problem. Write the fraction that answers the question.

Simon and Jessie shared a pizza.
Together they ate $\frac{3}{4}$ of the pizza.
How much of the pizza is left? _____

Sylvia baked a cherry pie. She gave $\frac{1}{3}$
to her grandmother and $\frac{1}{3}$ to a friend.
How much of the pie did she keep? _____

Ahmad erased $\frac{1}{2}$ of the blackboard
before the bell rang for recess.
How much of the blackboard does
he have left to erase? _____

Directions: Read the problem. Draw your own picture to help you solve the problem. Write the fraction that answers the question.

Yoko mowed $\frac{1}{4}$ of the yard before lunch.
How much does she have left to mow? _____

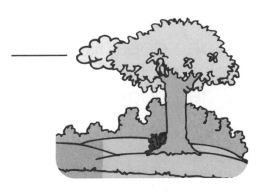

Problem Solving: Time

Directions: Solve each problem.

Addy wakes up at 7:00. She has 30 minutes before her bus comes. What time does her bus come?

_____ : _____

Vera walks her dog for 15 minutes after supper. She finishes supper at 6:30. When does she get home from walking her dog?

_____ : _____

Diego practices the piano for 30 minutes when he gets home from school. He gets home at 3:30. When does he stop practicing?

_____ : _____

Tanya starts mowing the grass at 4:30. She finishes at 5:00. For how many minutes does she mow the lawn?

_____ minutes

Aiden does his homework for 45 minutes. He starts his work at 7:15. When does he stop working?

_____ : _____

Problem Solving: Money

Directions: Read each problem. Use the pictures to help you solve the problems.

Ben bought a ball. He had 11¢ left.
How much money did he have at the start?

_____ ¢

Tara has 75¢. She buys a car.
How much money does she have left?

_____ ¢

Leah wants to buy a doll and a ball. She has 80¢.
How much more money does she need?

_____ ¢

Jacob has 95¢. He buys the car and the ball.
How much more money does he need to
buy a doll for his sister?

_____ ¢

Pilar paid three quarters, one dime,
and three pennies for a hat.
How much did it cost?

_____ ¢

Comprehensive Curriculum - **Grade 2**

GLOSSARY

Addition: Putting together or adding two or more numbers to find the sum.

Adjectives: Words that tell more about a person, place, or thing.

Alphabetical (ABC) Order: Putting letters or words in the order in which they appear in the alphabet.

Antonyms: Words that mean the opposite. Example: *big* and *small*

Articles: Small words that help us to better understand nouns. Example: *a* and *an*

Author: The person who wrote the words of a book.

Beginning Consonants: Consonant sounds that come at the beginning of words.

Blends: Two consonants put together to form a single sound.

Capital Letters: Letters that are used at the beginning of the names of people, places, days, months, and holidays. Capital letters are also used at the beginning of sentences. These letters are sometimes called uppercase or "big" letters.

Centimeter: A measurement of length in the metric system. There are $2\frac{1}{2}$ centimeters in an inch.

Chapters: Small sections of a book.

Characters: The people or animals in a story.

Circle: A figure that is round.

Classifying: Putting things that are alike into groups.

Closed Figures: Figures whose lines connect.

Commands: Sentences that tell someone to do something.

Commutative Property: The rule in addition that states that, even if the order of the numbers is changed, the sum will be the same.

Compound Predicate: Predicate of the sentence formed by joining two verbs that have the same subject.

Compound Subject: Subject of the sentence formed by joining two nouns that have the same predicate.

Compound Words: Two words that are put together to make one new word. Example: *house* + *boat* = *houseboat*

Comprehension: Understanding what you read.

Consonants: The letters *b, c, d, f, g, h, j, k, l, m, n, p, q, r, s, t, v,w, x, y*, and *z*.

Consonant Blends: Two or three consonant letters in a word whose sounds combine, or blend. Examples: *br, fr, gr, tr*

Consonant Teams: Two or three consonant letters that have a single sound. Examples: *sh* and *tch*

Contractions: A short way to write two words together. Example: *it is* = *it's*

Contrast: To discuss how things are different.

Decimal: A number with one or more places to the right of a decimal point, such as 6.5 or 3.78. Money amounts are written with two places to the right of a decimal point, such as $1.30.

Dictionary: A reference book that gives the meaning of words and how to pronounce them.

Difference: The answer in a subtraction problem.

Digit: The symbols used to write numbers: 0, 1, 2, 3, 4, 5, 6, 7, 8, and 9.

Dime: Ten cents. It is written 10¢ or $.10.

Dollar: A dollar is equal to one hundred cents. It is written $1.00.

Double Vowel Words: When two vowels appear together in a word. Examples: *tea, coat*

Ending Consonants: Consonant sounds that come at the end of words.

Fact: Something that can be proven.

Fiction: A make-believe story.

Fraction: A number that names part of a whole, such as   or   .

Geometry: Mathematics that has to do with lines and shapes.

Glossary: A little dictionary at the back of a book.

Graph: A drawing that shows information about numbers.

Guide Words: The words that appear at the top of a dictionary page to tell you what the first and the last words on that page will be.

Haiku: A Japanese form of poetry. Most have 5 syllables in the first and third lines, and 7 syllables in the middle line.

Half-Hour: Thirty minutes. It is written 0:30.

Hard and Soft c: In words where *c* is followed by *a* or *u*, the *c* usually has a hard sound (like a *k*). Examples: *cup, cart*. When *c* is followed by *e, i,* or *y*, it usually has a soft sound (like an *s*). Examples: *circle, fence*.

Hard and Soft g: When *g* is followed by *e, i,* or *y*, it usually has a soft sound (like *j*). Examples: *change* and *gentle*. The hard *g* sounds like the *g* in *girl* or *gate*.

Homophones: Words that sound the same but are spelled differently and mean different things. Example: *blue* and *blew*

Hour: Sixty minutes. The short hand of a clock tells the hour. It is written 1:00.

Illustrator: The person who drew pictures for a book.

Inch: A unit of length in the standard measurement system.

Inference: A conclusion arrived at by what is suggested in the text.

Joining Words: Words that combine ideas in a sentence, such as *and, but, or,* and *because*.

Letter Teams: Two letters put together to make one new sound.

Long Vowels: Long vowels say their names. Examples: Long *a* is the sound you hear in *hay*. Long *e* is the sound you hear in *me*. Long *i* is the sound you hear in *pie*. Long *o* is the sound you hear in *no*. Long *u* is the sound you hear in *cute*.

Main Idea: The most important point or idea in a story.

Making Deductions: Using reasoning skills to draw conclusions.

Metric System: A system of measuring in which length is measured in millimeters, centimeters, meters, and kilometers; capacity is measured in milliliters and liters; weight is measured in grams and kilograms; and temperature is measured in degrees Celsius.

Multiplication: A short way to find the sum of adding the same number a certain amount of times. For example, 7 x 4 = 28 instead of 7 + 7 + 7 + 7 = 28.

Nickel: Five cents. It is written 5¢ or $.05.

Nonfiction: A true story.

Nouns: Words that name a person, place, or thing.

Open Figures: Figures whose lines do not connect.

Opinion: A feeling or belief about something that cannot be proven.

Opposites: Words that are different in every way. Example: *black* and *white*

Ordinal Numbers: Numbers that indicate order in a series, such as *first*, *second* or *third*.

Pattern: Similar shapes or designs.

Penny: One cent. It is written 1¢ or $.01.

Place Value: The value of a digit, or numeral, shown by where it is in the number.

Plurals: Words that mean more than one. Examples: *shoes*, *ladies*, *dishes*, *foxes*

Predicate: The verb in the sentence that tells the main action.

Predicting: Telling what is likely to happen, based on the facts.

Prefix: A syllable added at the beginning of a word to change its meaning. Examples: *disappear*, *misplace*

Product: The answer of a multiplication problem.

Pronouns: Words that are used in place of nouns. *She*, *he*, *it*, and *they* are pronouns.

Proper Nouns: The names of specific people, places, and things. Proper nouns begin with a capital letter.

Quarter: Twenty-five cents. It is written 25¢ or $.25.

Questions: Sentences that ask something. A question begins with a capital letter and ends with a question mark.

R-Controlled Vowel: When *r* follows a vowel, it gives the vowel a different sound. Examples: *her, bark, bird*

Rectangle: A figure with four corners and four sides. Sides opposite each other are the same length.

Regroup: To use ten ones to form one ten, ten tens to form 100, and so on.

Rhyming Words: Words that end with the same sound. Example: *cat* and *rat*

Same and Different: Being able to tell how things are the same and how they are different.

Sentences: A group of words that tells a complete idea or asks a question.

Sequencing: Putting things in the correct order, such as 7, 8, 9, or small, medium, large.

Short Vowels: Vowels that make short sounds. Examples: Short *a* is the sound you hear in *cat*. Short *e* is the sound you hear in *leg*. Short *i* is the sound you hear in *pig*. Short *o* is the sound in *box*. Short *u* is the sound in *cup*.

Silent Letters: Letters you can't hear at all, such as the *gh* in *night*, the *w* in *wrong* and the *t* in *listen*.

Simile: A figure of speech that compares two things that are alike in some way. The words *like* and *as* are used in similes. Examples: as soft as a pillow, as light as a feather

Statements: Sentences that tell about something. Statements begin with a capital letter and end with a period.

Subtraction: Taking away or subtracting one number from another to find the difference.

Suffix: A syllable added at the end of a word to change its meaning. Examples: *small**er**, help**less***

Super Silent e: An *e* that you can't hear when it appears at the end of a word. It makes the other vowel have a long sound. Examples: *cape, robe, slide*

Surprising Sentences: Sentences that tell a strong feeling. Surprising sentences begin with a capital letter and end with an exclamation point.

Syllables: The parts of words that have vowel sounds. Examples: *Rab|bit* has two syllables. *Bas|ket|ball* has three syllables.

Synonyms: Words that mean the same or nearly the same. Example: *sleepy* and *tired*

Table of Contents: Sentences that tell a strong feeling. Telling sentences begin with a capital letter and end with an exclamation point.

Title: The name of a book.

Tracking: Following a path.

Triangle: A figure with three corners and three sides.

Venn Diagram: A diagram that shows how two things are the same and how they are different.

Verbs: Words that tell the action in a sentence. Example: The boy **ran** fast.

Vowel Team: Vowels that appear together in words. Usually, the first one says its name and the second one is silent. Examples: *leaf, soap, rain*

Vowels: The letters *a, e, i, o, u,* and sometimes *y.*

Y as a Vowel: When *y* comes at the end of a word, it is a vowel. Examples: *my, baby*

All About Me!

Directions: Fill in the blanks to tell all about you!
Answers will vary.

Name _____
(First)   (Last)
Address _____
City _____ State _____
Phone number _____
Age _____

Places I have visited: _____
_____
_____

My favorite vacation: _____
_____
_____

Page 6

Beginning Consonants: *B, C, D, F, G, H,* and *J*

Directions: Fill in the beginning consonant for each word.

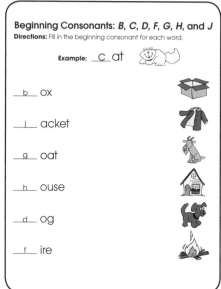

Example: _c_ at

_b_ ox

_j_ acket

_g_ oat

_h_ ouse

_d_ og

_f_ ire

Page 7

Beginning Consonants: *K, L, M, N, P, Q,* and *R*

Directions: Write the letter that makes the beginning sound for each picture.

_m_   _q_   _r_   _n_

_m_   _l_   _k_   _r_

_q_   _p_   _n_   _m_

_l_   _k_   _r_   _p_

Page 8

Beginning Consonants: *K, L, M, N, P, Q,* and *R*

Directions: Fill in the beginning consonant for each word.

Example: _r_ ose

_m_ oney

_q_ uilt

_l_ ion

_p_ an

_k_ ey

_n_ ose

Page 9

Beginning Consonants: *S, T, V, W, X, Y,* and *Z*

Directions: Write the letter that makes the beginning sound for each picture.

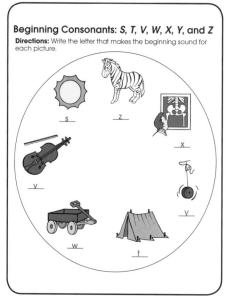

_s_   _z_

_x_

_v_   _y_

_w_   _t_

Page 10

Beginning Consonants: *S, T, V, W, X, Y,* and *Z*

Directions: Fill in the beginning consonant for each word.

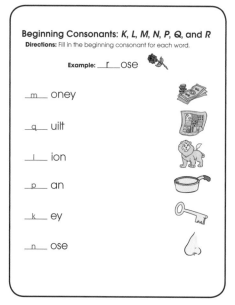

Example: _s_ ock

_z_ ipper

_t_ able

_x_ ray

_v_ ase

_y_ olk

_w_ and

Page 11

Ending Consonants: *B, D, F,* and *G*

Directions: Fill in the ending consonant for each word.

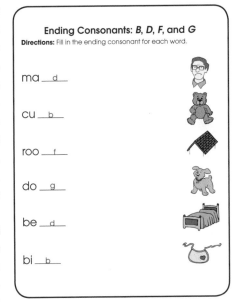

ma __d__

cu __b__

roo __f__

do __g__

be __d__

bi __b__

Page 12

Ending Consonants: *K, L, M, N, P,* and *R*

Directions: Fill in the ending consonant for each word.

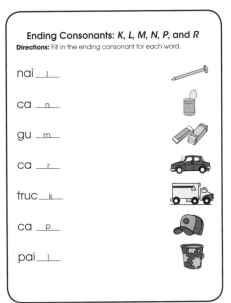

nai __l__

ca __n__

gu __m__

ca __r__

truc __k__

ca __p__

pai __l__

Page 13

Ending Consonants: *S, T,* and *X*

Directions: Fill in the ending consonant for each word.

ca __t__

bo __x__

bu __s__

fo __x__

boa __t__

ma __t__

Page 14

Consonant Blends

Consonant blends are two or three consonant letters in a word whose sounds combine, or blend. **Examples: br, fr, gr, pr, tr**

Directions: Look at each picture. Say its name. Write the blend you hear at the beginning of each word.

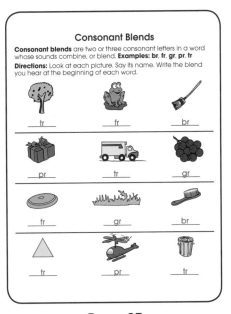

tr   fr   br

pr   tr   gr

fr   gr   br

tr   pr   tr

Page 15

Blends: *fl, br, pl, sk,* and *sn*

Directions: Look at the pictures, and say their names. Write the letters for the beginning sound in each word.

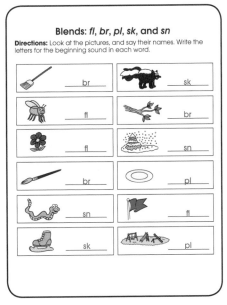

br   sk

fl   br

fl   sn

br   pl

sn   fl

sk   pl

Page 16

Blends: *bl, cl, cr,* and *sl*

Directions: Look at the pictures, and say their names. Write the letters for the beginning sound in each word.

__cl__ own   __bl__ anket   __cr__ ayon

__cl__ ock   __sl__ ide   __cl__ oud

__sl__ ed   __cr__ ab   __cr__ ocodile

Page 17

Comprehensive Curriculum - **Grade 2**

Page 18

Consonant Blends

Directions: Write a word from the word box to answer each riddle.

| clock | glass | blow | climb | slipper |
| sleep | gloves | clap | blocks | flashlight |

1. You need me when the lights go out. **What am I?** — flashlight
2. People use me to tell the time. **What am I?** — clock
3. You put me on your hands in the winter to keep them warm. **What am I?** — gloves
4. Cinderella lost one like me at midnight. **What am I?** — slipper
5. This is what you do with your hands when you are pleased. **What is it?** — clap
6. You can do this with a whistle or with bubble gum. **What is it?** — blow
7. These are what you might use to build a castle when you are playing. **What are they?** — blocks
8. You do this to get to the top of a hill. **What is it?** — climb
9. This is what you use to drink water or milk. **What is it?** — glass
10. You do this at night with your eyes closed. **What is it?** — sleep

Page 19

Consonant Blends

Directions: Read the words in the box. Write a word from the word box to finish each sentence. Circle the consonant blend in each word. **Hint:** There are three letters in each blend.

| splash | screen | spray | street | scream |
| screw | sprain | split | strong | string |

1. Did you **sprain** your ankle?
2. I tied a **string** to my tooth to help pull it out.
3. I have many friends who live on my **street**.
4. We always **scream** when we ride the roller coaster.
5. A **screen** helps keep bugs out of the house.
6. It is fun to **splash** in the water.
7. My father uses an ax to **split** the firewood.
8. We will need a **screw** to fix the chair.
9. You must be very **strong** to lift this heavy box.
10. The firefighters **spray** the fire with water.

Page 20

Consonant Teams

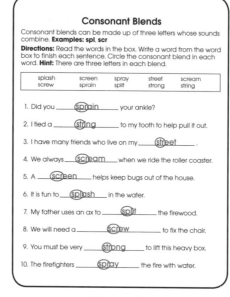

Page 21

Consonant Teams: *sh, ch, wh,* and *th*

Page 22

Consonant Teams: *sh, ch, wh,* and *th*

Page 23

Consonant Blends and Teams

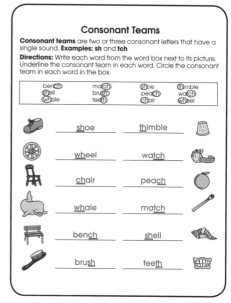

1. My **chicken** won't lay eggs.
2. I put a **chain** on my bicycle so nobody can take it.
3. We watched the big **ship** dock and let off its passengers.
4. It is my job to take out the **trash**.
5. I have to wear a **patch** over my eye until it is better.
6. The baby likes to **splash** in the bathtub.
7. Can you **catch** the ball with one hand?
8. Please **shut** the windows before it rains.
9. **When** are we going to leave for school?
10. I don't know **which** of these books is mine.

Consonant Blends and Teams

Directions: Look at the words in the word box. Write all of the words that end with the **ng** sound in the column under the picture of the **ring**. Write all of the words that end with the **nk** sound under the picture of the **sink**. Finish the sentences with words from the word box.

strong	rank	bring	bank	honk	hang	thank
long	hunk	song	stung	bunk	sang	junk

ng

strong	rank
bring	bank
hang	honk
long	thank
song	hunk
stung	bunk
sang	junk

1. _____Honk_____ your horn when you get to my house.
2. He was _____stung_____ by a bee.
3. We are going to put our money in a _____bank_____.
4. I want to _____thank_____ you for the birthday present.
5. My brother and I sleep in _____bunk_____ beds.

Page 24

Silent Letters

Some words have letters you can't hear at all, such as the **gh** in **night**, the **w** in **wrong**, the **l** in **walk**, the **k** in **knee**, the **b** in **climb**, and the **t** in **listen**.

Directions: Look at the words in the word box. Write the word under its picture. Underline the silent letters.

knife	light	calf	wrench	lamb	eight
wrist	whistle	comb	thumb	knob	knee

eight   wrist   knee   calf

lamb   knob   whistle   light

wrench   comb   thumb   knife

Page 25

Review

Directions: Read the story. Circle the consonant teams, consonant blends, and silent letters in the underlined words. Be sure to check for more than one team in a word! One has been done for you.

One day last spring, my family went on a picnic. My father picked out a pretty spot next to a stream. While my brother and I climbed a tree, my mother spread out a sheet and placed the food on it. But before we could eat, a skunk walked out of the woods! Mother screamed and scared the skunk. It sprayed us with a terrible smell! Now, we think it is a funny story. But that day, we ran!

Directions: Write the words with three-letter blends on the lines.

spring   stream   spread

screamed   sprayed

Page 26

Hard and Soft C

When **c** is followed by **e**, **i**, or **y**, it usually has a **soft** sound. The soft **c** sounds like **s**. For example, **c**ircle and fen**c**e. When **c** is followed by **a** or **u**, it usually has a **hard** sound. The **hard c** sounds like **k**, as in **c**up or **c**art.

Directions: Read the words in the word box. Write the words in the correct lists. One word will be in both. Write a word from the word box to finish each sentence.

pencil	cookie
dance	cent
popcorn	circus
carrot	mice
tractor	card

Words with soft c

pencil
dance
cent
circus
mice

Words with hard c

popcorn
carrot
tractor
cookie
circus
card

1. Another word for a penny is a _____cent_____.
2. A cat likes to chase _____mice_____.
3. You will see animals and clowns at the _____circus_____.
4. Will you please sharpen my _____pencil_____?

Page 27

Hard and Soft G

When **g** is followed by **e**, **i**, or **y**, it usually has a **soft** sound. The soft **g** sounds like **j**. **Example:** chan**g**e and **g**entle. When **g** is followed by **a**, **o**, or **u**, it usually has a **hard** sound, like the **g** in **g**o or **g**ate.

Directions: Read the words in the word box. Write the words in the correct lists. Write a word from the box to finish each sentence.

engine	glove	cage	magic	frog
giant	flag	large	glass	goose

Words with soft g

engine
giant
cage
large
magic

Words with hard g

glove
flag
glass
frog
goose

1. Our bird lives in a _____cage_____.
2. Pulling a rabbit from a hat is a good _____magic_____ trick.
3. A car needs an _____engine_____ to run.
4. A _____giant_____ is a huge person.
5. An elephant is a very _____large_____ animal.

Page 28

Hard and Soft C and G

Directions: Look at the **c** and **g** words at the bottom of the page. Cut them out, and glue them in the correct box below.

soft sound	hard sound
gem	jug
giant	crayon
age	grass
juice	goat
face	grow
engine	cart

Page 29

Short Vowels

Vowels can make **short** or **long** sounds. The short **a** sounds like the **a** in **cat**. The short **e** is like the **e** in **leg**. The short **i** sounds like the **i** in **pig**. The short **o** sounds like the **o** in **box**. The short **u** sounds like the **u** in **cup**.

Directions: Look at each picture. Write the missing short vowel.

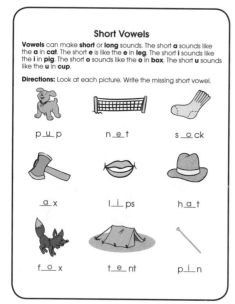

p_u_p   n_e_t   s_o_ck

_a_x   l_i_ps   h_a_t

f_o_x   t_e_nt   p_i_n

Page 31

Short Vowels

Vowels can make **short** or **long** sounds. The short **a** sounds like the **a** in **cat**. The short **e** is like the **e** in **leg**. The short **i** sounds like the **i** in **pig**. The short **o** sounds like the **o** in **box**. The short **u** is like the **u** in **cup**.

Directions: Look at the pictures. Their names all have short vowel sounds. But the vowels are missing. Fill in the missing vowels in each word.

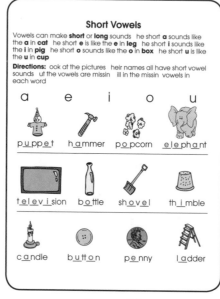

a   e   i   o   u

p_u_pp_e_t h_a_mmer p_o_pcorn el_e_ph_a_nt

telev_i_sion b_o_ttle sh_o_vel th_i_mble

c_a_ndle b_u_tt_o_n pe_n_ny l_a_dder

Page 32

Short Vowels

Directions: Cut out the giant vowels. Decorate them with pictures or words that have the short vowel sound.

Answers will vary.

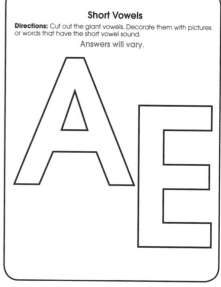

Page 33

Short Vowels

Answers will vary.

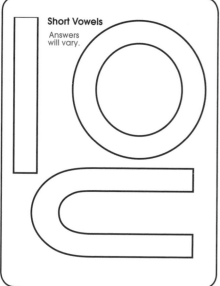

Page 35

Super Silent *E*

Long vowel sounds have the same sound as their names. When a **Super Silent e** appears at the end of a word, you can't hear it, but it makes the other vowel have a long sound. For example: **tub** has a **short** vowel sound, and **tube** has a **long** vowel sound.

Directions: Look at the following pictures. Decide if the word has a short or long vowel sound. Circle the correct word. Watch for the **Super Silent e**!

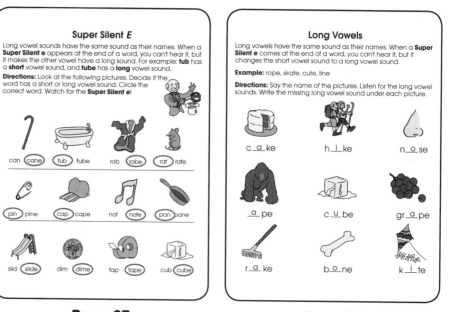

can (cane) (tub) tube rob (robe) (rat) rate

(pin) pine (cap) cape not (note) (pan) pane

slid (slide) dim (dime) tap (tape) cub (cube)

Page 37

Long Vowels

Long vowels have the same sound as their names. When a **Super Silent e** comes at the end of a word, you can't hear it, but it changes the short vowel sound to a long vowel sound.

Example: rope, skate, cute, line

Directions: Say the name of the pictures. Listen for the long vowel sounds. Write the missing long vowel sound under each picture.

c_a_ke   h_i_ke   n_o_se

_a_pe   c_u_be   gr_a_pe

r_a_ke   b_o_ne   k_i_te

Page 38

Review

Directions: Read the words in each box. Cross out the word that does not belong.

long vowels	short vowels
cube	man
~~cup~~	pet
rake	fix
me	~~ice~~

long vowels	short vowels
soap	cat
seed	pin
read	~~rain~~
~~mat~~	frog

Directions: Write **short** or **long** to label the words in each box.

<u>long</u> vowels	<u>short</u> vowels
hose	frog
take	hot
bead	sled
cube	lap
eat	block
see	sit

Page 39

R-Controlled Vowels

When a vowel is followed by the letter **r**, it has a different sound.

Example: he and **her**

Directions: Write a word from the word box to finish each sentence. Notice the sound of the vowel followed by an **r**.

park	chair	horse	bark	bird
hurt	girl	hair	store	ears

1. A dog likes to __bark__.
2. You buy food at a __store__.
3. Children like to play at the __park__.
4. An animal you can ride is a __horse__.
5. You hear with your __ears__.
6. A robin is a kind of __bird__.
7. If you fall down, you might get __hurt__.
8. The opposite of a boy is a __girl__.
9. You comb and brush your __hair__.
10. You sit down on a __chair__.

Page 40

R-Controlled Words

R-controlled vowel words are words in which the **r** that comes after the vowel changes the sound of the vowel. **Examples:** bird, star, burn

Directions: Write the correct word in the sentences below.

horse	purple
jar	bird
dirt	turtle

1. Jelly comes in one of these. __jar__
2. This creature has feathers and can fly. __bird__
3. This animal lives in a shell. __turtle__
4. This animal can pull wagons. __horse__
5. If you mix water and this, you will have mud. __dirt__
6. This color starts with the letter **p**. __purple__

Page 41

R-Controlled Vowels

Directions: Answer the riddles below. You will need to complete the words with the correct vowel followed by **r**.

1. I am something you may use to eat. What am I?   f__or__k
2. My word names the opposite of tall. What am I?   sh__or__t
3. I can be seen high in the sky. I twinkle. What am I?   st__ar__
4. I am a kind of clothing a girl might wear. What am I?   sk__ir__t
5. My word tells what a group of cows is called. What am I?   h__er__d
6. I am part of your body. What am I?   __ar__m

Page 42

Double Vowel Words

Usually when two vowels appear together, the first one says its name and the second one is silent. **Example: bean**

Directions: Unscramble the double vowel words below. Write the correct word on the line.

ocat   __coat__   etar   __tear__

mtea   __meat__   eetf   __feet__

teas   __seat__   otab   __boat__

ogat   __goat__   spea   __peas__

atli   __tail__   apil   __pail__

Page 43

Vowel Teams

The vowel teams **ou** and **ow** can have the same sound. You can hear it in the words **clown** and **cloud**. The vowel teams **au** and **aw** have the same sound. You hear it in the words **because** and **law**.

Directions: Look at the pictures. Write the correct vowel team to complete the words. The first one is done for you. You may need to use a dictionary to help you with the correct spelling.

auto   cl__ow__n   h__ou__se

fl__ow__er   s__aw__   __ow__l

p__ow__der   m__ou__th   j__aw__

p__aw__   m__ou__se   cl__ou__d

Page 44

Comprehensive Curriculum - **Grade 2**

Vowel Teams

The vowel team **ea** can have a short **e** sound, like in **head**, or a long **e** sound, like in **bead**. An **ea** followed by an **r** makes a sound like the one in **ear** or like the one in **heard**.

Directions: Read the story. Listen for the sound **ea** makes in the bold words.

Have you ever **read** a book or **heard** a story about a **bear**? You might have **learned** that bears sleep through the winter. Some bears may sleep the whole **season**. Sometimes, they look almost **dead**! But they are very much alive. As the cold winter passes and the spring **weather** comes **near**, they wake up. After such a nice rest, they must be **ready** to **eat** a **really** big **meal**!

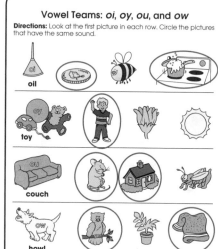

words with long **ea**	words with short **ea**	**ea** followed by **r**
season	read	heard
eat	dead	bear
really	weather	learned
meal	ready	near

Page 45

Vowel Teams

The vowel team **ie** makes the long **e** sound, as in **believe**. The team **ei** also makes the long **e** sound, as in **either**. But, **ei** can also make a long **a** sound, as in **vein**. The teams **eigh** and **ey** also make the long **a** sound.

Directions: Circle the words with the long **a** sound.

(neighbor)   (veil)

receive   (reindeer)

(reign)   ceiling

Directions: Finish the sentences with words from the word box.

chief   sleigh   obey   weigh   thief   field   ceiling

1. Eight reindeer pull Santa's ___sleigh___.
2. Rules are for us to ___obey___.
3. The bird got out of its cage and flew up to the ___ceiling___.
4. The leader of a tribe is the ___chief___.
5. How much do you ___weigh___?
6. They caught the ___thief___ who took my bike.
7. Corn grows in a ___field___.

Page 46

Vowel Teams: *oi*, *oy*, *ou*, and *ow*

Directions: Look at the first picture in each row. Circle the pictures that have the same sound.

oil

toy

couch

howl

Page 47

Vowel Teams: *ai* and *ee*

Directions: Write in the vowel team **ai** or **ee** to complete each word.

r _a_ _i_ n

f _e_ _e_ d

s _e_ _e_ d

p _a_ _i_ l

s _a_ _i_ l

cr _e_ _e_ k

Page 48

Review

Directions: Read the story. Fill in the blanks with words from the word box.

| cookies | Joe | bowl | tooth | flour | Layla |
| spoon | eats | enjoys | round | boy | chewy |

Do you like to cook? I know a ___boy___ named ___Joe___ who loves to cook. When Joe has a sweet ___tooth___, he makes healthy and tasty ___cookies___. He puts ___flour___ and applesauce in a ___bowl___ and stirs it with a ___spoon___. Then, he adds butter, oatmeal, raisins, and eggs. He makes cookies that are ___round___ and ___chewy___. Now is the part he ___enjoys___ the most: Joe ___eats___ the cookies. He shares them with his sister, ___Layla___.

Page 49

Y as a Vowel

When **y** comes at the end of a word, it is a vowel. When **y** is the only vowel at the end of a one-syllable word, it has the sound of a long **i** (as in **my**). When **y** is the only vowel at the end of a word with more than one syllable, it has the sound of long **e** (as in **baby**).

Directions: Look at the words in the word box. If the word has the sound of long **i**, write it under the word **my**. If the word has the sound of long **e**, write it under the word **baby**. Write the word from the word box that answers each riddle.

| happy | penny | fry | try | sleepy | dry |
| bunny | why | windy | sky | party | fly |

my	**baby**
fry	happy
try	penny
dry	sleepy
why	bunny
sky	windy
fly	party

1. It takes five of these to make a nickel. ___penny___
2. You might call it a rabbit. ___bunny___
3. It is often blue, and you can see it if you look up. ___sky___
4. You might have one of these on your birthday. ___party___
5. It is the opposite of wet. ___dry___
6. You might use this word to ask a question. ___why___

Page 50

Y as a Vowel

Directions: Read the rhyming story. Choose words from the box to fill in the blanks.

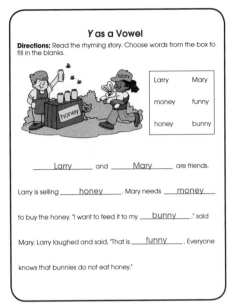

Larry	Mary
money	funny
honey	bunny

_____Larry_____ and _____Mary_____ are friends.

Larry is selling _____honey_____ . Mary needs _____money_____

to buy the honey. "I want to feed it to my _____bunny_____ ," said

Mary. Larry laughed and said, "That is _____funny_____ . Everyone

knows that bunnies do not eat honey."

Page 51

Y as a Vowel

Directions: Read the story. Choose words from the box to fill in the blanks.

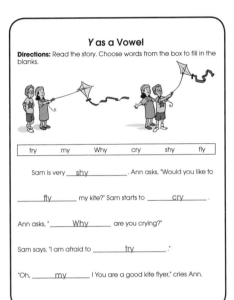

try	my	Why	cry	shy	fly

Sam is very _____shy_____ . Ann asks, "Would you like to

_____fly_____ my kite?" Sam starts to _____cry_____ .

Ann asks, "_____Why_____ are you crying?"

Sam says, "I am afraid to _____try_____ ."

"Oh, _____my_____ ! You are a good kite flyer," cries Ann.

Page 52

School Words

pencil	teacher	crayons
recess	lunchbox	play
fun	math	

Directions: Fill in the blanks with a word from the word box.

1. I need to sharpen my _____pencil_____ .

2. I like to _____play_____ at recess.

3. School is _____fun_____ !

4. My _____teacher_____ helps me learn.

5. I need to color the picture with _____crayons_____ .

6. I play kickball at _____recess_____ .

7. My sandwich is in my _____lunchbox_____ .

8. In _____math_____ , I can add and subtract.

Page 53

Days of the Week

Directions: Write the day of the week that answers each question.

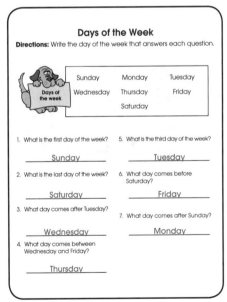

Sunday	Monday	Tuesday
Wednesday	Thursday	Friday
	Saturday	

1. What is the first day of the week?
   _____Sunday_____

2. What is the last day of the week?
   _____Saturday_____

3. What day comes after Tuesday?
   _____Wednesday_____

4. What day comes between Wednesday and Friday?
   _____Thursday_____

5. What is the third day of the week?
   _____Tuesday_____

6. What day comes before Saturday?
   _____Friday_____

7. What day comes after Sunday?
   _____Monday_____

Page 54

Compound Words

Compound words are two words that are put together to make one new word.

Directions: Help the cook brew her stew. Mix words from the first column with words from the second column to make new words. Write your new words on the lines at the bottom.

grand	brows
snow	light
eye	stairs
down	string
rose	book
shoe	mother
note	ball
moon	bud

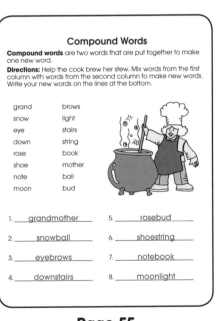

1. _____grandmother_____
2. _____snowball_____
3. _____eyebrows_____
4. _____downstairs_____
5. _____rosebud_____
6. _____shoestring_____
7. _____notebook_____
8. _____moonlight_____

Page 55

Compound Words

Directions: Read the sentences. Fill in the blank with a compound word from the box.

raincoat	bedroom	lunchbox	hallway	sandbox

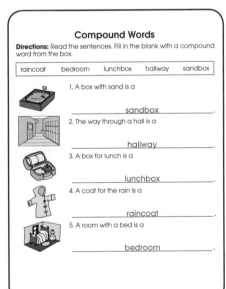

1. A box with sand is a
   _____sandbox_____ .

2. The way through a hall is a
   _____hallway_____ .

3. A box for lunch is a
   _____lunchbox_____ .

4. A coat for the rain is a
   _____raincoat_____ .

5. A room with a bed is a
   _____bedroom_____ .

Page 56

Compound Words

Directions: Cut out the words below. Glue them together in the box to make compound words.

— COMPOUND WORDS —

sunflower	sunscreen
mailbox	watermelon
football	bodyguard
airplane	classroom

Can you think of any more compound words?

Answers will vary.

Page 57

Compound Words

Directions: Draw a line under the compound word in each sentence. On the line, write the two words that make up the compound word.

1. A <u>firetruck</u> came to help put out the fire.   fire truck

2. I will be nine years old on my next <u>birthday</u>.   birth day

3. We built a <u>treehouse</u> in the oak tree.   tree house

4. Dad put a <u>scarecrow</u> in his garden.   scare crow

5. It is fun to make <u>footprints</u> in the snow.   foot prints

6. I like to read the comics in the <u>newspaper</u>.   news paper

7. <u>Cowboys</u> ride horses and use lassos.   cow boys

Page 59

Contractions

Contractions are a short way to write two words.

Examples: it is = it's, is not = isn't, I have = I've

Directions: Draw a line from each word pair to its contraction.

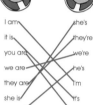

I am	she's
it is	they're
you are	we're
we are	he's
they are	I'm
she is	It's
he is	you're

Page 60

Contractions

Directions: Circle the contraction that should replace the underlined words.

Example: were not = weren't

1. The boy <u>was not</u> sad.
(wasn't) weren't

2. We <u>were not</u> working.
wasn't (weren't)

3. Jen and Caleb <u>have not</u> eaten lunch yet.
(haven't) hasn't

4. The mouse <u>has not</u> been here.
haven't (hasn't)

Page 61

Contractions

Directions: Match the words with their contractions.

would not	I've
was not	he'll
he will	wouldn't
could not	wasn't
I have	couldn't

Directions: Make the words at the end of each line into contractions to complete the sentences.

1. He ___didn't___ know the answer.   **did not**
2. ___It's___ a long way home.   **It is**
3. ___Here's___ my house.   **Here is**
4. ___We're___ not going to school today.   **We are**
5. ___They'll___ take the bus home tomorrow.   **They will**

Page 62

Contractions

Directions: Cut out the broken hearts, and put them together to show what two words make each contraction. Glue them over the contraction.

Page 63

Syllables

Words are made up of parts called **syllables**. Each syllable has a vowel sound. One way to count syllables is to clap as you say the word.

Example: cat   1 clap   1 syllable
       table   2 claps   2 syllables
       butterfly   3 claps   3 syllables

Directions: "Clap out" the words below. Write how many syllables each word has.

movie	2	dog	1
piano	3	basket	2
tree	1	swimmer	2
bicycle	3	rainbow	2
sun	1	paper	2
cabinet	3	picture	2
football	2	run	1
television	4	enter	2

Page 65

Syllables

Dividing a word into syllables can help you read a new word. You also might use syllables when you are writing if you run out of space on a line. Many words contain two consonants that are next to each other. A word can usually be divided between the consonants.

Directions: Divide each word into two syllables. The first one is done for you.

kitten	kit	ten
lumber	lum ber	
batter	bat ter	
winter	win ter	
funny	fun ny	
harder	har der	
dirty	dir ty	
sister	sis ter	
little	lit tle	
dinner	din ner	

Page 66

Syllables

One way to help you read a word you don't know is to divide it into parts called **syllables**. Every syllable has a vowel sound.

Directions: Say the words. Write the number of syllables. The first one is done for you.

straw • ber • ry

bird	1	rabbit	2
apple	2	elephant	3
balloon	2	family	3
basketball	3	fence	1
breakfast	2	ladder	2
block	1	open	2
candy	2	puddle	2
popcorn	2	Saturday	3
yellow	2	wind	1
understand	3	butterfly	3

Page 67

Syllables

When a double consonant is used in the middle of a word, the word can usually be divided between the consonants.
Directions: Look at the words in the word box. Divide each word into two syllables. Leave space between each syllable. One is done for you.

butter	puppy	kitten	yellow
dinner	chatter	ladder	happy
pillow	letter	mitten	summer

but ter	din ner	pil low
pup py	chat ter	let ter
kit ten	lad der	mit ten
yel low	hap py	sum mer

Many words are divided between two consonants that are not alike.
Directions: Look at the words in the word box. Divide each word into two syllables. One is done for you.

window	doctor	number	carpet
mister	winter	pencil	candle
barber	sister	picture	under

win dow	mis ter	bar ber
doc tor	win ter	sis ter
num ber	pen cil	pic ture
car pet	can dle	un der

Page 68

Syllables

Directions: Write 1 or 2 on the line to tell how many syllables are in each word. If the word has 2 syllables, draw a line between the syllables. **Example: sup|per**

dog	1	tim|ber	2
bed|room	2	cat	1
slip|per	2	street	1
tree	1	chalk	1
bat|ter	2	blan|ket	2
chair	1	mar|ker	2
fish	1	brush	1
mas|ter	2	rab|bit	2

Page 69

Haiku

A **haiku** is a form of Japanese poetry. Most haiku are about nature.

     first line – 5 syllables
     second line – 7 syllables
     third line – 5 syllables

Example: The squirrel is brown.
            He lives in a great big tree.
            He eats nuts all day.

Directions: Write your own haiku. Draw a picture to go with it.

Answers will vary.

Page 70

Suffixes

A **suffix** is a letter or group of letters that is added to the end of a word to change its meaning.

Directions: Add the suffixes to the root words to make new words. Use your new words to complete the sentences.

help + ful = _____helpful_____
care + less = _____careless_____
build + er = _____builder_____
talk + ed = _____talked_____
love + ly = _____lovely_____
loud + er = _____louder_____

1. My mother ___talked___ to my teacher about my homework.
2. The radio was ___louder___ than the television.
3. Madison is always ___helpful___ to her mother.
4. A ___builder___ put a new garage on our house.
5. The flowers are ___lovely___ .
6. It is ___careless___ to cross the street without looking both ways.

Page 71

Suffixes

An **ing** at the end of an action word shows that the action is happening now. An **ed** at the end shows that the action happened in the past.

Directions: Look at the words in the word box. Underline the root word in each one. Write a word to complete each sentence.

| <u>snow</u>ing | <u>wish</u>ed | <u>play</u>ed | <u>look</u>ing | <u>cry</u>ing |
| <u>talk</u>ing | <u>walk</u>ed | <u>eat</u>ing | <u>go</u>ing | <u>do</u>ing |

1. We like to play. We ___played___ yesterday.
2. Is that snow? Yes, it is ___snowing___ .
3. Do you want to go with me? No, I am ___going___ with my friend.
4. The baby will cry if we leave. The baby is ___crying___ .
5. We will walk home from school. We ___walked___ to school this morning.
6. Did you wish for a new bike? Yes, I ___wished___ for one.
7. Who is doing the dishes? I am ___doing___ them.
8. Did you talk to your friend? Yes, we are ___talking___ now.
9. Will you look at my book? I am ___looking___ at it now.
10. I like to eat pizza. We are ___eating___ it for lunch.

Page 72

Suffixes

Directions: Write a word from the word box next to its root word.

coming	running	sitting
lived	rained	swimming
visited	carried	racing
hurried		

run ___running___   come ___coming___
live ___lived___   carry ___carried___
hurry ___hurried___   race ___racing___
swim ___swimming___   rain ___rained___
visit ___visited___   sit ___sitting___

Directions: Write a word from the word box to finish each sentence.

1. I ___visited___ my grandmother during vacation.
2. Ava went ___swimming___ at the lake with her cousin.
3. Tyson ___carried___ the heavy package for his mother.
4. It ___rained___ and stormed all weekend.
5. Cars go very fast when they are ___racing___ .

Page 73

Suffixes

Directions: Read the story. Underline the words that end with **est**, **ed**, or **ing**. On the lines below, write the root word for each word you underlined.

The <u>funniest</u> book I ever read was about a girl <u>named</u> Nan. Nan did everything backward. She even <u>spelled</u> her name backward. Nan slept in the day and <u>played</u> at night. She <u>dried</u> her hair before <u>washing</u> it. She <u>turned</u> on the light after she <u>finished</u> her book—which she read from the back to the front! When it <u>rained</u>, Nan <u>waited</u> until she was inside before <u>opening</u> her umbrella. She even <u>walked</u> backward. The <u>silliest</u> part: The only thing Nan did forward was back up!

1. ___funny___   6. ___wash___   11. ___open___
2. ___name___   7. ___turn___   12. ___walk___
3. ___spell___   8. ___finish___   13. ___silly___
4. ___play___   9. ___rain___
5. ___dry___   10. ___wait___

Page 74

Prefixes: The Three Rs

A **prefix** is a letter or group of letters that is added to the beginning of a word to change its meaning. The prefix **re** means "again."

Directions: Read the story. Then, follow the instructions.

Kim wants to find ways she can help our planet. She studies the "three Rs"—reduce, reuse, and recycle. **Reduce** means "to make less." Both **reuse** and **recycle** mean "to use again."

Add **re** to the beginning of each word below. Use the new words to complete the sentences.

_re_ build   _re_ fill
_re_ read   _re_ tell
_re_ write   _re_ run

1. The race was a tie, so Sanj and Mia had to ___rerun___ it.
2. The block wall fell down, so Simon had to ___rebuild___ it.
3. The water bottle was empty, so Luna had to ___refill___ it.
4. Javier wrote a good story, but he wanted to ___rewrite___ it to make it better.
5. The teacher told a story, and students had to ___retell___ it.
6. Toni didn't understand the directions, so she had to ___reread___ them.

Page 75

Prefixes

Directions: Read the story. Change Unlucky Sam to Lucky Sam by removing the **un** prefix from the **bold** words. Write the new words in the new story.

Unlucky Sam

Sam was **unhappy** about a lot of things in his life. His parents were **uncaring**. His teacher was **unfair**. His big sister was **unkind**. His neighbors were **unfriendly**. He was **unhealthy**, too! How could one boy be as **unlucky** as Sam?

Lucky Sam

Sam was ___happy___ about a lot of things in his life. His parents were ___caring___ . His teacher was ___fair___ . His big sister was ___kind___ . His neighbors were ___friendly___ . He was ___healthy___ , too! How could one boy be as ___lucky___ as Sam?

Page 76

Prefixes

Directions: Change the meaning of the sentences by adding the prefixes to the **bold** words.

The boy was **lucky** because he guessed the answer **correctly**.

The boy was (un) ___unlucky___ because he guessed the answer (in) ___incorrectly___ .

When Jada **behaved**, she felt **happy**.

When Jada (mis) ___misbehaved___ , she felt (un) ___unhappy___ .

Mike wore his jacket **buttoned** because the dance was **formal**.

Mike wore his jacket (un) ___unbuttoned___ because the dance was (in) ___informal___ .

Cameron **understood** because he was **familiar** with the book.

Cameron (mis) ___misunderstood___ because he was (un) ___unfamiliar___ with the book.

Page 77

Prefixes

Directions: Read the story. Change the story by removing the prefix **re** from the **bold** words. Write the new words in the new story.

Repete is a **rewriter** who has to **redo** every story. He has to **rethink** up the ideas. He has to **rewrite** the sentences. He has to **redraw** the pictures. He even has to **retype** the pages. Who will **repay** **Repete** for all the work he **redoes**?

___Pete___ is a ___writer___ who has to ___do___ every story. He has to ___think___ up the ideas. He has to ___write___ the sentences.

He has to ___draw___ the pictures.

He even has to ___type___ the pages.

Who will ___pay___ ___Pete___ for all the work he ___does___ ?

Page 78

Review

Directions: Read each sentence. Look at the words in **bold**. Circle the prefix, and write the root word on the line.

1. The (pre)view of the movie was funny. ___view___
2. We always drink (non)fat milk. ___fat___
3. We will have to (re)schedule the trip. ___schedule___
4. Are you tired of (re)runs on television? ___run___
5. I have (out)grown my new shoes already. ___grown___
6. You must have (mis)placed the papers. ___place___
7. Police (en)force the laws of the city. ___force___
8. I (dis)liked that book. ___like___
9. The boy (dis)trusted the big dog. ___trust___
10. Try to (en)joy yourself at the party. ___joy___
11. Please try to keep the cat (in)side the house. ___side___
12. That song is total (non)sense! ___sense___
13. We will (re)place any parts that we lost. ___place___
14. Can you help me (un)zip this jacket? ___zip___
15. Let's (re)work today's arithmetic problems. ___work___

Page 79

Parts of a Book

A book has many parts. The **title** is the name of the book. The **author** is the person who wrote the words. The **illustrator** is the person who drew the pictures. The **table of contents** is located at the beginning to list what is in the book. The **glossary** is a little dictionary in the back to help you with unfamiliar words. Books are often divided into smaller sections of information called **chapters**.

Directions: Look at one of your books. Write the parts you see below.

Answers will vary.

The title of my book is _____

The author is _____

The illustrator is _____

My book has a table of contents.   Yes or No

My book has a glossary.   Yes or No

My book is divided into chapters.   Yes or No

Page 80

Recalling Details: Nikki's Pets

Directions: Read about Nikki's pets. Then, answer the questions.

Nikki has two cats, Tiger and Sniffer, and two dogs, Spot and Wiggles. Tiger is an orange striped cat who likes to sleep under a big tree and pretend she is a real tiger. Sniffer is a gray cat who likes to sniff the flowers in Nikki's garden. Spot is a Dalmatian with many black spots. Wiggles is a big, furry brown dog who wiggles all over when he is happy.

1. Which dog is brown and furry? ___Wiggles___
2. What color is Tiger? ___orange___
3. What kind of dog is Spot? ___a Dalmatian___
4. Which cat likes to sniff flowers? ___Sniffer___
5. Where does Tiger like to sleep? ___under a big tree___
6. Who wiggles all over when he is happy? ___Wiggles___

Page 82

Recalling Details: Pet Pests

Directions: Read the story. Then, answer the questions.

Sometimes, Marvin and Mugsy scratch and itch. Maggie knows that fleas or ticks are insect pests to her pets. Their bites are painful. Fleas suck the blood of animals. They don't have wings, but they can jump. Ticks are very flat, suck blood, and are related to spiders. They like to hide in dogs' ears. That is why Maggie checks Marvin and Mugsy every week for fleas and ticks.

1. What is a pest? ___an insect like a flea or a tick___

2. List three facts about fleas.
   a) ___Their bites are painful.___
   b) ___They suck the blood of animals.___
   c) ___They can jump.___

3. List three facts about ticks.
   a) ___Ticks are very flat.___
   b) ___They suck blood.___
   c) ___They are related to spiders.___

Page 83

Comprehensive Curriculum - **Grade 2**

Reading for Details

Directions: Read the story about baby animals. Answer the questions with words from the story.

Baby cats are called kittens. They love to play and drink lots of milk. A baby dog is a puppy. Puppies chew on old shoes. They run and bark. A lamb is a baby sheep. Lambs eat grass. A baby duck is called a duckling. Ducklings swim with their wide, webbed feet. Foals are baby horses. A foal can walk the day it is born! A baby goat is a kid. Some people call children kids, too!

1. A baby cat is called a ___kitten___.

2. A baby dog is a ___puppy___.

3. A ___lamb___ is a baby sheep.

4. ___Ducklings___ swim with their webbed feet.

5. A ___foal___ can walk the day it is born.

6. A baby goat is a ___kid___.

Page 84

Reading for Details

Directions: Read the story about bike safety. Answer the questions below the story.

Mike has a red bike. He likes his bike. Mike wears a helmet. Mike wears knee pads and elbow pads. They keep him safe. Mike stops at signs. Mike looks both ways. Mike is safe on his bike.

1. What color is Mike's bike? ___red___

2. Which sentence in the story tells why Mike wears pads and a helmet? Write it here.
   ___They keep him safe.___

3. What else does Mike do to keep safe?
   He ___stops___ at signs and ___looks___ both ways.

Page 85

Reading for Details

Directions: Read the story about different kinds of transportation. Answer the questions with words from the story.

People use many kinds of transportation. Boats float on the water. Some people fish in a boat. Airplanes fly in the sky. Flying in a plane is a fast way to get somewhere. Trains run on a track. The first car is the engine. The last car is the caboose. Some people even sleep in beds on a train! A car has four wheels. Most people have a car. A car rides on roads. A bus can hold many people. A bus rides on roads. Most children ride a bus to school.

1. A boat floats on the ___water___.

2. If you want to get somewhere fast, which form of transportation would you use? ___a plane___

3. The first car on a train is called an engine, and the last car is a ___caboose___.

4. ___Children___ ride on a bus.

5. A ___car___ has four wheels.

Page 86

Following Directions

Directions: Read the story. Answer the questions. Try the recipe.

Cows Give Us Milk

Cows live on a farm. The farmer milks the cow to get milk. Many things are made from milk. We make ice cream, sour cream, cottage cheese, and butter from milk. Butter is fun to make! You can learn to make your own butter. First, you need cream. Put the cream in a jar and shake it. Then, you need to pour off the liquid. Next, you put the butter in a bowl. Add a little salt and stir! Finally, spread it on crackers and eat!

1. What animal gives us milk? ___cows___

2. What 4 things are made from milk? ___cottage___
   ___ice cream___ ___sour cream___ ___cheese___ ___butter___

3. What did the story teach you to make? ___butter___

4. Put the steps in order. Place 1, 2, 3, or 4 by each sentence.

   ___4___ Spread the butter on crackers and eat!

   ___2___ Shake cream in a jar.

   ___1___ Start with cream.

   ___3___ Add salt to the butter.

Page 87

Following Directions: Parrot Art

Directions: Draw the missing parts on each parrot.

1. Draw the parrot's eye.

2. Draw the parrot's tail.

3. Draw the parrot's beak.

4. Draw the parrot's wings.

Page 88

Following Directions: How to Treat a Ladybug

Directions: Read about how to treat ladybugs. Then, follow the instructions.

Ladybugs are shy. If you see a ladybug, sit very still. Hold out your arm. Maybe the ladybug will fly to you. If it does, talk softly. Do not touch it. It will fly away when it is ready.

1. Complete the directions on how to treat a ladybug.

   a. Sit very still.

   b. ___Hold out your arm.___

   c. Talk softly.

   d. ___Do not touch it.___

2. Ladybugs are red. They have black spots. Color the ladybug.

Page 89

Following Directions: Insect Art

Directions: Read about insects. Then, follow the instructions.

All insects have these body parts:

Head at the front

Thorax in the middle

Abdomen at the back

Six legs—three on each side of the thorax

Two eyes on the head

Two antennae attached to the head

Some insects also have wings.

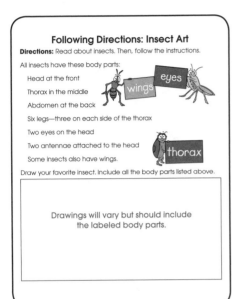

Draw your favorite insect. Include all the body parts listed above.

Drawings will vary but should include the labeled body parts.

Page 90

Sequencing: Packing Bags

Directions: Read about packing bags. Then, number the objects in the order they should be packed.

Cans are heavy. Put them in first. Then, put in boxes. Now, put in the apple. Put the bread in last.

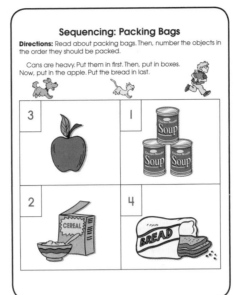

3 (apple)	1 (soup cans)
2 (cereal)	4 (bread)

Page 91

Sequencing: 1, 2, 3, 4!

Directions: Write numbers by each sentence to show the order of the story.

The pool is empty. __1__   Ben plays in the pool. __3__

Ben gets out. __4__   Ben fills the pool. __2__

Page 92

Sequencing/Predicting: A Game for Cats

Directions: Read about what cats like. Then, follow the instructions.

Cats like to play with paper bags. Pull a paper bag open. Take everything out. Now, lay the bag on its side.

1. Write 1, 2, and 3 to put the pictures in order.

2. In box 4, draw what you think the cat will do.

3	1
2	4 Answers will vary.

Page 93

Sequencing: Story Events

Spencer likes to make new friends. Today, he made friends with the dog in the picture.

Directions: Number the sentences in order to find out what Spencer did today.

__3__ Spencer kissed his mother good-bye.

__5__ Spencer saw the new dog next door.

__4__ Spencer went outside.

__6__ Spencer said hello.

__2__ Spencer got dressed and ate breakfast.

__1__ Spencer woke up.

Page 94

Sequencing: Yo-Yo Trick

Directions: Read about the yo-yo trick.

Wind up the yo-yo string. Hold the yo-yo in your hand. Now, hold your palm up. Throw the yo-yo downward on the string. Hold your palm down. Now, swing the yo-yo forward. Make it "walk." This yo-yo trick is called "walk the dog."

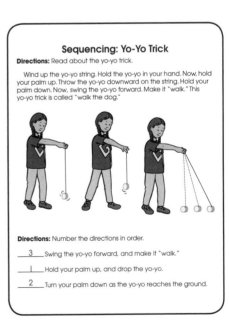

Directions: Number the directions in order.

__3__ Swing the yo-yo forward, and make it "walk."

__1__ Hold your palm up, and drop the yo-yo.

__2__ Turn your palm down as the yo-yo reaches the ground.

Page 95

Sequencing: Make a Hat

Mrs. Posey made a new hat, but she forgot how she did it. When she tried to tell her friend, she got all mixed up.

Directions: Read Mrs. Posey's story. Write her story on the lines in the order you think it happened. Then, color the picture.

I glued flowers on it. Then, I bought this straw hat. Now, I am wearing my hat. Then, I added ribbon around the flowers. I tried on many hats at the store.

The real story:

_____

I tried on many hats at the store.

Then, I bought this straw hat.

I glued flowers on it.

Then, I added ribbon around the flowers.

Now, I am wearing my hat.

_____

_____

Page 96

Sequencing: Follow a Recipe

Here is a recipe for guacamole. When you use a recipe, you must follow the directions carefully. The sentences below are not in the correct order.

Directions: Write number 1 to show what you would do first. Then, number each step to show the correct sequence.

__2__ Cut the avocado in half, and squeeze the flesh into a bowl.

__6__ Eat and enjoy!

__4__ Add lime juice, salt, and garlic powder to the mashed avocado.

__1__ First, wash the avocado.

__5__ Mix all the ingredients together, and serve with corn chips.

__3__ Mash the avocado in the bowl with a fork until only a few small chunks remain.

Try the recipe with an adult.

Do you like to cook? <u>Answers will vary.</u>

Page 97

Sequencing: Follow a Recipe

Alana and Marcus are hungry for a snack. They want to make nacho chips and cheese. The steps they need to follow are all mixed up.

Directions: Read the steps. Number them in 1, 2, 3 order. Then, color the picture.

__5__ Bake the chips in the oven for 2 minutes.

__2__ Get a cookie sheet to bake on.

__1__ Get out the nacho chips and cheese.

__6__ Eat the nachos.

__3__ Put the chips on the cookie sheet.

__4__ Put grated cheese on the chips.

Page 98

Sequencing: Making a Snowman

Directions: Read about how to make a snowman. Then, follow the instructions.

It is fun to make a snowman. First, find things for the snowman's eyes and nose. Dress warmly. Then, go outdoors. Roll a big snowball. Then, roll another to put on top of it. Now, roll a small snowball for the head. Put on the snowman's face.

1. Number the pictures in order.

2. Write two things to do before going outdoors.

a) <u>First, find things for the snowman's eyes and nose.</u>

b) <u>Dress warmly.</u>

Page 99

Sequencing: Baking a Cake

Directions: Read about baking a cake. Then, write the missing steps.

Dylan, Dana, and Dad are baking a cake. Dad turns on the oven. Dana opens the cake mix. Dylan adds the eggs. Dad pours in the water. Dana stirs the batter. Dylan pours the batter into a cake pan. Dad puts it in the oven.

1. Turn on the oven.

2. <u>Open the cake mix.</u>

3. Add the eggs.

4. <u>Pour in the water.</u>

5. Stir the batter.

6. <u>Pour the batter into a cake pan.</u>

7. <u>Put the cake in the oven.</u>

Page 100

Sequencing: Story Events

Mari was sick yesterday.

Directions: Number the events in 1, 2, 3 order to tell the story about Mari.

__2__ She went to the doctor's office.

__9__ Mari felt much better.

__1__ Mari felt very hot and tired.

__6__ Mari's mother went to the drugstore.

__4__ The doctor wrote down something.

__3__ The doctor looked in Mari's ears.

__7__ Mari took a pill.

__5__ The doctor gave Mari's mother the piece of paper.

__8__ Mari drank some water with her pill.

Page 101

Sequencing: Making a Card

Directions: Read about how to make a card. Then, follow the instructions.

You will need scissors, glue, old greeting cards, and colored paper. First, look at all your old cards. Then, cut out what you like. Now, fold the colored paper in half. Glue the cut-outs to the front of your card. Write your name inside.

1. Write the steps in order for making a card.

a) Look at all your old cards.

b) Cut out what you like.

c) Fold the colored paper in half.

d) Glue the cut-outs to the front of your card.

e) Write your name inside.

Page 102

Sequencing: Making Clay

Directions: Read about making clay. Then, follow the instructions.

It is fun to work with clay. Here is what you need to make it:

1 cup salt
2 cups flour
3/4 cup water

Mix the salt and flour. Then, add the water. DO NOT eat the clay. It tastes bad. Use your hands to mix and mix. Now, roll it out. What can you make with your clay?

1. Circle the main idea:

Do not eat clay.

~~Mix salt, flour, and water to make clay.~~

2. Write the steps for making clay.

a. Mix the salt and flour.

b. Add the water.

c. Mix the clay.

d. Roll it out.

3. Write why you should not eat clay. It tastes bad.

Page 103

Sequencing: Play a Game

Children all around the world like to play games. Think about your favorite game. Maybe you could teach your friends to play it.

Directions: Write, in order, how to play your game.
Answers will vary.

Directions: Draw a picture of you playing your favorite game.

Drawings will vary.

Page 104

Sequencing: A Visit to the Zoo

Directions: Read the story. Then, follow the instructions.

One Saturday morning in May, Olivia and Anna went to the zoo. First, they bought tickets to get into the zoo. Second, they visited the Gorilla Garden and had fun watching the gorillas stare at them. Then, they went to Tiger Town and watched the tigers as they slept in the sunshine. Fourth, they went to Hippo Haven and laughed at the hippos cooling off in their pool. Next, they visited Snake Station and learned about poisonous and nonpoisonous snakes. It was noon, and they were hungry, so they ate lunch at Parrot Patio.

Write **first**, **second**, **third**, **fourth**, **fifth**, and **sixth** to put the events in order.

fourth They went to Hippo Haven.

first Olivia and Anna bought zoo tickets.

third They watched the tigers sleep.

sixth They ate lunch at Parrot Patio.

second The gorillas stared at them.

fifth They learned about poisonous and nonpoisonous snakes.

Page 105

Sequencing: Why Does It Rain?

Directions: Read about rain. Then, follow the instructions.

Clouds are made of little drops of ice and water. They push and bang into each other. Then, they join together to make bigger drops and begin to fall. More raindrops cling to them. They become heavy and fall quickly to the ground.

Write **first**, **second**, **third**, **fourth**, and **fifth** to put the events in order.

fourth More raindrops cling to them.

first Clouds are made of little drops of ice and water.

third They join together and make bigger drops that begin to fall.

second The drops of ice and water bang into each other.

fifth The drops become heavy and fall quickly to the ground.

Page 106

Sequencing: Make a Pencil Holder

Directions: Read how to make a pencil holder. Then, follow the instructions.

You can use "junk" to make a pencil holder! First, you need a clean can with one end removed. Make sure there are no sharp edges. Then, you need glue, scissors, and paper. Find colorful paper, such as wrapping paper, wallpaper, or construction paper. Cut the paper to fit the can. Glue the paper around the can. Decorate can with glitter, buttons, and stickers. Then, put your pencils inside!

Write **first**, **second**, **third**, **fourth**, **fifth**, **sixth**, and **seventh** to put the steps in order.

second Make sure there are no sharp edges.

third Get glue, scissors, and paper.

fourth Cut the paper to fit the can.

seventh Put your pencils in the can!

fifth Glue colorful paper to the can.

first Remove one end of a clean can.

sixth Decorate the can with glitter and stickers.

Page 107

Tracking: Where Does She Go?

Every morning when Ivana wakes up, she goes somewhere. Find out where she goes.

Directions:
Read the sentences. Follow the instructions.

1. On Monday, Ivana needs bread. Use a red crayon to mark her path from her house to the place she buys bread. Where does she go? ___bakery___

2. On Tuesday, Ivana wants to read books. Use a green crayon to mark her path. Where does she go? ___library___

3. On Wednesday, Ivana wants to swing. Use a yellow crayon to mark her path. Where does she go? ___park___

4. On Thursday, Ivana wants to buy stamps. Use a black crayon to mark her path. Where does she go? ___post office___

5. On Friday, Ivana wants to get money. Use a purple crayon to mark her path. Where does she go? ___bank___

Page 108

Tracking: Sequencing

Directions: Look at the paths you drew for Ivana on page 108. Number, in order, the places that she went each day. Draw a line to connect the place with the day of the week.

_5_	Bank	Monday
_3_	Park	Tuesday
_2_	Library	Wednesday
_1_	Bakery	Thursday
_4_	Post Office	Friday

Page 109

Tracking: With a Map

Greg and Tess walk to and from school together each day. After school, they stop at the park to play. Then, they go home.

Directions: Read the sentences. Draw Greg's path in red and Tess's path in blue.

Greg starts at his home.
He walks to school.
When he leaves school, he stops at the park.
Then, he goes home.
Tess goes the same places that Greg goes.
Some of their paths will be the same.

Page 110

Tracking: With a Map

Directions: Study the map of the United States. Follow the instructions.

1. Draw a star on the state where you live.
2. Draw a line from your state to the Atlantic Ocean.
3. Draw a triangle in the Gulf of Mexico.
4. Draw a circle in the Pacific Ocean.
5. Color each state that borders your state a different color.
   Answers 1, 2, and 5 will vary.

CANADA

Pacific Ocean

Atlantic Ocean

Gulf of Mexico

N
W—E
S

Page 111

Tracking: Alternate Paths

Look at Spotty Dog's home. Look at the paths he takes to the oven and the back door. The numbers by each path show how many steps Spotty must take to get there.

Directions: Follow the instructions.

1. Spotty Dog's casserole is done. Trace Spotty's path from his chair to the oven.

2. How many steps does Spotty take? ___5___

3. While Spotty is looking in his oven, he hears a noise in the backyard. Trace Spotty's path to the door.

4. How many steps has Spotty taken in all? ___9___

5. Spotty goes back to his chair. How many steps must he take? ___7___

6. How many steps has he taken in all? ___16___

7. Spotty's path has made a shape. What shape is it? ___a triangle___

Page 112

Same/Different: Objects

Directions: Look at the pictures. Draw an **X** on the picture in each row that is different.

Page 113

Same/Different: Stuffed Animals

Kate and Oralia like to collect and trade stuffed animals.

Directions: Draw two stuffed animals that are alike and two that are different.

Drawings will vary.

Alike

Different

Page 114

Same/Different: Shell Homes

Directions: Read about shells. Then, answer the questions.

Shells are the homes of some animals. Snails live in shells on land. Clams live in shells in the water. Clam shells open. Snail shells stay closed. Both shells keep the animals safe.

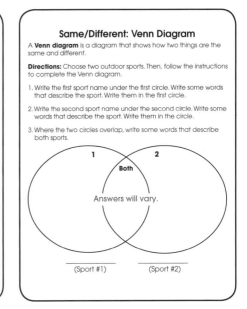

1. (Circle the correct answer.) Snails live in shells

   in the water. (on land.)

2. (Circle the correct answer.)
   Clam shells are different from snail shells because

   (they open.)

   they stay closed.

3. Write one way all shells are the same. <u>Shells keep the</u>
   <u>animals inside safe.</u>

Page 115

Same/Different: Venn Diagram

A **Venn diagram** is a diagram that shows how two things are the same and different.

Directions: Choose two outdoor sports. Then, follow the instructions to complete the Venn diagram.

1. Write the first sport name under the first circle. Write some words that describe the sport. Write them in the first circle.

2. Write the second sport name under the second circle. Write some words that describe the sport. Write them in the circle.

3. Where the two circles overlap, write some words that describe both sports.

```
        1           2
           Both
      Answers will vary.

_____     _____
 (Sport #1)      (Sport #2)
```

Page 116

Same/Different: Dina and Dina

Directions: Read the story. Then, complete the Venn diagram, telling how Dina, the duck, is the same or different than Dina, the girl.

One day in the library, Dina found a story about a duck named Dina!

My name is Dina. I am a duck, and I like to swim. When I am not swimming, I walk on land or fly. I have two feet and two eyes. My feathers keep me warm. Ducks can be different colors. I am gray, brown, and black. I really like being a duck. It is fun.

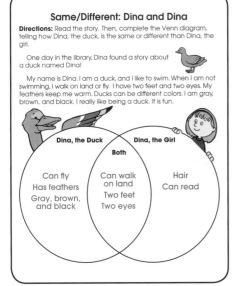

```
Dina, the Duck      Dina, the Girl
              Both

Can fly      Can walk     Hair
Has feathers on land      Can read
Gray, brown, Two feet
and black    Two eyes
```

Page 117

Same/Different: Emma and Lee Have Fun

Directions: Read about Emma and Lee. Then, write how they are the same and different in the Venn diagram.

Emma and Lee like to play ball. They like to jump rope. Lee likes to play a card game called "Old Maid." Emma likes to play a card game called "Go Fish." What do you do to have fun?

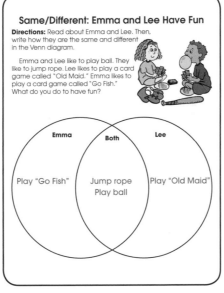

```
Emma        Both        Lee

Play "Go Fish"  Jump rope  Play "Old Maid"
                Play ball
```

Page 118

Same/Different: Cats and Tigers

Directions: Read about cats and tigers. Then, complete the Venn diagram, telling how they are the same and different.

Tigers are a kind of cat. Pet cats and tigers both have fur. Pet cats are small and tame. Tigers are large and wild.

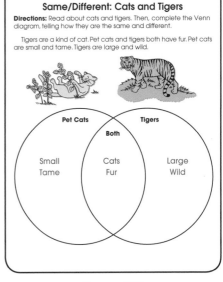

```
Pet Cats        Tigers
          Both

Small      Cats      Large
Tame       Fur       Wild
```

Page 119

Same/Different: Marvin and Mugsy

Directions: Read about Marvin and Mugsy. Then, complete the Venn diagram, telling how they are the same and different.

Maggie has two dogs, Marvin and Mugsy. Marvin is a black-and-white spotted Dalmatian. Marvin likes to run after balls in the backyard. His favorite food is Canine Crunchy Crunch. Maggie likes to take Marvin for walks, because dogs need exercise. Marvin loves to sleep in his doghouse. Mugsy is a big, furry brown dog who wiggles when she is happy. Since she is big, she needs lots of exercise. Maggie takes her for walks in the park. Her favorite food is Canine Crunchy Crunch. Mugsy likes to sleep on Maggie's bed.

Marvin
- Black-and-white Dalmatian
- Likes to run after balls
- Likes to sleep in his doghouse

Both
- Eats Canine Crunchy Crunch
- Likes to go for walks

Mugsy
- Big, furry brown dog
- Wiggles when happy
- Needs lots of exercise
- Sleeps on Maggie's bed

Page 120

Same/Different: Bluebirds and Parrots

Directions: Read about parrots and bluebirds. Then, complete the Venn diagram, telling how they are the same and different.

Bluebirds and parrots are both birds. Bluebirds and parrots can fly. They both have beaks. Parrots can live inside a cage. Bluebirds must live outdoors.

Bluebirds
- Must live outdoors

Both
- Birds
- Can fly
- Have beaks

Parrots
- Can live inside a cage

Page 121

Same/Different: Sleeping Whales

Directions: Read about whales. Then, complete the Venn diagram, telling how whales and people are the same and different.

Whales do not sleep like we do. They take many short naps. Like us, whales breathe air. Whales live in very cold water, but they have fat that keeps them warm.

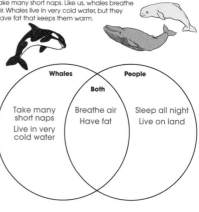

Whales
- Take many short naps
- Live in very cold water

Both
- Breathe air
- Have fat

People
- Sleep all night
- Live on land

Page 122

Similes

A **simile** is a figure of speech that compares two different things. The words **like** and **as** are used in similes.

Directions: Draw a line to the picture that goes with each set of words.

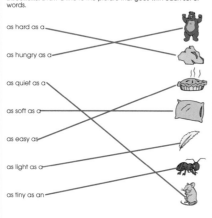

as hard as a

as hungry as a

as quiet as a

as soft as a

as easy as

as light as a

as tiny as an

Page 123

Classifying: A Rainy Day

Directions: Read the story. Then, circle the objects Jonathan needs to stay dry.

It is raining. Jonathan wants to play outdoors. What should he wear to stay dry? What should he carry to stay dry?

Page 124

Classifying: Outdoor/Indoor Games

Classifying is putting things that are alike into groups.

Directions: Read about games. Draw an **X** on the games you can play indoors. Circle the objects used for outdoor games.

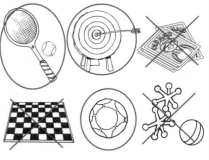

Some games are outdoor games. Some games are indoor games. Outdoor games are active. Indoor games are quiet.

Which do you like best? _____ Answers will vary. _____

Page 125

Classifying: Art Tools

Directions: Read about art tools. Then, color only the art tools.

Andrea uses different art tools to help her design her masterpieces. To cut, she needs scissors. To draw, she needs a pencil. To color, she needs crayons. To paint, she needs a brush.

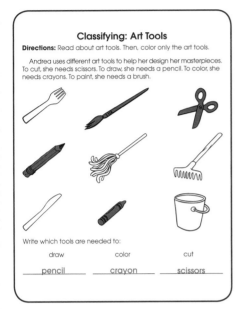

Write which tools are needed to:

draw	color	cut
pencil	crayon	scissors

Page 126

Classifying

Classifying is putting similar things into groups.
Directions: Write each word from the word box on the correct line.

baby	donkey	whale	family	fox
uncle	goose	grandfather	kangaroo	policeman

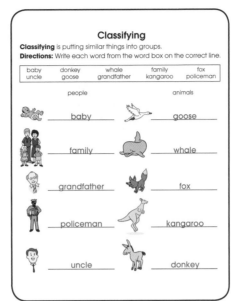

people	animals
baby	goose
family	whale
grandfather	fox
policeman	kangaroo
uncle	donkey

Page 127

Classifying

Directions: Read the sentences. Write the words from the word box where they belong.

bush	rocket	strawberries	thunder	bicycle	Danger
airplane	wind	honey	rain	car	grass
Stop	truck	Poison	flower	apple juice	bird

1. These things taste sweet.

   strawberries   honey   apple juice

2. These things come when it storms.

   wind   rain   thunder

3. These things have wheels.

   car   bicycle   truck

4. These are words you see on signs.

   Stop   Danger   Poison

5. These things can fly.

   airplane   rocket   bird

6. These things grow in the ground.

   bush   flower   grass

Page 128

Classifying: Animals

Directions: Use a red crayon to circle the names of three animals that would make good pets. Use a blue crayon to circle the names of three wild animals. Use an orange crayon to circle the two animals that live on a farm.

| BEAR | CAT | LION | SHEEP | BIRD | DOG | COW | TIGER |

A	M	E	O	W	W	N	L	I	O	N
B	M	D	O	G	G	X	I	I	S	O
A	B	E	A	R	R	V	L	M	H	R
R	M	R	M	O	O	U	S	E	E	K
K	C	A	B	B	I	R	D	S	E	M
I	O	T	T	I	G	E	R	M	P	Q
B	W	N	O	W	W	R	Q	N	E	N
D	N	C	P	H	H	I	D	U	D	N
F	K	C	A	T	T	R	O	A	R	M

Page 129

Classifying

Directions: The words in each box form a group. Choose the word from the word box that describes each group, and write it on the line.

clothes	family	noises	colors	flowers
fruits	animals	coins	toys	

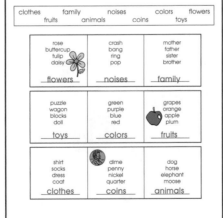

rose buttercup tulip daisy	crash bang ring pop	mother father sister brother
flowers	noises	family
puzzle wagon blocks doll	green purple blue red	grapes orange apple plum
toys	colors	fruits
shirt socks dress coat	dime penny nickel quarter	dog horse elephant moose
clothes	coins	animals

Page 130

Classifying

Living things need air, food, and water to live. **Non-living** things are not alive.
Directions: Cut out the words on the bottom. Glue each word in the correct column.

Living	Non-living
flower	book
boy	chair
dog	bread
tree	camera
horse	car
ant	shoe

Page 131

Classifying: Foods

Darcy likes fruit and things made from fruit. She also likes bread.

Directions: Circle the things on the menu that Darcy will eat.

MENU
- (apple pie)
- peas
- beans
- (oranges)
- chicken
- corn
- (rolls)
- (banana bread)
- (grape juice)

Page 133

Classifying: Words

Dapper Dog is going camping.

Directions: Draw an **X** on the word in each row that does not belong in that group.

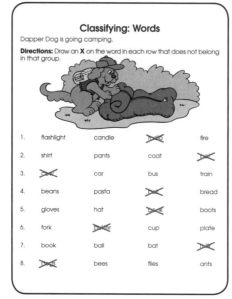

1. flashlight   candle   ~~tent~~   fire
2. shirt   pants   coat   ~~X~~
3. ~~X~~   car   bus   train
4. beans   pasta   ~~X~~   bread
5. gloves   hat   ~~X~~   boots
6. fork   ~~X~~   cup   plate
7. book   ball   bat   ~~X~~
8. ~~X~~   bees   flies   ants

Page 134

Classifying: Leaves

Directions: Look at each leaf, and read its name. Write the name of each leaf on the line. Then, color the leaves.

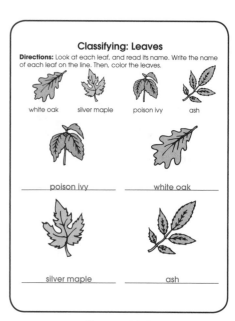

white oak   silver maple   poison ivy   ash

poison ivy   white oak

silver maple   ash

Page 135

Classifying: Leaves

This tricky tree has four different kinds of leaves: ash, poison ivy, silver maple, and white oak.

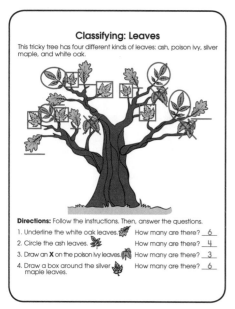

Directions: Follow the instructions. Then, answer the questions.

1. Underline the white oak leaves.   How many are there? 6
2. Circle the ash leaves.   How many are there? 4
3. Draw an **X** on the poison ivy leaves.   How many are there? 3
4. Draw a box around the silver maple leaves.   How many are there? 6

Page 136

Classifying: Watch Out for Poison Ivy!

Poison ivy is not safe. If you touch it, it can make your skin red and itchy. It can hurt. It grows on the ground. It has three leaves. It can be green or red. Watch out, Jay! There is poison ivy in these woods.

Directions: Color the poison ivy leaves red. Then, color the "safe" leaves other colors.

Page 137

Classifying: Leaves

Directions: Gather some leaves. Put your leaves into groups by type. Then, answer the questions.

white oak   red oak   pine   ash

elm   silver maple   red maple

Answers will vary.

1. How many white oak leaves did you find?_____
2. How many red oak leaves did you find?_____
3. How many pine needles did you find?_____
4. How many ash leaves did you find?_____
5. How many elm leaves did you find?_____
6. How many silver maple leaves did you find?_____
7. How many red maple leaves did you find?_____
8. What other kinds of leaves did you find? Go online with an adult or use a book to help you name them. Write their names on the lines._____

Page 138

Classifying: Animal Habitats

Directions: Read the story. Then, write each animal's name under **Water** or **Land** to tell where it lives.

Animals live in different habitats. A habitat is the place of an animal's natural home. Many animals live on land, and others live in water. Most animals that live in water breathe with gills. Animals that live on land breathe with lungs.

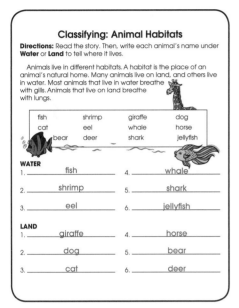

fish	shrimp	giraffe	dog
cat	eel	whale	horse
bear	deer	shark	jellyfish

WATER
1. fish
2. shrimp
3. eel
4. whale
5. shark
6. jellyfish

LAND
1. giraffe
2. dog
3. cat
4. horse
5. bear
6. deer

Page 139

Review

Directions: Compare the leaves on the left to the pictures of the other leaves. Write the missing names under the leaves.

ash — red oak — poison ivy — ash

silver maple — silver maple — elm — white oak

Directions: Color the pictures that are fruits.

apple — carrot — peach — corn

Directions: Draw an **X** on the word in each group that does not belong.

night — black — dark — sun

rose — ash — oak — elm

muffin — banana — rolls — bread

Page 140

Comprehension: Ladybugs

Directions: Read about ladybugs. Then, answer the questions.

Have you ever seen a ladybug? Ladybugs are red. They have black spots. They have six legs. Ladybugs are pretty!

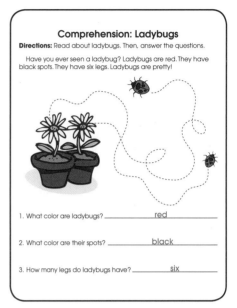

1. What color are ladybugs? red

2. What color are their spots? black

3. How many legs do ladybugs have? six

Page 141

Comprehension: Playful Cats

Directions: Read about cats. Then, follow the instructions.

Cats make good pets. They like to play. They like to jump. They like to run. Do you?

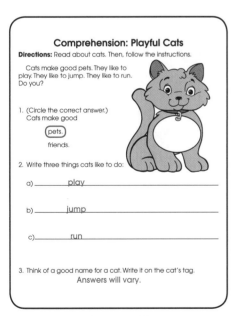

1. (Circle the correct answer.) Cats make good
   (pets.)
   friends.

2. Write three things cats like to do:
   a) play
   b) jump
   c) run

3. Think of a good name for a cat. Write it on the cat's tag.
   Answers will vary.

Page 142

Comprehension: Types of Tops

The **main idea** is the most important point or idea in a story.

Directions: Read about tops. Then, answer the questions.

Tops come in all sizes. Some tops are made of wood. Some tops are made of tin. All tops do the same thing. They spin! Do you have a top?

1. Circle the main idea:
   (There are many kinds of tops.)
   Some tops are made of wood.

2. What are some tops made of? wood, tin

3. What do all tops do? spin

Page 143

Comprehension: Playing Store

Directions: Read about playing store. Then, answer the questions.

Tyson and his friends like to play store. They use boxes and cans. They line them up. Then, they put them in bags.

Grocery Bag — Grocery Bag — Cereal — CAKE MIX — Soup

1. Circle the main idea:
   (Tyson and his friends use boxes, cans, and bags to play store.)
   You need bags to play store.

2. (Circle your answer.) Who likes to play store?
   all kids — (some kids)

3. Do you like to play store? Answers will vary.

Page 144

ANSWER KEY

Comprehension: Singing Whales

Directions: Read about singing whales. Then, follow the instructions.

Some whales can sing! We cannot understand the words. But, we can hear the tune of the humpback whale. Each season, humpback whales sing a different song.

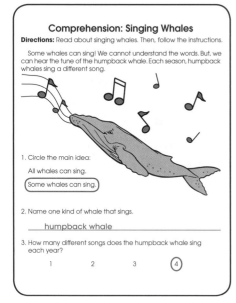

1. Circle the main idea:

   All whales can sing.

   (Some whales can sing.)

2. Name one kind of whale that sings.

   humpback whale

3. How many different songs does the humpback whale sing each year?

   1   2   3   (4)

Page 145

Comprehension: Paper-Bag Puppets

Directions: Read about paper-bag puppets. Then, follow the instructions.

It is easy to make a hand puppet. You need a small paper bag. You need colored paper. You need glue. You need scissors. Are you ready?

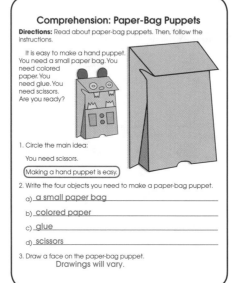

1. Circle the main idea:

   You need scissors.

   (Making a hand puppet is easy.)

2. Write the four objects you need to make a paper-bag puppet.

   a) a small paper bag

   b) colored paper

   c) glue

   d) scissors

3. Draw a face on the paper-bag puppet.
   Drawings will vary.

Page 146

Comprehension: Sea Horses Look Strange!

Directions: Read about sea horses. Then, answer the questions.

Sea horses are fish, not horses. A sea horse's head looks a little like a horse's head. It has a tail like a monkey's tail. A sea horse looks very strange!

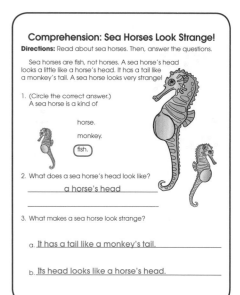

1. (Circle the correct answer.)
   A sea horse is a kind of

   horse.

   monkey.

   (fish.)

2. What does a sea horse's head look like?

   a horse's head

3. What makes a sea horse look strange?

   a. It has a tail like a monkey's tail.

   b. Its head looks like a horse's head.

Page 147

Comprehension: Carla and Tony Jump Rope

Directions: Read about jumping rope. Then, follow the instructions.

Carla and Tony like to jump rope. Carla likes to jump rope alone. Tony likes to have two people turn the rope for him. Carla and Tony can jump slowly. They can also jump fast.

1. Name another way to jump rope.

   a. Have two people turn the rope.

   b. Jump rope alone.

2. Name two speeds for jumping rope.

   a) slow   b) fast

3. Do you like to jump rope? Answers will vary.

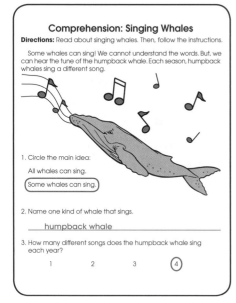

Page 148

Comprehension: How to Stop a Dog Fight

Directions: Read about how to stop a dog fight. Then, answer the questions.

Sometimes, dogs fight. They bark loudly. They may bite. Do not try to pull apart fighting dogs. Turn on a hose, and spray them with water. This will stop the fight.

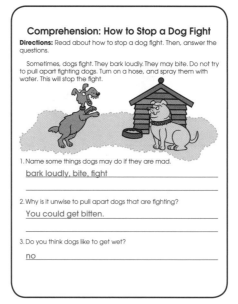

1. Name some things dogs may do if they are mad.

   bark loudly, bite, fight

2. Why is it unwise to pull apart dogs that are fighting?

   You could get bitten.

3. Do you think dogs like to get wet?

   no

Page 149

Comprehension: Training a Dog

Directions: Read about how to train dogs. Then, answer the questions.

A dog has a ball in his mouth. You want the ball. What should you do? Do not pull on the ball. Hold out something else for the dog. The dog will drop the ball to take it!

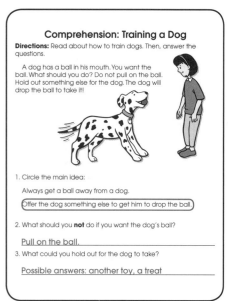

1. Circle the main idea:

   Always get a ball away from a dog.

   (Offer the dog something else to get him to drop the ball.)

2. What should you **not** do if you want the dog's ball?

   Pull on the ball.

3. What could you hold out for the dog to take?

   Possible answers: another toy, a treat

Page 150

Comprehension: How to Meet a Dog

Directions: Read about how to meet a dog. Then, follow the instructions.

Do not try to pet a dog right away. First, let the dog sniff your hand. Do not move quickly. Do not talk loudly. Just let the dog sniff.

1. Predict what the dog will let you do if it likes you.
   The dog will let you pet it.

2. What should you let the dog do? Sniff your hand.

3. Name three things you should not do when you meet a dog.

   a) Do not pet the dog.

   b) Do not move quickly.

   c) Do not talk loudly.

Page 151

Comprehension: Dirty Dogs

Directions: Read about dogs. Then, answer the questions.

Like people, dogs get dirty. Some dogs get a bath once a month. Baby soap is a good soap for cleaning dogs. Fill a tub with warm water. Get someone to hold the dog still in the tub. Then, wash the dog quickly.

1. How often do some dogs get a bath? once a month

2. What is a good soap to use on dogs? baby soap

3. Do you think most dogs like to take baths? Answers will vary.

Page 152

Comprehension: Pretty Parrots

Directions: Read about parrots. Then, follow the instructions.

Big parrots are pretty. Their feet have four toes each. Two toes are in front. Two toes are in back. Parrots use their feet to climb. They use them to hold food.

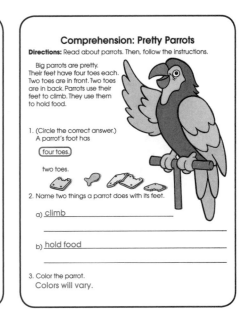

1. (Circle the correct answer.)
   A parrot's foot has

   four toes.

   two toes.

2. Name two things a parrot does with its feet.

   a) climb

   b) hold food

3. Color the parrot.
   Colors will vary.

Page 153

Comprehension: A Winter Story

Directions: Read about parrots. Then, follow the instructions.

It is cold in winter. Snow falls in some parts of the country. Water freezes. Most kids like to play outdoors. Some kids make a snowman. Some kids skate. What do you do in winter?

1. Circle the main idea:

   Snow falls in winter.

   In winter, there are many things to do outside.

2. Write two things about winter weather.

   a) Answers will vary.

   b)

3. Write what you like to do in winter.
   Answers will vary.

Page 154

Comprehension: The Puppet Play

Directions: Read the play out loud with a friend. Then, answer the questions.

Pip: Hey, Pep. What kind of turkey eats very fast?

Pep: Uh, I don't know.

Pip: A gobbler!

Pep: I have a good joke for you, Pip. What kind of burger does a polar bear eat?

Pip: Uh, a cold burger?

Pep: No, an iceberg-er!

Pip: Hey, that was a great joke!

1. Who are the characters in the play? Pip and Pep

2. Who are the jokes about? a turkey and a polar bear

3. What are the characters in the play doing? telling jokes

Page 155

Comprehension: Just Junk?

Directions: Read about saving things. Then, follow the instructions.

Do you save old crayons? Do you save old buttons or cards? Some people call these things junk. They throw them out. Leah saves these things. She likes to use them for art projects. She puts them in a box. What kinds of things do you save?

1. Circle the main idea:

   Everyone has junk.

   People have different ideas about what junk is.

2. Name two kinds of junk.

   a) Answers will vary.

   b)

3. What are two things you can do with old things?
   Possible answers:
   a) Turn them into art projects.

   b) Recycle them.

Page 156

Comprehension: Snakes!

Directions: Read about snakes. Then, answer the questions.

There are many facts about snakes that might surprise someone. A snake's skin is dry. Most snakes are shy. They will hide from people. Snakes eat mice and rats. They do not chew them up. Snakes' jaws drop open so they can swallow their food whole.

1. How does a snake's skin feel? __dry__

2. Most snakes are __shy__

3. What do snakes eat?

   a. __mice__

   b. __rats__

Page 157

Comprehension: More About Snakes!

Directions: Read more about snakes. Then, follow the instructions.

Unlike people, snakes have cold blood. They like to be warm. They hunt for food when it is warm. They lie in the sun. When it is cold, snakes curl up into a ball.

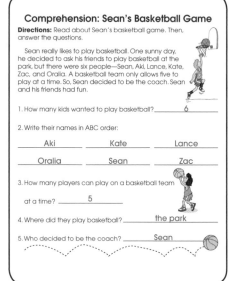

1. What do snakes do when it is warm?

   a. __Hunt for food.__

   b. __Lie in the sun.__

2. Why do you think snakes curl up when it is cold? __to keep themselves warm__

3. (Circle the correct answer.)
   People have:

   cold blood.   (warm blood.)

Page 158

Comprehension: Sean's Basketball Game

Directions: Read about Sean's basketball game. Then, answer the questions.

Sean really likes to play basketball. One sunny day, he decided to ask his friends to play basketball at the park, but there were six people—Sean, Aki, Lance, Kate, Zac, and Oralia. A basketball team only allows five to play at a time. So, Sean decided to be the coach. Sean and his friends had fun.

1. How many kids wanted to play basketball? ___6___

2. Write their names in ABC order:

   | Aki | Kate | Lance |
   | Oralia | Sean | Zac |

3. How many players can play on a basketball team at a time? ___5___

4. Where did they play basketball? __the park__

5. Who decided to be the coach? __Sean__

Page 159

Comprehension: Outdoor/Indoor Games

Directions: Read the story. Then, answer the questions.

Derrick likes to play outdoor and indoor games. His favorite outdoor game is baseball because he likes to hit the ball with the bat and run around the bases. He plays this game in the park with the neighborhood kids.

When it rains, he plays checkers with Lorenzo on the dining-room table in his apartment. He likes the game, because he has to use his brain to think about his next move, and the rules are easy to follow.

Answers will vary.

1. What is your favorite outdoor game? _____

2. Why do you like this game? _____

3. Where is this game played? _____

4. What is your favorite indoor game? _____

5. Why do you like this game? _____

6. Where is this game played? _____

Page 160

Reading Comprehension

Directions: Read the story. Then, complete the sentences with words from the story.

Mike lives on a farm. There are many animals on the farm: birds, cows, pigs, goats, and chickens. But Mike likes his horse best. His horse's name is Stormy. Stormy stays in a barn. For fun, Mike rides Stormy to the lake. Stormy helps Mike, too. Stormy pulls a cart to carry weeds from the garden. After a hard day, Mike feeds Stormy corn and hay. For a treat, Stormy gets a pear.

1. Mike lives on a __farm__
2. His favorite animal is a __horse__
3. The horse's name is __Stormy__
4. Stormy stays in a __barn__
5. It is fun to ride to the __lake__
6. Stormy eats __corn__ and __hay__
7. Stormy's treat is a __pear__

Write 5 words from the story that have an **r-controlled vowel**.

Possible answers:

| __farm__ | __are__ | __birds__ |
| __horse__ | __Stormy__ | |

Now, write 5 words from the story that have a **long vowel sound**.

| __Mike__ | __goats__ | __likes__ |
| __lake__ | __hay__ | |

Page 161

Comprehension: Ant Farms

Directions: Read about ant farms. Then, answer the questions.

Ant farms are sold at toy stores and pet stores. Ant farms come in a flat frame. The frame has glass on each side. Inside the glass is sand. The ants live in the sand.

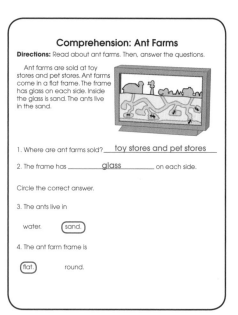

1. Where are ant farms sold? __toy stores and pet stores__

2. The frame has __glass__ on each side.

Circle the correct answer.

3. The ants live in

   water.   (sand.)

4. The ant farm frame is

   (flat.)   round.

Page 162

Comprehension: Amazing Ants

Directions: Read about ants. Then, answer the questions.

Ants are insects. Ants live in many parts of the world and make their homes in soil, sand, wood, and leaves. Most ants live for about 6 to 10 weeks. But the queen ant, who lays the eggs, can live for up to 15 years!

The largest ant is the bulldog ant. This ant can grow to be 5 inches long, and it eats meat! The bulldog ant can be found in Australia.

1. Where do ants make their homes? soil, sand, wood, and leaves

2. How long can a queen ant live? up to 15 years

3. What is the largest ant? the bulldog ant

4. What does it eat? meat

Page 163

Comprehension: Sharks Are Fish, Too!

Directions: Read the story. Then, follow the instructions.

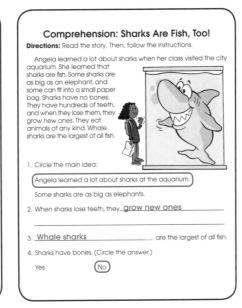

Angela learned a lot about sharks when her class visited the city aquarium. She learned that sharks are fish. Some sharks are as big as an elephant, and some can fit into a small paper bag. Sharks have no bones. They have hundreds of teeth, and when they lose them, they grow new ones. They eat animals of any kind. Whale sharks are the largest of all fish.

1. Circle the main idea:

   (Angela learned a lot about sharks at the aquarium.)

   Some sharks are as big as elephants.

2. When sharks lose teeth, they grow new ones

3. Whale sharks are the largest of all fish.

4. Sharks have bones. (Circle the answer.)

   Yes   (No)

Page 164

Comprehension: Fish

Directions: Read about fish. Then, follow the instructions.

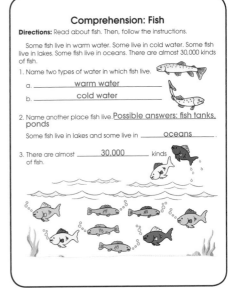

Some fish live in warm water. Some live in cold water. Some fish live in lakes. Some fish live in oceans. There are almost 30,000 kinds of fish.

1. Name two types of water in which fish live.

   a. warm water

   b. cold water

2. Name another place fish live. Possible answers: fish tanks, ponds

   Some fish live in lakes and some live in oceans.

3. There are almost 30,000 kinds of fish.

Page 165

Comprehension: Fish Come in Many Colors

Directions: Read about the color of fish. Then, follow the instructions.

All fish live in water. Fish that live at the top are blue, green, or black. Fish that live down deep are silver or red. The colors make it hard to see the fish.

1. List the colors of fish at the top.

   blue   green   black

2. List the two colors of fish that live down deep.

   silver   red

3. Color the top fish and the bottom fish the correct colors.

Page 166

Comprehension: Fish Can Protect Themselves

Directions: Read about two fish. Then, follow the instructions.

Most fish have ways to protect themselves from danger. Two of these fish are the trigger fish and the porcupine fish. The trigger fish lives on the ocean reef. When it sees danger, it swims into its private hole and puts its top fin up and squeezes itself in tight. Then, it cannot be taken from its hiding place. The porcupine fish also lives on the ocean reef. When danger comes, it puffs up like a balloon by swallowing air or water. When it puffs up, poisonous spikes stand out on its body. When danger is past, it deflates its body.

1. Circle the main idea:

   Trigger fish and porcupine fish can be dangerous.

   (Some fish have ways to protect themselves from danger.)

2. Trigger fish and porcupine fish live on the ocean reef

3. The porcupine fish puffs up by swallowing air

   or water.

Page 167

Comprehension: Ideas Come from Books

Directions: Read the story. Then, follow the instructions.

Zoe has many books. She gets different ideas from these books. Some of her books are about fish. Some are about cardboard and paper crafts. Some are about nature. Others are about reusing junk. Zoe wants to make a paper airplane. She reads about it in one of her books. Then, she asks an adult to help her.

1. Circle the main idea:

   (Zoe learns about different ideas from books.)

   Zoe likes crafts.

2. (Circle the correct answer.) Zoe is:

   (a person who likes to read.)

   a person who doesn't like books.

3. What does Zoe want to make from paper? a paper airplane

4. Write two ways to learn how to do something.

   a) Read about it.

   b) Ask someone to show you.

Page 168

Predicting: A Rainy Game

Predicting is telling what is likely to happen based on the facts.

Directions: Read the story. Then, check each sentence below that tells how the story could end.

One cloudy day, Juan and his baseball team, the Bears, played the Crocodiles. In the last half of the fifth inning, it started to rain. The coaches and umpires had to decide what to do.

✔ They kept playing until nine innings were finished.

✔ They ran for cover and waited until the rain stopped.

_____ Each player grabbed an umbrella and returned to the field to finish the game.

✔ They canceled the game and played it another day.

_____ They acted like crocodiles and slid around the wet bases.

_____ The coaches played the game while the players sat in the dugout.

Page 169

Predicting: Oops!

Directions: Look at the pictures on the left. On the right, draw and write what you predict will happen next.

Answers and drawings will vary.

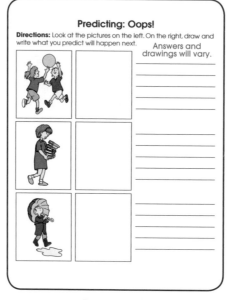

Page 170

Predicting: Dog Derby

Directions: Read the story. Then, answer the questions.

Maggie had a great idea for a game to play with her dogs, Marvin and Mugsy. The game was called "Dog Derby." Maggie would stand at one end of the driveway and hold on to the dogs by their collars. Her friend Mitch would stand at the other end of the driveway. When he said, "Go!" Maggie would let go of the dogs and they would race to Mitch. The first one there would get a dog biscuit. If there was a tie, both dogs would get a biscuit.

Answers will vary.

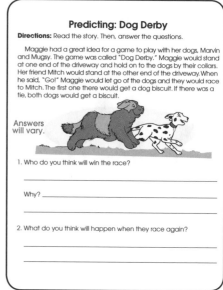

1. Who do you think will win the race?

_____

Why? _____

_____

2. What do you think will happen when they race again?

_____

_____

Page 171

Predicting: What Will Bobby Do?

Directions: Read about Bobby the cat. Then, write what you think will happen.

One sunny spring day, Bobby was sleeping under her favorite tree. She was dreaming about her favorite food—tuna. Suddenly, she became hungry for a treat. Bobby woke up and listened when she heard someone call her name.

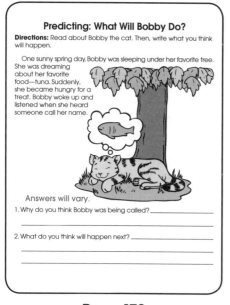

Answers will vary.

1. Why do you think Bobby was being called? _____

_____

2. What do you think will happen next? _____

_____

_____

Page 172

Predicting: Dog-Gone!

Directions: Read the story. Then, follow the instructions.

Scotty and Simone were washing their dog, Willis. His fur was wet. Their hands were wet. Willis did NOT like to be wet. Scotty dropped the soap. Simone picked it up and let go of Willis. Uh-oh!

1. Write what happened next.
Answers will vary.

_____

_____

2. Draw what happened next.

Drawings will vary.

Page 173

Predicting Outcome

Directions: Read the story. Complete the story in the last box.

1. A cat is playing with a ball of yarn.

3. The mouse tiptoes past the playful cat.

Answers will vary.

2. A mouse peeks around the corner.

4. _____

_____

Drawings will vary.

Page 174

Predicting Outcome

Directions: Read the story. Complete the story in the last box.

1. "Look at that elephant! He sure is big!"

3. "Stop, Amy! Look at that sign!"

Don't feed the animals

2. "I'm hungry." "I bet that elephant is, too."

4. Answers will vary.

POPCORN

Drawings will vary.

Page 175

Predicting Outcome

Directions: Read the story. In the last box, draw what you think will happen next. Then, write the words for the end of the story.

1. "Do you want to go to the library with me?" "Yes, I want a book about seashells."

3. "Excuse me. Where can I find a book about seashells?"

READ

2. "Have you found your book?" "No. I can't find it." "Why don't you ask someone?"

4. Answers will vary.

Drawings will vary.

Page 176

Predicting Outcome

Directions: Complete the story. Then, draw pictures to match the four parts. Answers and drawings will vary.

1. Grace and Jazmin are flying a kite.

3._____

Beginning

Middle

2. The kite gets stuck in a tree.

4._____

Middle

End

Page 177

Predicting Outcome

Directions: Create your own story in the squares. Show the beginning in box 1, the middle in boxes 2 and 3, and the end in box 4. Drawings will vary.

Beginning (Setting) | Middle (Problem)

1.

3.

2.

4.

Middle (Problem) | End (Solution)

Page 178

Predicting Outcome

Kelly and Gina always have fun at the fair.

Directions: Read the sentences. Write what you think will happen next. Answers will vary.

1. Kelly and Gina are riding the Ferris wheel. It stops when they are at the top.

2. As they walk into the animal barn, a little piglet runs toward them.

3. Snow cones are their favorite way to cool off. The ones they bought are made from real snow.

4. They play a "toss the ring over the bottle" game, but when the ring goes around the bottle, it disappears.

Page 179

Predicting: Puff and Trigg

Directions: Read about Puff and Trigg. Then, write what happens next in the story.

It was a sunny, warm day in the Pacific Ocean. Puff, the happy porcupine fish, and Trigg, the jolly trigger fish, were having fun playing fish tag. They were good friends. Suddenly, they saw the shadow of a giant fish! It was coming right at them! They knew the giant fish might like eating smaller fish! What did they do?

What did Puff and Trigg do to get away from the giant fish? Answers will vary.

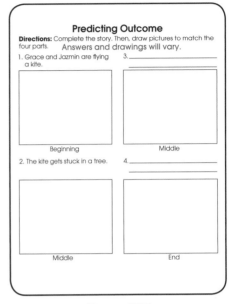

Page 180

Comprehensive Curriculum - **Grade 2**

Fact and Opinion: Games!

A **fact** is something that can be proven. An **opinion** is a feeling or belief about something and cannot be proven.

Directions: Read these sentences about different games. Then, write **F** next to each fact and **O** next to each opinion.

- O 1. Tennis is cool!
- F 2. There are red and black markers in a checkers game.
- F 3. In football, a touchdown is worth six points.
- O 4. Being a goalie in soccer is easy.
- F 5. A yo-yo moves on a string.
- O 6. June's sister looks like the queen on the card.
- F 7. The six kids need three more players for a baseball team.
- O 8. Table tennis is more fun than court tennis.
- F 9. Hide-and-seek is a game that can be played outdoors or indoors.
- F 10. Play money is used in many board games.

Page 181

Fact and Opinion: Recycling

Directions: Read about recycling. Then, follow the instructions.

What do you throw away every day? What could you do with these things? You could change an old greeting card into a new card. You could make a puppet with an old paper bag. Old buttons make great refrigerator magnets. You can plant seeds in plastic cups. Cardboard tubes make perfect rockets. So, use your imagination!

1. Write **F** next to each fact and **O** next to each opinion.

- O Cardboard tubes are ugly.
- F Buttons can be made into refrigerator magnets.
- F An old greeting card can be changed into a new card.
- O Paper-bag puppets are cute.
- F Seeds can be planted in plastic cups.
- F Rockets can be made from cardboard tubes.

2. What could you do with a cardboard tube? _____

make a rocket _____

Page 182

Fact and Opinion: An Owl Story

Directions: Read the story. Then, follow the instructions.

My name is Owen Owl, and I am a bird. I go to Nocturnal School. Our teacher is Mr. Screech Owl. In his class, I learned that owls are birds that can sleep all day and hunt at night. Some of us live in nests in trees. In North America, it is against the law to harm owls. I like being an owl!

Write **F** next to each fact and **O** next to each opinion.

- F 1. No one can harm owls in North America.
- O 2. It would be great if owls could talk.
- F 3. Owls sleep all day.
- F 4. Some owls sleep in nests.
- O 5. Mr. Screech Owl is a good teacher.
- F 6. Owls are birds.
- O 7. Owen Owl would be a good friend.
- F 8. Owls hunt at night.
- O 9. Nocturnal School is a good school for smart owls.
- O 10. This story is for the birds.

Page 183

Fact and Opinion: A Bounty of Birds

Directions: Read the story. Then, follow the instructions.

Tashi's family likes to go to the zoo. Her favorite animals are all the different kinds of birds. Tashi likes birds because they can fly, they have colorful feathers, and they make funny noises.

Write **F** next to each fact and **O** next to each opinion.

- F 1. Birds have two feet.
- F 2. All birds lay eggs.
- O 3. Parrots are too noisy.
- F 4. All birds have feathers and wings.
- O 5. It would be great to be a bird and fly south for the winter.
- F 6. Birds have hard beaks or bills instead of teeth.
- O 7. Pigeons are fun to watch.
- F 8. Some birds cannot fly.
- O 9. Parakeets make good pets.
- F 10. A penguin is a bird.

Page 184

Fact and Opinion: Henrietta the Humpback

Directions: Read the story. Then, follow the instructions.

My name is Henrietta, and I am a humpback whale. I live in cold seas in the summer and warm seas in the winter. My long flippers are used to move forward and backward. I like to eat fish. Sometimes, I show off by leaping out of the water. Would you like to be a humpback whale?

Write **F** next to each fact and **O** next to each opinion.

- O 1. Being a humpback whale is fun.
- F 2. Humpback whales live in cold seas during the summer.
- O 3. Whales are fun to watch.
- F 4. Humpback whales use their flippers to move forward and backward.
- O 5. Henrietta is a great name for a whale.
- O 6. Leaping out of water would be hard.
- F 7. Humpback whales like to eat fish.
- F 8. Humpback whales show off by leaping out of the water.

Page 185

Making Inferences: Ryan's Top

Directions: Read about Ryan's top. Then, follow the instructions.

Ryan got a new top. He wanted to place it where it would be safe. He asked his dad to put it up high. Where can his dad put the top?

1. Write where Ryan's dad can put the top. _____

Answers will vary.

Draw a place Ryan's dad can put the top.

Drawings will vary.

Page 186

Making Inferences: Down on the Ant Farm

Directions: Read about ant farms. Then, answer the questions.

Ants are busy on the farm. They dig in the sand. They make roads in the sand. They look for food in the sand. When an ant dies, other ants bury it.

1. Where do you think ants are buried? _in the sand_

2. Is it fair to say ants are lazy? _no_

3. Write a word that tells about ants. _Possible answers: busy, hardworking_

Page 187

Making Inferences: Monty's Trip

Directions: Read Monty's answer. Then, circle the answer to each question. Color the pictures.

Monty says, "I want to learn more about big cats. Someday, I would like to be an animal trainer or a zoo director. Where can we learn about big cats?"

1. What cat does Monty want to learn about?

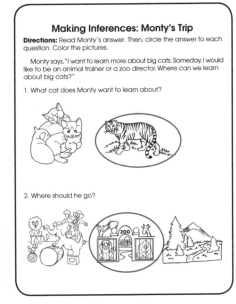

2. Where should he go?

Page 188

Making Inferences

Directions: Read the story. Then, answer the questions.

Jeff is baking cookies. He wears special clothes when he bakes. He puts flour, sugar, eggs, and butter into a bowl. He mixes everything together. He puts the cookies in the oven at 11:15 A.M. It takes 15 minutes for the cookies to bake. Jeff wants something cold and white to drink when he eats his cookies.

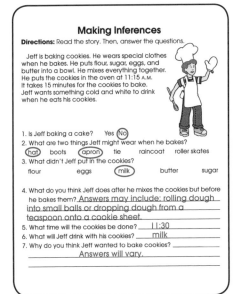

1. Is Jeff baking a cake?   Yes (No)
2. What are two things Jeff might wear when he bakes?
   (hat)   boots   (apron)   tie   raincoat   roller skates
3. What didn't Jeff put in the cookies?
   flour   eggs   (milk)   butter   sugar

4. What do you think Jeff does after he mixes the cookies but before he bakes them? _Answers may include: rolling dough into small balls or dropping dough from a teaspoon onto a cookie sheet._
5. What time will the cookies be done? _11:30_
6. What will Jeff drink with his cookies? _milk_
7. Why do you think Jeff wanted to bake cookies? _____
   Answers will vary.

Page 189

Making Inferences

Directions: Read the story. Then, answer the questions.

Shawn and his family are on a trip. It is very sunny. Shawn loves to swim. He also likes the waves. There is something else he likes even more. Shawn builds drip castles. He makes drips by using very wet sand. He lets it drip out of his hand into a tall pile. He makes the drip piles as high as he can.

1. Where is Shawn? _at the beach_

2. What does Shawn wear on his trip? _a swimsuit_

3. Is Shawn hot or cold? _hot_

4. What does Shawn like to do best? _build sandcastles_

5. What are drip castles made from? _very wet sand_

6. What do you think happens when drip castles get too big?

They fall over.

7. If Shawn gets too hot, what do you think he will do?

go swimming

Page 190

Making Inferences

Directions: Read the story. Then, answer the questions.

Mrs. Sweet looked forward to a visit from her niece, Candy. In the mor ning, she cleaned her house. She also baked some banana bread. An hour before Candy was to arrive, the phone rang. Mrs. Sweet said, "I understand." When she hung up the phone, she looked very sad.

1. Who do you think called Mrs. Sweet?

Candy

2. How do you know that?

Mrs. Sweet probably said, "I understand" when

Candy said she wouldn't visit today.

3. Why is Mrs. Sweet sad?

Her niece, Candy, probably can't come visit today.

Page 191

Making Inferences: Sea Horses

Directions: Read more about sea horses. Then, answer the questions.

A father sea horse helps the mother. He has a small sack, or pouch, on the front of his body. The mother sea horse lays the eggs. She does not keep them. She gives the eggs to the father.

1. What does the mother sea horse do with her eggs?

She gives them to the father.

2. Where does the father sea horse put the eggs?

in his pouch

3. Sea horses can change color. Color the sea horses.

Page 192

Comprehensive Curriculum - **Grade 2**

Making Inferences: Using Pictures

Directions: Draw a picture for each idea. Then, write two sentences that tell about it.

Answers and drawings will vary.

You and a friend are playing your favorite game.

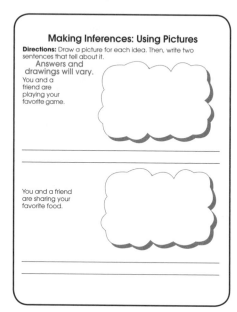

You and a friend are sharing your favorite food.

Page 193

Making Inferences: Visualizing

Directions: Read this story about Ling and Bradley. Draw pictures for the beginning and middle to describe each part of the story.

Beginning: One sunny day, Ling and Bradley, wearing their empty backpacks, rode their bikes down the street to the park.

Drawings will vary.

Middle: They stopped by an oak tree with many acorns under it. They picked up some and stuffed them into their backpacks.

Directions: Draw an ending for this story that tells what you think they did with the acorns.

End: With the heavy backpacks strapped on their backs, they pedaled home.

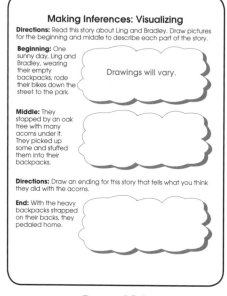

Page 194

Making Inferences: Visualizing

Directions: Read the story about Melinda. Then, draw pictures that describe each part of the story.

Beginning: It was Halloween. Melinda's costume was a black cat with super-duper polka-dot sunglasses.

Drawings will vary.

Middle: Her little brown dog, Marco, yelped and ran under a big red chair when he saw her come into the room.

End: Melinda took off her black cat mask and sunglasses. Then, she held out a dog biscuit. She picked Marco up and hugged him. Then, he was happy.

Page 195

Making Inferences: Visualizing

Directions: Read the story about Chad and Leon. Then, draw pictures that describe each part of the story.

Beginning: One chilly morning, Chad and Leon rolled two big snowballs to make a snowman in Chad's front yard.

Drawings will vary.

Middle: Chad put his big snowball on top of the bigger one. Leon added a carrot nose, two charcoal eyes, a stick mouth, and a cowboy hat. Then, they went into the house.

End: Later, when they looked out the window, they saw the snowman dancing around. "Thank you!" he shouted to the boys.

Page 196

Making Inferences: Point of View

Juniper has three problems to solve. She needs your help.

Directions: Read each problem. Write what you think she should do.

1. Juniper is watching her favorite TV show when the power goes out.

Answers will vary.

2. Juniper is riding her bike to school when the front tire goes flat.

3. Juniper loses her father while shopping in the supermarket.

Page 197

Making Inferences: Point of View

Toran also has three problems. Now that you have helped Juniper, he would like you to help him, too.

Directions: Read each problem. Write what you think he should do.

Answers will vary.

1. The class is having a picnic, and Toran left his lunch at home.

2. Toran wants to buy a special video game, but he needs three more dollars.

3. Toran's best friend, Felix, made the third out, and their team lost the kickball game.

Page 198

Making Inferences: Sequencing

Directions: Draw three pictures to tell a story about each topic.
Drawings will vary.

1. Feeding a pet

| Beginning | Middle | End |

2. Playing with a friend

| Beginning | Middle | End |

Page 199

Making Inferences: Sequencing

Help make a doggie pizza for Spotty Dog. The steps to follow are all mixed up. Three of the steps are not needed.

Directions: Number the steps in order from 1 to 7. Draw a dog bone by the 3 steps that are not needed.

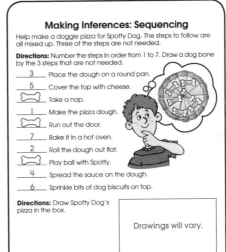

- 3 Place the dough on a round pan.
- 5 Cover the top with cheese.
- 🦴 Take a nap.
- 1 Make the pizza dough.
- 🦴 Run out the door.
- 7 Bake it in a hot oven.
- 2 Roll the dough out flat.
- 🦴 Play ball with Spotty.
- 4 Spread the sauce on the dough.
- 6 Sprinkle bits of dog biscuits on top.

Directions: Draw Spotty Dog's pizza in the box.

Drawings will vary.

Page 200

Making Deductions: Find the Books

Directions: Use the clues to help the children find their books. Draw a line from each child's name to the correct book.

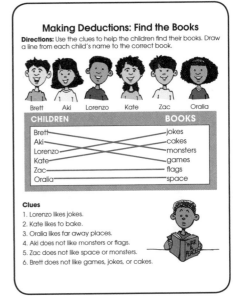

Brett   Aki   Lorenzo   Kate   Zac   Oralia

CHILDREN	BOOKS
Brett	jokes
Aki	cakes
Lorenzo	monsters
Kate	games
Zac	flags
Oralia	space

Clues

1. Lorenzo likes jokes.
2. Kate likes to bake.
3. Oralia likes far away places.
4. Aki does not like monsters or flags.
5. Zac does not like space or monsters.
6. Brett does not like games, jokes, or cakes.

Page 201

Making Deductions: Travel

Six children from the same neighborhood each travel to school in a different way. Can you find out how each one gets to school?

Directions: Read the clues. Draw a dot to show how each child travels to school. Draw **X**'s on the remaining boxes.

	Brian	Gina	Lawrence	Luna	Taylor	Marianna
car	X	X	X	X	•	X
bus	•	X	X	X	X	X
walk	X	X	•	X	X	X
bicycle	X	•	X	X	X	X
truck	X	X	X	X	X	•
van	X	X	X	•	X	X

Clues:

1. Lawrence likes to walk to school.
2. Taylor hates to walk, so his mother takes him in the car.
3. Luna lives next door to Lawrence and waves to Gina as Gina goes by in a pickup truck.
4. Brian joins his pals on the bus.
5. Gina's friend, who lives next door to Lawrence, rides a bike to school.
6. Marianna likes to sit in the middle seat while riding to school.

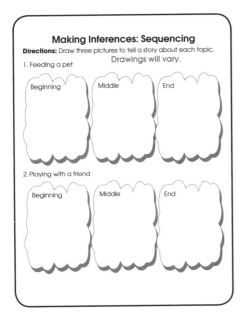

Page 202

Making Deductions: Sports

Children all over the world like to play sports. They like many different kinds of sports: football, soccer, basketball, softball, in-line skating, swimming, and more.

Directions: Read the clues. Draw dots and **X**'s on the chart to match the children with their sports.

	swimming	football	soccer	basketball	baseball	in-line skating
J.J.	X	•	X	X	X	X
Zoe	X	X	X	X	X	•
Andy	X	X	X	•	X	X
Amber	X	X	•	X	X	X
Raul	X	X	X	X	•	X
Sierra	•	X	X	X	X	X

Clues

1. Zoe hates football.
2. Andy likes basketball.
3. Raul likes to pitch in his favorite sport.
4. J.J. likes to play what Zoe hates.
5. Amber is good at kicking the ball to her teammates.
6. Sierra needs a pool for her favorite sport.

Page 203

Making Deductions: What Day Is It?

Dad is cooking dinner tonight. Find out what day of the week it is.

Directions: Read the clues. Complete the menu. Answer the question.

Menu

Monday	pizza
Tuesday	chicken
Wednesday	tacos
Thursday	soup
Friday	pasta
Saturday	fish
Sunday	salad

1. Mom fixed pizza on Monday.
2. Dad fixed a salad the day before that.
3. Tess made soup three days after Mom fixed pizza.
4. Tom fixed tacos the day before Tess made soup.
5. Mom fixed pasta the day after Tess made soup.
6. Tess cooked fish the day before Dad fixed a salad.
7. Dad is making chicken today. What day is it? __Tuesday__

Page 204

Review

Directions: Read the story. Then, answer the questions.

Randa, Emily, Ali, Dave, Liesl, and Deana all love to read. Every Tuesday, they all go to the library together and pick out their favorite books. Randa likes books about fish. Emily likes books about sports and athletes. Ali likes books about art. Dave likes books about wild animals. Liesl likes books with riddles and puzzles. Deanna likes books about cats and dogs.

1. Circle the main idea:

   Randa, Emily, Ali, Dave, Liesl, and Deana are good friends.

   ⟨Randa, Emily, Ali, Dave, Liesl, and Deana all like books.⟩

2. Who do you think might grow up to be an artist?
   _____Ali_____

3. Who do you think might grow up to be an oceanographer (someone who studies the ocean)?
   _____Randa_____

4. Who do you think might grow up to be a veterinarian (an animal doctor)?
   _____Deanna_____

5. Who do you think might grow up to be a zookeeper (someone who cares for zoo animals)?
   _____Dave_____

Page 205

Fiction/Nonfiction: Heavy Hitters

Stories that are **fiction** are make-believe. Stories that are **non-fiction** are true stories.

Directions: Read the stories about two famous baseball players. Then, write **fiction** or **nonfiction** in the baseball bats.

Even if you are not a baseball fan, you might know who Jackie Robinson was. African American players were not allowed to play in the major leagues. Then, in 1947, Jackie joined the Brooklyn Dodgers. He was the first African American player in the major leagues. People said hateful things to him. But Jackie was strong and did not fight back. He made history and became one of the best major league players ever!

nonfiction

The Mighty Casey played baseball for the Mudville Nine and was the greatest of all baseball players. He could hit the cover off the ball with the power of a hurricane. But, when the Mudville Nine was behind 4 to 2 in the championship game, Mighty Casey struck out with the bases loaded. There was no joy in Mudville that day, because the Mudville Nine had lost the game.

fiction

Page 206

Nonfiction: Tornado Tips

Directions: Read about tornadoes. Then, follow the instructions.

A tornado begins over land with strong winds and thunderstorms. The spinning air becomes a funnel. It can cause damage. If you are inside, go to the lowest floor of the building. A basement is a safe place. A bathroom or closet in the middle of a building can be a safe place, too. If you are outside, lie in a ditch. Remember, tornadoes are dangerous.

Answers may vary.
Possible answers:
Write five facts about tornadoes.

1. _A tornado begins over land ._

2. _The spinning air becomes a funnel._

3. _It can cause damage._

4. _A basement is a safe place._

5. _Tornadoes are dangerous._

Page 207

Fiction: Hercules

The **setting** is where a story takes place. The characters are the people in a story or play.

Directions: Read about Hercules. Then, answer the questions.

Hercules was born in the warm Atlantic Ocean. He was a very small and weak baby. He wanted to be the strongest hurricane in the world. But he had one problem. He couldn't blow 75-mile-per-hour winds. Hercules blew and blew in the ocean, until one day, his sister, Hola, told him it would be more fun to be a breeze than a hurricane. Hercules agreed. It was a breeze to be a breeze!

1. What is the setting of the story? _the Atlantic Ocean_

2. Who are the characters? _Hercules and Hola_

3. What is the problem? _He couldn't blow hard enough to be the strongest hurricane in the world._

4. How does Hercules solve his problem? _____

   He decides to be a breeze.

Page 208

Fiction/Nonfiction: The Fourth of July

Directions: Read each story. Then, write whether it is fiction or nonfiction.

One sunny day in July, a dog named Stan ran away from home. He went up one street and down the other looking for fun, but all the yards were empty. Where was everybody? Stan kept walking until he heard the sound of band music and happy people. Stan walked faster until he got to Central Street. There he saw men, women, children, and dogs getting ready to walk in a parade. It was the Fourth of July!

Fiction or nonfiction? _____fiction_____

Americans celebrate the Fourth of July every year because it is the birthday of the United States of America. On July 4, 1776, the United States won its independence from Great Britain. Today, Americans celebrate this holiday with parades, picnics, and fireworks as they proudly wave the red, white, and blue American flag.

Fiction or nonfiction? _____nonfiction_____

Page 209

Fiction and Nonfiction: Which Is It?

Directions: Read about fiction and nonfiction books. Then, follow the instructions.

There are many kinds of books. Some books have make-believe stories about princesses and dragons. Some books contain poetry and rhymes, like Mother Goose. These are fiction.

Some books contain facts about space and plants. And still other books have stories about famous people in history, like Abraham Lincoln. These are nonfiction.

Write **F** for fiction and **NF** for nonfiction.

_F_ 1. nursery rhyme

_F_ 2. fairy tale

_NF_ 3. true life story of a famous athlete

_F_ 4. Aesop's fables

_NF_ 5. dictionary entry about foxes

_NF_ 6. weather report

_F_ 7. story about a talking tree

_NF_ 8. text about how a tadpole becomes a frog

_NF_ 9. text about animal habitats

_F_ 10. riddles and jokes

Page 210

Writing: My Snake Story

Directions: Write a fictional (make-believe) story about a snake. Make sure to include details and a title.

Stories will vary.

title

Page 211

Review: All About You!

Directions: What are some of your interests? Write a story telling what you like to do. Then, on another sheet of paper, draw a picture to go with your story.

Stories and drawings will vary.

Page 212

ABC Order

Directions: Put the words in ABC order on the bags.

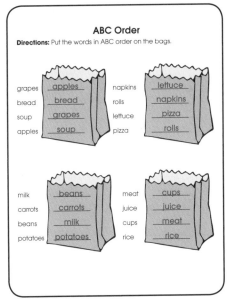

grapes	apples	napkins	lettuce
bread	bread	rolls	napkins
soup	grapes	lettuce	pizza
apples	soup	pizza	rolls

milk	beans	meat	cups
carrots	carrots	juice	juice
beans	milk	cups	meat
potatoes	potatoes	rice	rice

Page 214

Alphabetical Order

Directions: Cut out the scoops of ice cream on the bottom. Place them on the correct cone in alphabetical order.

apple   dog   frost

house   lemon   ring   truck

Page 215

ABC Order

Directions: Write each group of words in alphabetical order. If two words start with the same letter, look at the second letter in each word.

Example: lamb   **Lamb** comes first because **a** comes before **i**
light   in the alphabet.

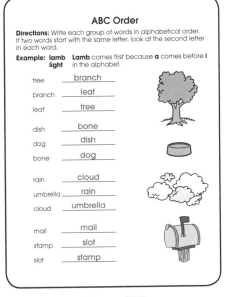

tree	branch
branch	leaf
leaf	tree

dish	bone
dog	dish
bone	dog

rain	cloud
umbrella	rain
cloud	umbrella

mail	mail
stamp	slot
slot	stamp

Page 217

Sequencing: ABC Order

Directions: Write 1, 2, 3, or 4 on the lines in each row to put the words in ABC order.

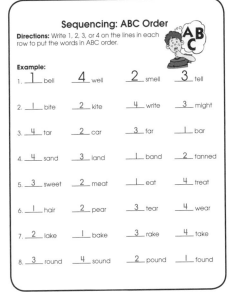

Example:
1. _1_ bell   _4_ well   _2_ smell   _3_ tell
2. _1_ bite   _2_ kite   _4_ write   _3_ might
3. _4_ tar   _2_ car   _3_ far   _1_ bar
4. _4_ sand   _3_ land   _1_ band   _2_ fanned
5. _3_ sweet   _2_ meat   _1_ eat   _4_ treat
6. _1_ hair   _2_ pear   _3_ tear   _4_ wear
7. _2_ lake   _1_ bake   _3_ rake   _4_ take
8. _3_ round   _4_ sound   _2_ pound   _1_ found

Page 218

Comprehensive Curriculum - **Grade 2**

Sequencing: ABC Order

If the first letters of two words are the same, look at the second letters in both words. If the second letters are the same, look at the third letters.

Directions: Write 1, 2, 3, or 4 on the lines in each row to put the words in ABC order.

Example:

1. _1_ candle   _2_ carrot   _4_ duck   _3_ dance

2. _2_ cold   _4_ hot   _1_ carry   _3_ hit

3. _2_ flash   _1_ fan   _3_ fun   _4_ garden

4. _2_ seat   _4_ sun   _1_ saw   _3_ sit

5. _3_ row   _1_ ring   _2_ rock   _4_ run

6. _2_ truck   _3_ turn   _4_ twin   _1_ talk

7. _1_ seven   _2_ shoe   _4_ soup   _3_ smell

Page 219

Sequencing: ABC Order

Directions: Write the following names in ABC order: Oscar, Ali, Lance, Kim, Zane, and Bonita.

Ali
Bonita
Kim
Lance
Oscar
Zane

Directions: Write the names of six friends or family members in ABC order.

Answers will vary.

Page 220

Sequencing: ABC Order

Kwan likes to make rhymes. Help Kwan think of rhyming words.

Directions: Write three words in ABC order that rhyme with each word Kwan wrote.

Possible answers:

cap	bet	bill
gap	get	dill
lap	let	fill
rap	met	hill
dog	man	hat
fog	pan	mat
hog	ran	pat
log	tan	rat

Directions: Write a short poem using some of the rhyming words you wrote.

Poems will vary.

Page 221

Synonyms

Words that mean the same or nearly the same are called **synonyms**.

Directions: Read the sentence that tells about the picture. Draw a circle around the word that means the same as the **bold** word.

The child is **unhappy**.
(sad)   hungry

The flowers are **lovely**.
(pretty)   green

The baby was very **tired**.
(sleepy)   hurt

The **funny** clown made us laugh.
(silly)   glad

The ladybug is so **tiny**.
(small)   red

We saw a **scary** tiger.
(frightening)   ugly

Page 222

Synonyms

Synonyms are words that have almost the same meaning.

Directions: Read the story. Then, fill in the blanks with the synonyms.

funny	unhappy
windy	little

A New Balloon

It was a breezy day. The wind blew the small child's balloon away. The child was sad. A silly clown gave him a new balloon.

1. It was a ___windy___ day.

2. The wind blew the ___little___ child's balloon away.

3. The child was ___unhappy___ .

4. A ___funny___ clown gave him a new balloon.

Page 223

Synonyms

Directions: Read each sentence. Fill in the blanks with the synonyms.

friend	tired	story
	presents	little

I want to go to bed because I am very <u>sleepy</u>.
___tired___

On my birthday, I like to open my <u>gifts</u>.
___presents___

My <u>pal</u> and I like to play together.
___friend___

My favorite <u>tale</u> is Cinderella.
___story___

The mouse was so <u>tiny</u> that it was hard to catch him.
___little___

Page 224

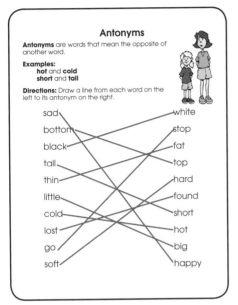

Page 225

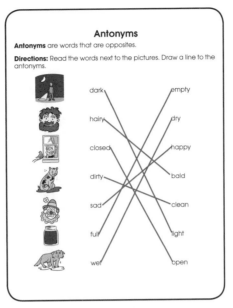

Page 226

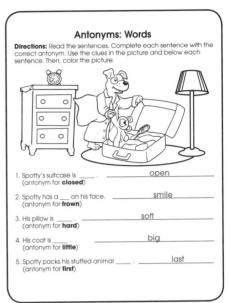

Page 227

Page 228

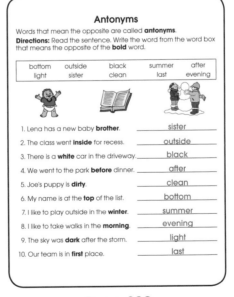

Page 229

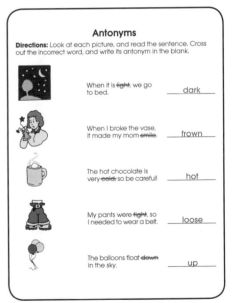

Page 230

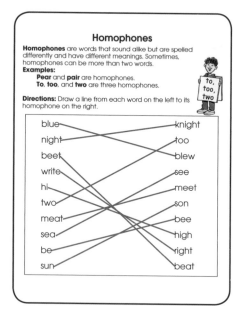

Page 231

Page 232

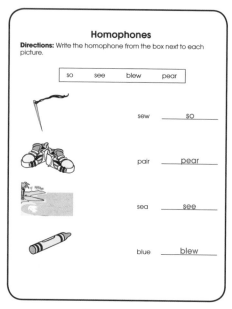

Page 233

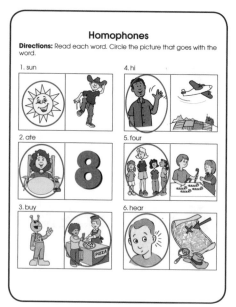

Page 234

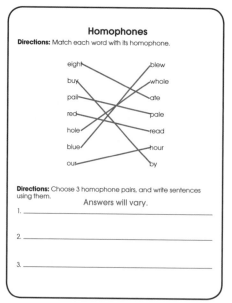

Page 235

Homophones: Doggy Birthday Cake

Homophones are words that sound alike but have different spellings and meanings.

Directions: Read the sentences. The bold words are homophones. Then, follow the directions for a doggy birthday cake.

1. The baker **read** a recipe to bake a doggy cake. Color the plate he put it on **red**.

2. Draw a **hole** in the middle of the doggy cake. Then, color the **whole** cake yellow.

3. Look **for** the top of the doggy cake. Draw **four** candles there.

4. In the hole, draw what you think the doggy would really like.

5. Write a sentence using the words **hole** and **whole**.
   Answers will vary.

6. Write a sentence using the words **read** and **red**.
   Answers will vary.

Page 236

Nouns

A **noun** is the name of a person, place, or thing.

Directions: Read the story, and circle all the nouns. Then, write the nouns next to the pictures below.

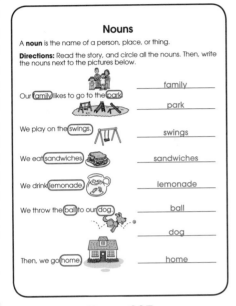

Our (family) likes to go to the (park).   family

                                               park

We play on the (swings).   swings

We eat (sandwiches).   sandwiches

We drink (lemonade).   lemonade

We throw the (ball) to our (dog).   ball

                                               dog

Then, we go (home).   home

Page 237

Nouns

Directions: Look through a magazine. Cut out pictures of nouns, and glue them below. Write the name of the noun next to the picture.

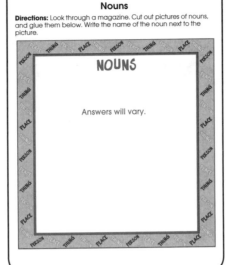

NOUNS

Answers will vary.

Page 238

Proper Nouns

Proper nouns are the names of specific people, places, and things. Proper nouns begin with a capital letter.

Directions: Write the proper nouns on the lines below. Use capital letters at the beginning of each word.

logan, utah   mike smith

Logan, Utah   Mike Smith

lynn cramer   buster

Lynn Cramer   Buster

fluffy   chicago, illinois

Fluffy   Chicago, Illinois

Page 239

Proper Nouns

The days of the week and the months of the year are always capitalized.

Directions: Circle the words that are written correctly. Write the words that need capital letters on the lines below.

sunday	(July)	(Wednesday)	may	december
friday	tuesday	june	august	(Monday)
january	(February)	(March)	(Thursday)	(April)
(September)	saturday	(October)		

Days of the Week   **Months of the Year**

1. Sunday   1. May

2. Friday   2. December

3. Tuesday   3. June

4. Saturday   4. August

                              5. January

Page 240

Capitalization

The first word and all of the important words in a title begin with a capital letter.

Directions: Write the book titles on the lines below. Use capital letters.

1. Dinosaurs

2. Lizards Everywhere

3. The Magic Cat

4. All About Presidents

5. The Space Dog

6. Gerbil Care

Page 241

Review

Directions: Write capital letters where they should appear in the sentences below.

Example: joe can play in january.
           Joe can play in January.

1. we celebrate thanksgiving on the fourth thursday in november.
We celebrate Thanksgiving on the fourth Thursday in November.

2. in june, michelle and mark will go camping every friday.
In June, Michelle and Mark will go camping every Friday.

3. on mondays in october, i will take piano lessons.
On Mondays in October, I will take piano lessons.

Page 242

ANSWER KEY

Plural Nouns

Plural nouns name more than one person, place, or thing.

Directions: Read the words in the box. Write the words in the correct column.

| hats | girl | cows | kittens | melon |
| spoons | glass | book | horse | trees |

one   more than one

girl	hats
melon	cows
glass	kittens
book	spoons
horse	trees

Page 243

Plurals

Plurals are words that mean more than one. To make a word plural, add **s** or **es** to it. In some words ending in **y**, the **y** changes to an **i** before adding **es**. For example, **baby** changes to **babies**.

Directions: Look at the following lists of plural words. Next to each, write the word that means one. The first one has been done for you.

foxes	fox	balls	ball
bushes	bush	candies	candy
dresses	dress	wishes	wish
chairs	chair	boxes	box
shoes	shoe	ladies	lady
stories	story	bunnies	bunny
puppies	puppy	desks	desk
matches	match	dishes	dish
cars	car	pencils	pencil
glasses	glass	trucks	truck

Page 244

Pronouns

Pronouns are words that can be used instead of nouns. **She**, **he**, **it**, and **they** are pronouns.

Directions: Read the sentence. Then, write the sentence again, using **she**, **he**, **it**, or **they** in the blank.

1. Dan likes funny jokes. _____He_____ likes funny jokes.

2. Mei and Sam went to the zoo. _____They_____ went to the zoo.

3. My dog likes to dig in the yard. ___It___ likes to dig in the yard.

4. Sara is a very good dancer. ___She___ is a very good dancer.

5. Levi and Leo are twins. _____They_____ are twins.

Page 245

Subjects

The **subject** of a sentence is the person, place, or thing the sentence is about.

Directions: Underline the subject in each sentence.

Example: Mom read a book.
(Think: Who is the sentence about? Mom)

1. The bird flew away.

2. The kite was high in the air.

3. The children played a game.

4. The books fell down.

5. The monkey climbed a tree.

Page 246

Compound Subjects

Two similar sentences can be joined into one sentence if the predicate is the same. A **compound subject** is made of two subjects joined together by a conjunction, such as **and**.

Example: Jamie can sing.
Sofia can sing.
Jamie **and** Sofia can sing.

Directions: Combine the sentences. Write the new sentence on the line.

1. The cats are my pets.
The dogs are my pets.

The cats and the dogs are my pets.

2. Chairs are in the store.
Tables are in the store.

Chairs and tables are in the store.

3. Myles can ride a bike.
Jack can ride a bike.

Myles and Jack can ride a bike.

Page 247

Verbs

A **verb** is the action word in a sentence. Verbs tell what something does.

Example: **Run**, **sleep**, and **jump** are verbs.

Directions: Circle the verbs in the sentences below.

1. We play baseball every day.

2. Maddy pitches the ball very well.

3. Marco swings the bat harder than anyone.

4. Chris slides into home base.

5. Laura hit a home run.

Page 248

Verbs

Verbs tell when something happens. Add **ed** to verbs to tell that something has already happened.

Example: Today, we will **play**. Yesterday, we **played**.

Directions: Write the correct verb in the blank.

1. Today, I will ____wash____ my dog, Fritz.
wash   washed

2. Last week, Fritz ____cried____ when we said, "Bath time, Fritz."
cry   cried

3. My sister likes to ____help____ wash Fritz.
help   helped

4. One time she ____cleaned____ Fritz by herself.
clean   cleaned

5. Fritz will ____look____ a lot better after his bath.
look   looked

Page 249

Verbs

Directions: Write each verb in the correct column.

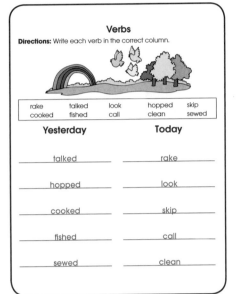

| rake | talked | look | hopped | skip |
| cooked | fished | call | clean | sewed |

Yesterday	Today
talked	rake
hopped	look
cooked	skip
fished	call
sewed	clean

Page 250

Predicates

The **predicate** is the part of the sentence that tells about the action.

Directions: Circle the predicate in each sentence.

Example: The boys ran on the playground.
(Think: The boys did what? Ran)

1. The woman painted a picture.

2. The puppy chases his ball.

3. The students went to school.

4. Butterflies fly in the air.

5. The baby wants a drink.

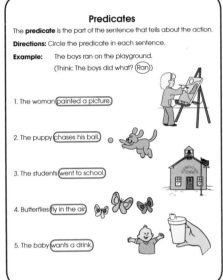

Page 251

Compound Predicates

A **compound predicate** is made by joining two sentences that have the same subject. The predicates are usually joined together by the word **and**.

Example: Evan can jump.
Evan can run.
Evan can run **and** jump.

Directions: Combine the sentences. Write the new sentence on the line.

1. The dog can roll over.
The dog can bark.

The dog can roll over and bark.

2. My mom plays with me.
My mom reads with me.

My mom plays and reads with me.

3. Tara is tall.
Tara is smart.

Tara is tall and smart.

Page 252

Subjects and Predicates

The **subject** of the sentence is the person, place, or thing the sentence is about. The **predicate** is the part of the sentence that describes the subject or tells what the subject does.

Directions: Draw a line between the subject and the predicate. Underline the noun in the subject, and circle the verb in the predicate.

Example: The furry cat | ate food.

1. Hannah | walks to school.

2. The bus driver | drove the children.

3. The school bell | rang very loudly.

4. The teacher | spoke to the students.

5. The girls | opened their books.

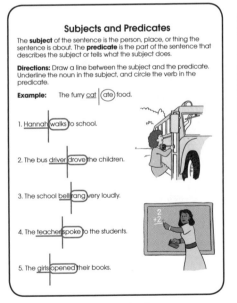

Page 253

Compound Subjects and Predicates

The following sentences have either a compound subject or a compound predicate.

Directions: If the sentence has a compound subject (more than one thing doing the action), **underline** the subject. If it has a compound predicate (more than one action), **circle** the predicate.

Examples: Bats and owls like the night.
The fox slinks and spies.

1. Raccoons and mice steal food.

2. Monkeys and birds sleep in trees.

3. Elephants wash and play in the river.

4. Bears eat honey and scratch trees.

5. Owls hoot and hunt.

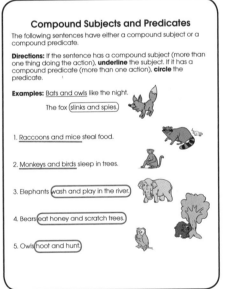

Page 254

Compound Subjects and Predicates

Directions: Write one new sentence using a compound subject or predicate.

Example: The boy will jump. The girl will jump.
The boy and girl will jump.

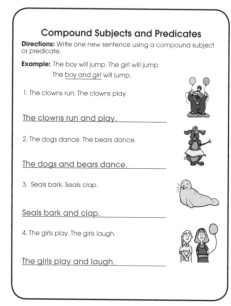

1. The clowns run. The clowns play.

The clowns run and play.

2. The dogs dance. The bears dance.

The dogs and bears dance.

3. Seals bark. Seals clap.

Seals bark and clap.

4. The girls play. The girls laugh.

The girls play and laugh.

Page 255

Parts of a Sentence

Directions: Draw a circle around the noun, the naming part of the sentence. Draw a line under the verb, the action part of the sentence.

Example: (John) drinks juice every morning. ♫

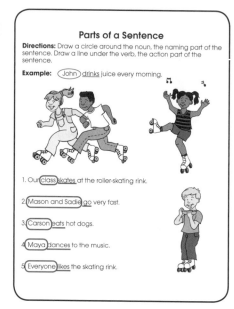

1. Our (class) skates at the roller-skating rink.

2. (Mason and Sadie) go very fast.

3. (Carson) eats hot dogs.

4. (Maya) dances to the music.

5. (Everyone) likes the skating rink.

Page 256

Parts of a Sentence

Directions: Look at the pictures. Draw a line from the naming part of the sentence to the action part to complete the sentence.

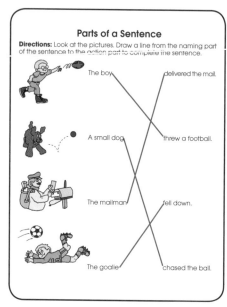

The boy — threw a football.
A small dog — chased the ball.
The mailman — delivered the mail.
The goalie — fell down.

Page 257

Adjectives

Adjectives are words that tell more about a person, place, or thing.

Examples: cold, fuzzy, dark

Directions: Circle the adjectives in the sentences.

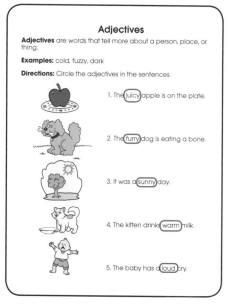

1. The (juicy) apple is on the plate.

2. The (furry) dog is eating a bone.

3. It was a (sunny) day.

4. The kitten drinks (warm) milk.

5. The baby has a (loud) cry.

Page 258

Adjectives

Directions: Choose an adjective from the box to fill in the blanks.

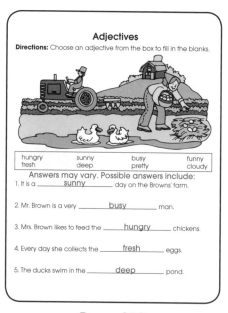

| hungry | sunny | busy | funny |
| fresh | deep | pretty | cloudy |

Answers may vary. Possible answers include:

1. It is a ____sunny____ day on the Browns' farm.

2. Mr. Brown is a very ____busy____ man.

3. Mrs. Brown likes to feed the ____hungry____ chickens.

4. Every day she collects the ____fresh____ eggs.

5. The ducks swim in the ____deep____ pond.

Page 259

Adjectives

Directions: Think of your own adjectives. Write a story about Fluffy the cat.

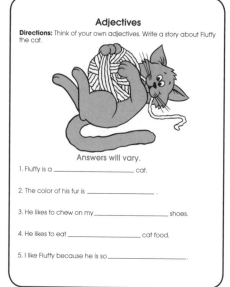

Answers will vary.

1. Fluffy is a _____ cat.

2. The color of his fur is _____.

3. He likes to chew on my_____ shoes.

4. He likes to eat _____ cat food.

5. I like Fluffy because he is so _____.

Page 260

Articles

Articles are small words that help us to better understand nouns. **A** and **an** are articles. We use **an** before a word that begins with a vowel. We use **a** before a word that begins with a consonant.

Example: We looked in **a** nest. It had **an** eagle in it.

Directions: Read the sentences. Write **a** or **an** in the blank.

1. I found ___a___ book.

2. It had a story about ___an___ ant in it.

3. In the story, ___a___ lion gave three wishes to ___an___ ant.

4. The ant's first wish was to ride ___an___ elephant.

5. The second wish was to ride ___an___ alligator.

6. The last wish was ___a___ wish for three more wishes.

Page 261

Sentences and Non-Sentences

A **sentence** tells a complete idea. It has a noun and a verb. It begins with a capital letter and has punctuation at the end.

Directions: Circle the group of words if it is a sentence.

1. (Grass is a green plant.)

2. Mowing the lawn.

3. (Grass grows in fields and lawns.)

4. Tickle the feet.

5. (Sheep, cows, and horses eat grass.)

6. We like to play in.

7. (My sister likes to mow the lawn.)

8. A picnic on the grass.

9. (My dog likes to roll in the grass.)

10. Plant flowers around.

Page 262

Sentences and Non-Sentences

Directions: Circle the group of words if it tells a complete idea.

1. (A secret is something you know.)

2. (My mom's birthday gift is a secret.)

3. No one else.

4. If you promise not to.

5. (I'll tell you a secret.)

6. Something nobody knows.

Page 263

Statements

Statements are sentences that tell us something. They begin with a capital letter and end with a period.

Directions: Write the sentences on the lines below. Begin each sentence with a capital letter, and end it with a period.

1. we like to ride our bikes

We like to ride our bikes.

2. we go down the hill very fast

We go down the hill very fast.

3. we keep our bikes shiny and clean

We keep our bikes shiny and clean.

4. we know how to change the tires

We know how to change the tires.

Page 264

Surprising Sentences

Surprising sentences tell a strong feeling and end with an exclamation point. A surprising sentence may be only one or two words showing fear, surprise, or pain. **Example: Oh, no!**

Directions: Put a period at the end of the sentences that tell something. Put an exclamation point at the end of the sentences that tell a strong feeling. Put a question mark at the end of the sentences that ask a question.

1. The cheetah can run very fast.

2. Wow!

3. Look at that cheetah go!

4. Can you run fast?

5. Oh, my!

6. You're faster than I am.

7. Let's run together.

8. We can run as fast as a cheetah.

9. What fun!

10. Do you think cheetahs get tired?

Page 265

Commands

Commands tell someone to do something. **Example: Be careful.** It can also be written as "Be careful!" if it tells a strong feeling.

Directions: Put a period at the end of the command sentences. Use an exclamation point if the sentence tells a strong feeling. Write your own commands on the lines below.

1. Clean your room.

2. Now!

3. Be careful with your goldfish.

4. Watch out!

5. Be a little more careful!

Answers will vary.

_____

_____

Page 266

Comprehensive Curriculum - **Grade 2**

Questions

Questions are sentences that ask something. They begin with a capital letter and end with a question mark.

Directions: Write the questions on the lines below. Begin each sentence with a capital letter, and end it with a question mark.

1. will you be my friend

Will you be my friend?

2. what is your name

What is your name?

3. are you eight years old

Are you eight years old?

4. do you like rainbows

Do you like rainbows?

Page 267

Making Inferences: Writing Questions

Tommy likes to answer questions. He knows the answers, but you need to write the questions.

Directions: Write two questions for each answer.

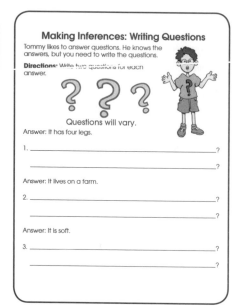

Questions will vary.

Answer: It has four legs.

1. _____?
   _____?

Answer: It lives on a farm.

2. _____?
   _____?

Answer: It is soft.

3. _____?
   _____?

Page 268

Making Inferences: Writing Questions

Toban and Sean use many colors when they paint.

Directions: Write two questions for each answer.

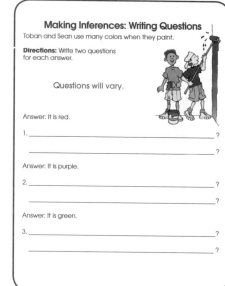

Questions will vary.

Answer: It is red.

1. _____?
   _____?

Answer: It is purple.

2. _____?
   _____?

Answer: It is green.

3. _____?
   _____?

Page 269

Making Inferences: Writing Questions

Tomas likes sports. He enjoys meeting athletes. He would like to be a sports reporter someday.

Directions: Write a question Tomas could ask each of these athletes.

Questions will vary.

1. An Olympic champion skier _____

2. An All-Star basketball player _____
   _____

3. The Quarterback of the Year _____
   _____

4. The winner of the Indy 500 _____
   _____

5. The top home-run hitter _____
   _____

6. An Olympic champion runner _____
   _____

7. A first-place winner in diving _____
   _____

Page 270

Making Inferences: Writing Questions

Erin found many solid shapes in her house.

Directions: Write two questions for each answer.

Questions will vary.

Answer: It is a cube.

1. _____?
   _____?

Answer: It is a cylinder.

2. _____?
   _____?

Answer: It is a sphere.

3. _____?
   _____?

Page 271

Making Inferences: Point of View

Chelsea likes to pretend she will meet famous people someday. She would like to ask them many questions.

Directions: Write a question you think Chelsea would ask if she met these people.

Questions will vary.

1. an actor in a popular, new film _____

2. an Olympic gold medal winner _____

3. an alien from outer space _____
   _____?

Directions: Now, write the answers these people might have given to Chelsea's questions.

Answers will vary.

4. an actor in a popular, new film _____
   _____

5. an Olympic gold medal winner _____
   _____

6. an alien from outer space _____
   _____

Page 272

Making Inferences: Point of View

Ellen likes animals. Someday, she might want to be a veterinarian.

Directions: Write one question you think Ellen would ask each of these animals if she could speak their language.
Questions will vary.

1. a giraffe _____?
2. a mouse _____?
3. a shark _____?
4. a hippopotamus _____?
5. a penguin _____?
6. a gorilla _____?
7. an eagle _____?

Directions: Now, write the answers you think these animals might have given Ellen. **Answers will vary.**

8. a giraffe _____
9. a mouse _____
10. a shark _____
11. a hippopotamus _____
12. a penguin _____
13. a gorilla _____
14. an eagle _____

Page 273

Creative Writing

Directions: Look at the picture below. Write a story about the picture.

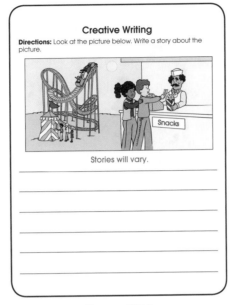

Stories will vary.

_____
_____
_____
_____
_____
_____
_____

Page 274

Ownership

Add **'s** to nouns (people, places, or things) to tell who or what owns something.

Directions: Read the sentences. Fill in the blanks to show ownership.

Example: The doll belongs to **Sara**.
It is **Sara's** doll.

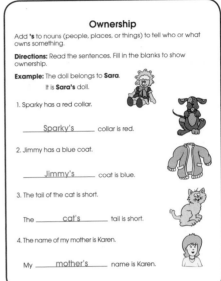

1. Sparky has a red collar.

    _____Sparky's_____ collar is red.

2. Jimmy has a blue coat.

    _____Jimmy's_____ coat is blue.

3. The tail of the cat is short.

    The _____cat's_____ tail is short.

4. The name of my mother is Karen.

    My _____mother's_____ name is Karen.

Page 275

Ownership

Directions: Read the sentences. Choose the correct word, and write it in each sentence below.

1. The _____boy's_____ lunchbox is broken.   boys   boy's
2. The _____gerbils_____ played in the cage.   gerbil's   gerbils
3. _____Ann's_____ hair is brown.   Anns   Ann's
4. The _____horses_____ ran in the field.   horse's   horses
5. My _____sister's_____ coat is torn.   sister's   sisters
6. The _____cat's_____ fur is brown.   cats   cat's
7. Three _____birds_____ flew past our window.   birds   bird's
8. The _____dog's_____ paws are muddy.   dogs   dog's
9. The _____giraffe's_____ neck is long.   giraffes   giraffe's
10. The _____lions_____ are big and powerful.   lion's   lions

Page 276

Is, Are, and Am

Is, **are**, and **am** are special action words that tell us something is happening now.

Use **am** with **I. Example: I am.**
Use **is** to tell about one person or thing. **Example: He is.**
Use **are** to tell about more than one. **Example: We are.**
Use **are** with you. **Example: You are.**

Directions: Write **is**, **are**, or **am** in the sentences below.

1. My friends _____are_____ helping me build a tree house.

2. It _____is_____ in my backyard.

3. We _____are_____ using hammers, wood, and nails.

4. It _____is_____ a very hard job.

5. I _____am_____ lucky to have good friends.

Page 277

Was and Were

Was and **were** tell about something that already happened.
Use **was** to tell about one person or thing. **Example: I was, he was.** Use **were** to tell about more than one person or thing or when using the word **you. Example: We were, you were.**

Directions: Write **was** or **were** in each sentence.

1. Lily _____was_____ eight years old on her birthday.

2. Colin and Charley _____were_____ happy to be at the party.

3. Megan _____was_____ too shy to sing "Happy Birthday."

4. Ben _____was_____ sorry he dropped his cake.

5. All of the children _____were_____ happy to be invited.

Page 278

Comprehensive Curriculum - Grade 2

Go, Going, and Went

Use **go** or **going** to tell about now or later. Sometimes, **going** is used with the words **am** or **are**. Use **went** to tell about something that already happened.

Directions: Write **go**, **going**, or **went** in the sentences below.

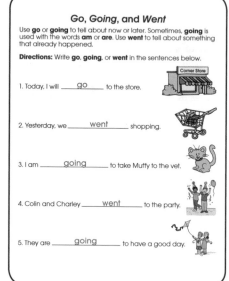

1. Today, I will _____go_____ to the store.

2. Yesterday, we _____went_____ shopping.

3. I am _____going_____ to take Muffy to the vet.

4. Colin and Charley _____went_____ to the party.

5. They are _____going_____ to have a good day.

Page 279

Have, Has, and Had

Use **have** and **has** to tell about now. Use **had** to tell about something that already happened.

Directions: Write **has**, **have**, or **had** in the sentences below.

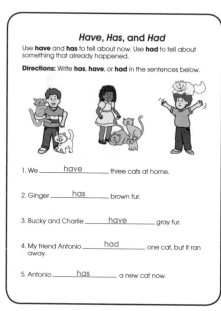

1. We _____have_____ three cats at home.

2. Ginger _____has_____ brown fur.

3. Bucky and Charlie _____have_____ gray fur.

4. My friend Antonio _____had_____ one cat, but it ran away.

5. Antonio _____has_____ a new cat now.

Page 280

See, Saw, and Sees

Use **see** or **sees** to tell about now. Use **saw** to tell about something that already happened.

Directions: Write **see**, **sees**, or **saw** in the sentences below.

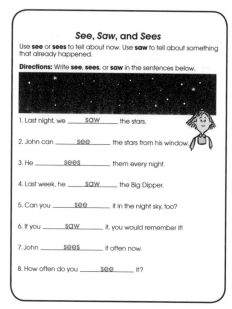

1. Last night, we _____saw_____ the stars.

2. John can _____see_____ the stars from his window.

3. He _____sees_____ them every night.

4. Last week, he _____saw_____ the Big Dipper.

5. Can you _____see_____ it in the night sky, too?

6. If you _____saw_____ it, you would remember it!

7. John _____sees_____ it often now.

8. How often do you _____see_____ it?

Page 281

Eat, Eats, and Ate

Use **eat** or **eats** to tell about now. Use **ate** to tell about what already happened.

Directions: Write **eat**, **eats**, or **ate** in the sentences below.

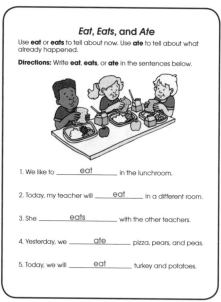

1. We like to _____eat_____ in the lunchroom.

2. Today, my teacher will _____eat_____ in a different room.

3. She _____eats_____ with the other teachers.

4. Yesterday, we _____ate_____ pizza, pears, and peas.

5. Today, we will _____eat_____ turkey and potatoes.

Page 282

Leave, Leaves, and Left

Use **leave** and **leaves** to tell about now. Use **left** to tell about what already happened.

Directions: Write **leave**, **leaves**, or **left** in the sentences below.

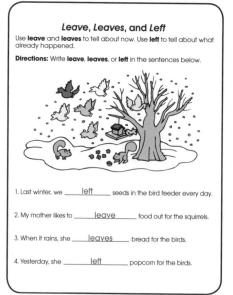

1. Last winter, we _____left_____ seeds in the bird feeder every day.

2. My mother likes to _____leave_____ food out for the squirrels.

3. When it rains, she _____leaves_____ bread for the birds.

4. Yesterday, she _____left_____ popcorn for the birds.

Page 283

Learning Dictionary Skills

A **dictionary** is a book that gives the meaning of words. It also tells how words sound. Words in a dictionary are in ABC order. That makes them easier to find. A picture dictionary lists a word, a picture of the word, and its meaning.

Directions: Look at this page from a picture dictionary. Then, answer the questions.

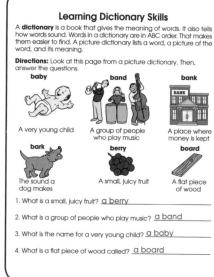

baby — A very young child

band — A group of people who play music

bank — A place where money is kept

bark — The sound a dog makes

berry — A small, juicy fruit

board — A flat piece of wood

1. What is a small, juicy fruit? _a berry_

2. What is a group of people who play music? _a band_

3. What is the name for a very young child? _a baby_

4. What is a flat piece of wood called? _a board_

Page 284

Learning Dictionary Skills

Directions: Look at this page from a picture dictionary. Then, answer the questions.

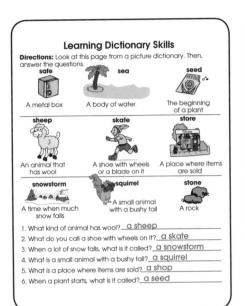

safe — A metal box

sea — A body of water

seed — The beginning of a plant

sheep — An animal that has wool

skate — A shoe with wheels or a blade on it

store — A place where items are sold

snowstorm — A time when much snow falls

squirrel — A small animal with a bushy tail

stone — A rock

1. What kind of animal has wool? <u>a sheep</u>
2. What do you call a shoe with wheels on it? <u>a skate</u>
3. When a lot of snow falls, what is it called? <u>a snowstorm</u>
4. What is a small animal with a bushy tail? <u>a squirrel</u>
5. What is a place where items are sold? <u>a shop</u>
6. When a plant starts, what is it called? <u>a seed</u>

Page 285

Learning Dictionary Skills

Directions: Look at this page from a picture dictionary. Then, answer the questions.

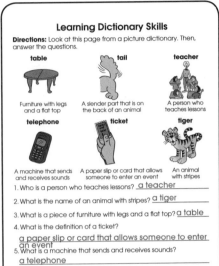

table — Furniture with legs and a flat top

tail — A slender part that is on the back of an animal

teacher — A person who teaches lessons

telephone — A machine that sends and receives sounds

ticket — A paper slip or card that allows someone to enter an event

tiger — An animal with stripes

1. Who is a person who teaches lessons? <u>a teacher</u>
2. What is the name of an animal with stripes? <u>a tiger</u>
3. What is a piece of furniture with legs and a flat top? <u>a table</u>
4. What is the definition of a ticket?
<u>a paper slip or card that allows someone to enter an event</u>
5. What is a machine that sends and receives sounds?
<u>a telephone</u>

Page 286

Learning Dictionary Skills

The **guide words** at the top of a page in a dictionary tell you what the first and last words on the page will be. Only words that come in ABC order between those two words will be on that page. **Guide words** help you find the page you need to look up a word.

Directions: Write each word from the box in ABC order between each pair of guide words.

faint	far	fence	feed	farmer
fan	feet	farm	family	face

face   **fence**

face	farm
faint	farmer
family	feed
fan	feet
far	fence

Page 287

Learning Dictionary Skills

Directions: Write each word from the box in ABC order between each pair of guide words.

fierce	fix	fight	first	few
fish	fill	flush	flat	finish

few   **flush**

few	first
fierce	fish
fight	fix
fill	flat
finish	flush

Page 288

Learning Dictionary Skills

Directions: Create your own dictionary page. Include guide words at the top. Write the words with their meanings in ABC order.

Answers will vary.

guide word	guide word
1. _____ word	4. _____ word
2. _____ word	5. _____ word
3. _____ word	6. _____ word

Page 289

Learning Dictionary Skills

When words have more than one meaning, the meanings are numbered in a dictionary.

Directions: Read the meanings of **tag**. Write the number of the correct definition after each sentence.

tag
1. A small strip or tab attached to something else
2. To label
3. To follow closely and constantly
4. A game of chase

1. We will play a game of tag after we study. <u>4</u>
2. I will tag this coat with its price. <u>2</u>
3. My little brother will tag along with us. <u>3</u>
4. My mother already took off the price tag. <u>1</u>
5. The tag on the toy said, "For Sale." <u>1</u>
6. Do not tag that tree. <u>2</u>

Page 290

Number Words

Directions: Write each number word beside the correct picture. Then, write it again.

Example: six six

| one | two | three | four | five | six | seven | eight | nine | ten |

one one
three three
two two
nine nine
four four
seven seven
five five
ten ten
eight eight

Page 296

Number Words

Directions: Write the correct number words in the blanks.

| one | two | three | four | five | six | seven | eight | nine | ten |

Add a letter to each of these words to make a number word.

Example:

even — seven
on — one
tree — three

Change a letter to make these words into number words.

Example:

live — five
fix — six
line — nine

Write the number words that sound the same as these.

Example:

ate — eight
to — two
for — four

Write the number word you did not use: ten

Page 297

Number Words: Asking Sentences

Directions: Write an asking sentence about each picture. Begin each sentence with **How many**. Then, answer your question. Begin each sentence with a capital letter, and end it with a period or a question mark.

| one | two | three | four | five | six | seven | eight | nine | ten |

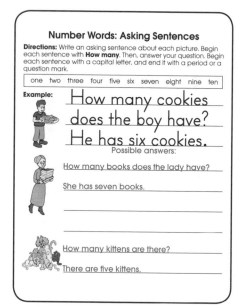

Example: How many cookies does the boy have? He has six cookies.

Possible answers:

How many books does the lady have?

She has seven books.

How many kittens are there?

There are five kittens.

Page 298

Number Words: Sentences

Directions: Change the telling sentences into asking sentences. Change the asking sentences into telling sentences. Begin each one with a capital letter, and end it with a period or a question mark.

Examples:

Is she eating the grapes?

She is eating the grapes.

He is bringing one truck.

Is he bringing one truck?

1. Is he painting two blue birds?

He is painting two blue birds.

2. Did she find four apples?

She found four apples.

3. She will be six on her birthday.

Will she be six on her birthday?

Page 299

Short *A* Words: Rhyming Words

Short a is the sound you hear in the word **math**.

Directions: Use the **short a** words in the box to write rhyming words.

lamp	fat	bat	van
path	can	cat	Dan
math	stamp	fan	sat

1. Write four words that rhyme with **mat**.

fat cat
bat sat

2. Write two words that rhyme with **bath**.

path math

3. Write two words that rhyme with **damp**.

lamp stamp

4. Write four words that rhyme with **pan**.

can fan
van Dan

Page 300

Short *A* Words: Sentences

Directions: Use a word from the box to complete each sentence.

fat	path	lamp	can
van	stamp	Dan	math
sat	cat	fan	bat

Example:

1. The lamp had a pink shade.
2. The bike path led us to the park.
3. I like to add in math class.
4. The cat is very fat.
5. The can of beans was hard to open.
6. The envelope needed a stamp.
7. He swung the bat and hit the ball.
8. The fan blew air around.
9. My mom drives a blue van.
10. I sat in the backseat.

Page 301

Long *A* Words

Long a is a vowel sound that says its own name. **Long a** can be spelled **ai**, as in the word **mail**, **ay**, as in the word **say**, and **a** with a **silent e** at the end of a word, as in the word **same**.

Directions: Say each word, and listen for the **long a** sound. Then, write each word, and underline the letters that make the **long a** vowel sound.

mail	bake	train
game	day	sale
paint	play	name
made	gray	tray

1. m<u>ai</u>l
2. g<u>a</u>m<u>e</u>
3. p<u>ai</u>nt
4. m<u>a</u>d<u>e</u>
5. b<u>a</u>k<u>e</u>
6. d<u>ay</u>
7. pl<u>ay</u>
8. gr<u>ay</u>
9. tr<u>ai</u>n
10. s<u>a</u>l<u>e</u>
11. n<u>a</u>m<u>e</u>
12. tr<u>ay</u>

Page 302

Long *A* Words: Rhyming Words

Long a is the vowel sound you hear in the word **cake**.

Directions: Use the **long a** words in the box to write rhyming words.

paint	gray	train	tray
mail	day	sale	play
game	made	name	bake

1. Write the word that rhymes with **make**.
   bake
2. Write the words that rhyme with **hail**.
   mail   sale
3. Write the words that rhyme with **say**.
   gray   tray
   day   play
4. Write the word that rhymes with **shade**.
   made
5. Write the words that rhyme with **same**.
   game   name

Page 303

Long *A* Words: Sentence Order

Directions: Write the words in order so that each sentence tells a complete idea. Begin each sentence with a capital letter, and end it with a period or a question mark.

1. plate was on the cake a

   The cake was on a plate.

2. like you would to play a game

   Would you like to play a game?

3. gray around the a corner train came

   A gray train came around the corner.

4. was on mail Bob's name the

   Bob's name was on the mail.

5. sail for on day we went a nice a

   On a nice day, we went for a sail.

Page 304

Short *O* Words

Short o is the vowel sound you hear in the word **pot**.

Directions: Say each word, and listen for the **short o** sound. Then, write each word, and underline the letter that makes the **short o** sound.

hot	box	sock	mop
stop	not	fox	cot
Bob	rock	clock	lock

1. h<u>o</u>t
2. st<u>o</u>p
3. B<u>o</u>b
4. b<u>o</u>x
5. n<u>o</u>t
6. r<u>o</u>ck
7. s<u>o</u>ck
8. f<u>o</u>x
9. cl<u>o</u>ck
10. m<u>o</u>p
11. c<u>o</u>t
12. l<u>o</u>ck

Page 305

Short *O* Words: Rhyming Words

Short o is the vowel sound you hear in the word **got**.

Directions: Use the **short o** words in the box to write rhyming words.

hot	rock	lock	cot
stop	sock	fox	mop
box	mob	clock	Bob

1. Write the words that rhyme with **dot**.
   hot   cot
2. Write the words that rhyme with **socks**.
   box   fox
3. Write the words that rhyme with **hop**.
   stop   mop
4. Write the words that rhyme with **dock**.
   rock   lock
   sock   clock
5. Write the words that rhyme with **cob**.
   mob   Bob

Page 306

Long *O* Words

Long o is a vowel sound that says its own name. **Long o** can be spelled **oa**, as in the word **float**, or **o** with a **silent e** at the end, as in **cone**.

Directions: Say each word, and listen for the **long o** sound. Then, write each word, and underline the letters that make the **long o** sound.

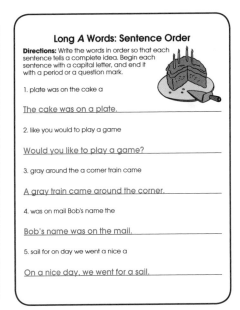

rope	coat	soap	wrote
note	hope	boat	cone
bone	pole	phone	hole

1. r<u>o</u>p<u>e</u>
2. n<u>o</u>t<u>e</u>
3. b<u>o</u>n<u>e</u>
4. c<u>oa</u>t
5. h<u>o</u>p<u>e</u>
6. p<u>o</u>l<u>e</u>
7. s<u>oa</u>p
8. b<u>oa</u>t
9. ph<u>o</u>n<u>e</u>
10. wr<u>o</u>t<u>e</u>
11. c<u>o</u>n<u>e</u>
12. h<u>o</u>l<u>e</u>

Page 307

Comprehensive Curriculum - **Grade 2**

Long O Words: Rhyming Words

Long o is the vowel sound you hear in the word **home**.

Directions: Use the **long o** words in the box to write rhyming words.

rope	soap	coat	wrote
note	boat	hope	cone
bone	phone	pole	hole

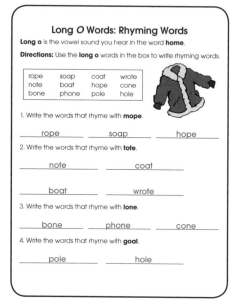

1. Write the words that rhyme with **mope**.

___rope___   ___soap___   ___hope___

2. Write the words that rhyme with **tote**.

___note___   ___coat___

___boat___   ___wrote___

3. Write the words that rhyme with **lone**.

___bone___   ___phone___   ___cone___

4. Write the words that rhyme with **goal**.

___pole___   ___hole___

Page 308

Long O Words: Sentences

Directions: Draw a line from the first part of the sentence to the part that completes the sentence.

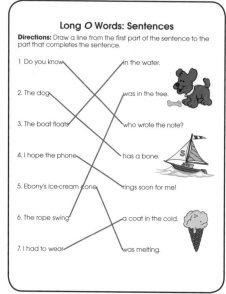

1. Do you know
2. The dog
3. The boat floats
4. I hope the phone
5. Ebony's ice-cream cone
6. The rope swing
7. I had to wear

in the water.
was in the tree.
who wrote the note?
has a bone.
rings soon for me!
a coat in the cold.
was melting.

Page 309

Animal Words

Directions: Write the animal names twice beside each picture.

| fox | rabbit | bear | squirrel | mouse | deer |

Example:

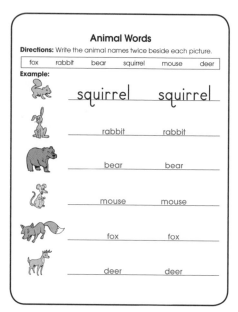

squirrel   squirrel

rabbit   rabbit

bear   bear

mouse   mouse

fox   fox

deer   deer

Page 310

Animal Words

Directions: Circle the word in each sentence that is not spelled correctly. Then, write it correctly.

| squirrel | bears | rabbit | deer | fox | mouse |

Example:
Animals like to live in (threes.)   trees

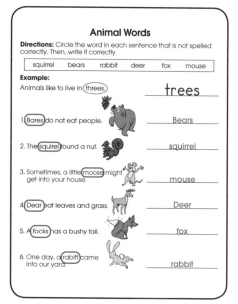

1. (Bares) do not eat people.   Bears

2. The (squirel) found a nut.   squirrel

3. Sometimes, a little (moose) might get into your house.   mouse

4. (Dear) eat leaves and grass.   Deer

5. A (focks) has a bushy tail.   fox

6. One day, a (rabitt) came into our yard.   rabbit

Page 311

Animal Words: More Than One

To show more than one of something, add **s** to most words.

Example: one dog – **two dogs**   one book – **two books**
But some words are different. For words that end with **x**, use **es** to show two.

Example: one fox – **two foxes**   one box – **two boxes**
The spelling of some words changes a lot when there are two.

Example: one mouse – **two mice**
Some words stay the same, even when you mean two of something.

Example: one deer – **two deer**   one fish – **two fish**

Directions: Complete the sentences below with the correct word.

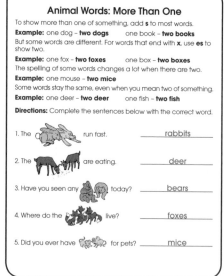

1. The _____ run fast.   rabbits

2. The _____ are eating.   deer

3. Have you seen any _____ today?   bears

4. Where do the _____ live?   foxes

5. Did you ever have _____ for pets?   mice

Page 312

Animal Words: More Than One

Directions: Write the two sentences below as one sentence. Remember the special spelling of **fox**, **mouse**, and **deer** when there are more than one.

Example:
I saw a mouse. You saw a mouse.

We saw two mice.

1. Julie petted a deer.
   Matt petted a deer.

Julie and Matt petted the deer.

2. Avi colored a fox.
   Nora colored a fox.

Avi and Nora colored foxes.

Page 313

Animal Words: Kinds of Sentences

Another name for an asking sentence is a **question**.

Directions: Use the words in the box to write a telling sentence. Then, use the words to write a question.

Example:

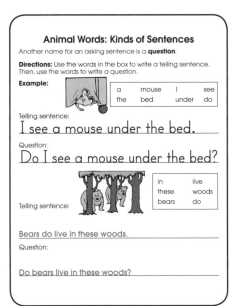

a	mouse	I	see
the	bed	under	do

Telling sentence:

I see a mouse under the bed.

Question:

Do I see a mouse under the bed?

in	live
these	woods
bears	do

Telling sentence:

Bears do live in these woods.

Question:

Do bears live in these woods?

Page 314

Animal Words: Sentences

Directions: Read the sentences on each line, and draw a line between them. Then, write each sentence again on the lines below. Begin each one with a capital letter, and put a period or question mark at the end.

Example:

why do squirrels hide nuts | they eat them in the winter

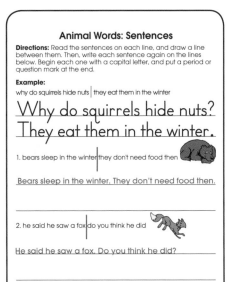

Why do squirrels hide nuts?
They eat them in the winter.

1. bears sleep in the winter | they don't need food then

Bears sleep in the winter. They don't need food then.

2. he said he saw a fox | do you think he did

He said he saw a fox. Do you think he did?

Page 315

Review

Directions: Complete each line of the poem below with a word from the box. Make sure each line rhymes.

deer	fox	house	here	mouse	box

A little gray _____ mouse

Once ran through my _____ house .

Then, a bushy-tailed _____ fox

Ran into a _____ box .

Last came a _____ deer

What was he doing _____ here ?

Now, make your own poem using the words **bear** and **there**.

Poems will vary.

Page 316

Family Words

Directions: This is Andy's **family tree**. It shows all the people in his family. Use the words in the box to finish writing the names in Andy's family tree.

grandmother	mother
grandfather	father
aunt	uncle
brother	sister

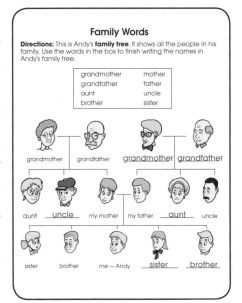

grandmother grandfather grandmother grandfather

aunt uncle my mother my father aunt uncle

sister brother me — Andy sister brother

Page 317

Family Words

Some words tell how a person looks or feels. These are called **describing** words, or **adjectives**.

Directions: Help Andy write about the people in his family. In each box, cross out the word that does not tell about the picture next to it. Finish the sentence using the other two describing words.

Example:

~~asleep~~
funny
tall

My aunt

is tall and funny.

1. My grandmother

is smiling and happy.

~~broken~~
happy
smiling

2. My uncle

is hot and tired.

hot
~~broken~~
tired

3. My little brother

is hungry and thirsty.

thirsty
hungry
~~hard~~

Page 318

Family Words: Joining Words

Joining words often join two sentences to make one long sentence. Three words help do this:

and — if both sentences are much the same.
Example: I took my dog for a walk, **and** I played with my cat.

but — if the second sentence says something different from the first sentence. Sometimes, the second sentence tells why you can't do the first sentence.
Example: I want to play outside, **but** it is raining.

or — if each sentence names a different choice.
Example: You could eat your cookie, **or** you could give it to me.

Directions: Use the word given to join the two short sentences into one longer sentence.

Example: (but)
My aunt lives far away. She calls me often.

My aunt lives far away but she calls me often.

1. **(and)**
My sister had a birthday. She got a new bike.

My sister had a birthday, and she got a new bike.

2. **(or)**
We can play outside. We can play inside.

We can play outside, or we can play inside.

Page 319

Family Words: Joining Words

Directions: Read each pair of sentences. Then, join them with **and**, **but**, or **or**.

1. My uncle likes popcorn.
   He does not like peanuts.

My uncle likes popcorn, but he does not like peanuts.

_____

2. He could read a book.
   He could tell me his own story.

He could read a book, or he could tell me his own

story.

3. My little brother is sleepy.
   He wants to go to bed.

My little brother is sleepy, and he wants to go to bed.

_____

Page 320

Family Words: Completing a Story

Directions: Write family words in the blanks to complete the story.

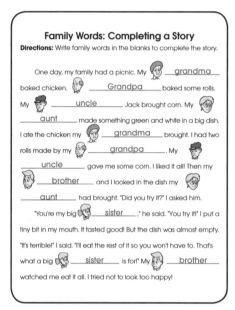

One day, my family had a picnic. My __grandma__

baked chicken. __Grandpa__ baked some rolls.

My __uncle__ Jack brought corn. My

__aunt__ made something green and white in a big dish.

I ate the chicken my __grandma__ brought. I had two

rolls made by my __grandpa__. My

__uncle__ gave me some corn. I liked it all! Then my

__brother__ and I looked in the dish my

__aunt__ had brought. "Did you try it?" I asked him.

"You're my big __sister__," he said. "You try it!" I put a

tiny bit in my mouth. It tasted good! But the dish was almost empty.

"It's terrible!" I said. "I'll eat the rest of it so you won't have to. That's

what a big __sister__ is for!" My __brother__

watched me eat it all. I tried not to look too happy!

Page 321

Short *E* Words

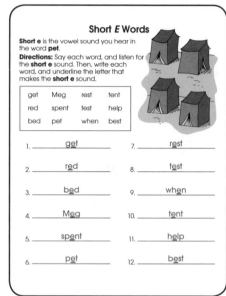

Short e is the vowel sound you hear in the word **pet**.

Directions: Say each word, and listen for the **short e** sound. Then, write each word, and underline the letter that makes the **short e** sound.

get	Meg	rest	tent
red	spent	test	help
bed	pet	when	best

1. __g<u>e</u>t__   7. __r<u>e</u>st__

2. __r<u>e</u>d__   8. __t<u>e</u>st__

3. __b<u>e</u>d__   9. __wh<u>e</u>n__

4. __M<u>e</u>g__   10. __t<u>e</u>nt__

5. __sp<u>e</u>nt__   11. __h<u>e</u>lp__

6. __p<u>e</u>t__   12. __b<u>e</u>st__

Page 322

Short *E* Words: Rhyming Words

Short e is the vowel sound you hear in the word **egg**.

Directions: Use the **short e** words in the box to write rhyming words.

get	test	pet	help
let	head	spent	red
best	tent	rest	bed

1. Write the words that rhyme with **fed**.

__head__   __red__   __bed__

2. Write the words that rhyme with **bent**.

__tent__   __spent__

3. Write the words that rhyme with **west**.

__best__   __test__   __rest__

4. Write the words that rhyme with **bet**.

__get__   __let__   __pet__

Page 323

Short *E* Words: Sentences

Directions: Write the correct **short e** word in each sentence.

get	Meg	rest	bed	spent	best
test	help	head	pet	red	tent

1. Of all my crayons, I like the color __red__

the __best__!

2. I always make my __bed__ when I __get__ up.

3. My new hat keeps my __head__ warm.

4. __Meg__ wanted a dog for a __pet__.

5. When we go camping, my job is to __help__ put up

the __tent__.

6. I have a __test__ in math tomorrow, so I want to get

a good night's __rest__.

Page 324

Long *E* Words

Long e is the vowel sound that says its own name. **Long e** can be spelled **ee**, as in the word **teeth**, **ea**, as in the word **meat**, or **e**, as in the word **me**.

Directions: Say each word, and listen for the **long e** sound. Then, write the words, and underline the letters that make the **long e** sound.

street	neat	treat	feet
sleep	keep	deal	meal
mean	clean	beast	feast

1. __str<u>ee</u>t__   7. __tr<u>ea</u>t__

2. __sl<u>ee</u>p__   8. __d<u>ea</u>l__

3. __m<u>ea</u>n__   9. __b<u>ea</u>st__

4. __n<u>ea</u>t__   10. __f<u>ee</u>t__

5. __k<u>ee</u>p__   11. __m<u>ea</u>l__

6. __cl<u>ea</u>n__   12. __f<u>ea</u>st__

Page 325

Long *E* Words: Rhyming Words

Long e is the vowel sound you hear in the word **meet**.

Directions: Use the **long e** words in the box to write rhyming words.

street	feet	neat	treat
keep	deal	sleep	meal
mean	beast	clean	feast

1. Write the words that rhyme with **beat**.

___street___ ___neat___

___feet___ ___treat___

2. Write the words that rhyme with **deep**.

___keep___ ___sleep___

3. Write the words that rhyme with **feel**.

___deal___ ___meal___

4. Write the words that rhyme with **bean**.

___mean___ ___clean___

5. Write the words that rhyme with **least**.

___beast___ ___feast___

Page 326

Long *E* Words: Sentences

Directions: Write a word from the box to complete each sentence.

street	feet	neat	treat
keep	deal	sleep	meal
mean	beast	clean	feast

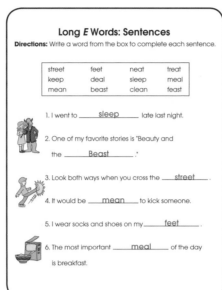

1. I went to ___sleep___ late last night.

2. One of my favorite stories is "Beauty and the ___Beast___."

3. Look both ways when you cross the ___street___.

4. It would be ___mean___ to kick someone.

5. I wear socks and shoes on my ___feet___.

6. The most important ___meal___ of the day is breakfast.

Page 327

Verbs

Verbs are words that tell the action in the sentence.

Directions: Draw a line from each sentence to its picture. Then, finish the sentence with the verb or action word that is under each picture.

Example:

He will ___help___ the baby.

1. I can ___fix___ my book.

2. It is time to ___clean___ up.

3. That chair might ___break___.

4. They ___build___ houses.

5. I ___cut___ this out myself.

6. Is that too heavy to ___carry___?

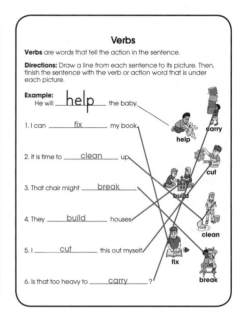

carry
help
cut
build
clean
fix
break

Page 328

Verbs: Sentences

Directions: Read the two sentences in each story below. Then, write one more sentence to tell what happened next. Use the verbs from the box.

break	build	fix	clean	cut	carry

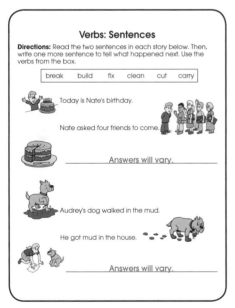

Today is Nate's birthday.

Nate asked four friends to come.

___Answers will vary.___

Audrey's dog walked in the mud.

He got mud in the house.

___Answers will vary.___

Page 329

Verbs: Sentences

Directions: Join each pair of sentences to make one longer sentence. Use one of the **joining** words: **and**, **but**, or **or**. In the second part of the sentence, use **he**, **she**, or **they** in place of the person's name.

Example: I asked Tim to help me. Tim wanted to play.

I asked Tim to help me, but he wanted to play.

1. Kelly dropped a glass. Kelly cut her finger.

Kelly dropped a glass, and she cut her finger.

_____

2. Linda and Allen got a new dog. Linda and Allen named it Baby.

Linda and Allen got a new dog, and they named it Baby.

Page 330

Verbs: Word Endings

Most **verbs** end with **s** when the sentence tells about one thing. The **s** is taken away when the sentence tells about more than one thing.

Example:

One dog walks.   One boy runs.
Two dogs **walk**.   Three boys **run**.

The spelling of some **verbs** changes when the sentence tells about only one thing.

Example:

One girl carries her lunch.   The boy fixes his car.
Two girls **carry** their lunches.   Two boys **fix** their cars.

Directions: Write the missing verbs in the sentences.

Example:

Alma works hard. She and Peter ___work___ all day.

1. The father bird builds a nest.

The mother and father ___build___ it together.

2. The girls clean their room. Jenny ___cleans___ under her bed.

3. The children cut out their pictures. Henry ___cut___ his slowly.

4. These workers fix things. This man ___fixes___ televisions.

5. Two trucks carry horses. One truck ___carries___ pigs.

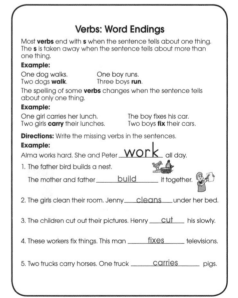

Page 331

Verbs: Completing a Story

Directions: Write a sentence that tells what happens in each picture. Use the **verb** under the picture.

Example:

fall   break   clean

A glass falls off the table.
Answers will vary. Possible answers:

The glass breaks.

The girl cleans up the mess.

fix   cut   carry

Dad fixes the mower.

The girl cuts the grass.

The boy carries the bag.

Page 332

Verbs

Directions: Circle the words in each sentence that are not spelled correctly. Then, write the sentence correctly.

Example:
I need to (klean) the cage my (mouses) live in.

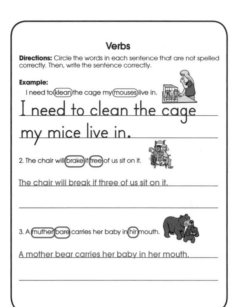

I need to clean the cage my mice live in.

2. The chair will (brake) if (tree) of us sit on it.

The chair will break if three of us sit on it.

3. A (muther) (bare) carries her baby in (hir) mouth.

A mother bear carries her baby in her mouth.

Page 333

Short *I* Words

Short i is the vowel sound you hear in the word **pig**.

Directions: Say each word, and listen for the **short i** sound. Then, write each word, and underline the letter that makes the **short i** sound.

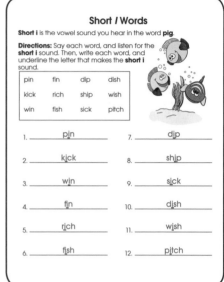

pin	fin	dip	dish
kick	rich	ship	wish
win	fish	sick	pitch

1. p<u>i</u>n   7. d<u>i</u>p

2. k<u>i</u>ck   8. sh<u>i</u>p

3. w<u>i</u>n   9. s<u>i</u>ck

4. f<u>i</u>n   10. d<u>i</u>sh

5. r<u>i</u>ch   11. w<u>i</u>sh

6. f<u>i</u>sh   12. p<u>i</u>tch

Page 334

Short *I* Words: Rhyming Words

Short i is the sound you hear in the word **pin**.

Directions: Use the **short i** words in the box to write rhyming words.

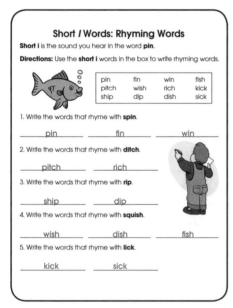

pin	fin	win	fish
pitch	wish	rich	kick
ship	dip	dish	sick

1. Write the words that rhyme with **spin**.

pin   fin   win

2. Write the words that rhyme with **ditch**.

pitch   rich

3. Write the words that rhyme with **rip**.

ship   dip

4. Write the words that rhyme with **squish**.

wish   dish   fish

5. Write the words that rhyme with **lick**.

kick   sick

Page 335

Short *I* Words: Sentences

Directions: Complete the sentences by matching the words to the correct sentence.

1. I made a _____ on a star.   fin

2. All we could see was the shark's _____ above the water.   fish

3. I like to eat vegetables with _____   kick

4. We saw lots of _____ in the water.   win

5. The soccer player will _____ the ball and score a goal.   dish

6. If you feel _____, see a doctor.   dip

7. Did Kenji _____ the race?   wish

8. The _____ was full of candy.   sick

Page 336

Long *I* Words

Long i is the vowel sound that says its own name. **Long i** can be spelled **igh**, as in **sight**, **i** with a **silent e** at the end, as in **mine**, and **y** at the end, as in **fly**.

Directions: Say each word, and listen for the **long i** sound. Then, write each word, and underline the letters that make the **long i** sound.

bike	fry	ride	line
glide	ripe	nine	pipe
fight	high	light	sigh

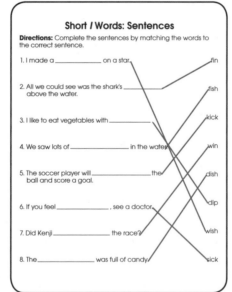

1. b<u>i</u>k<u>e</u>   7. r<u>i</u>d<u>e</u>

2. gl<u>i</u>d<u>e</u>   8. n<u>i</u>n<u>e</u>

3. f<u>igh</u>t   9. l<u>igh</u>t

4. fr<u>y</u>   10. l<u>i</u>n<u>e</u>

5. r<u>i</u>p<u>e</u>   11. p<u>i</u>p<u>e</u>

6. h<u>igh</u>   12. s<u>igh</u>

Page 337

Long *I* Words: Rhyming Words

Long **i** is the sound you hear in the word **fight**.

Directions: Use the **long i** words in the box to write rhyming words.

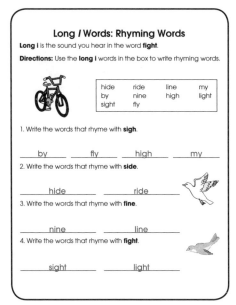

hide	ride	line	my
by	nine	high	light
sight	fly		

1. Write the words that rhyme with **sigh**.

by   fly   high   my

2. Write the words that rhyme with **side**.

hide   ride

3. Write the words that rhyme with **fine**.

nine   line

4. Write the words that rhyme with **fight**.

sight   light

Page 338

Review

Directions: Write **igh** in each blank below. Then, read the words.

Example:

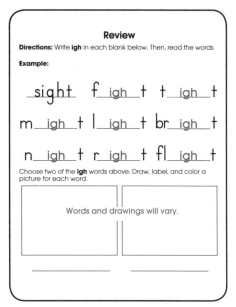

sight   f_igh_t   t_igh_t

m_igh_t   l_igh_t   br_igh_t

n_igh_t   r_igh_t   fl_igh_t

Choose two of the **igh** words above. Draw, label, and color a picture for each word.

Words and drawings will vary.	

Page 339

Location Words

Directions: Use one of the location words from the box to complete each sentence.

between	around	inside	outside	beside	across

Example:
She will hide **under** the basket.

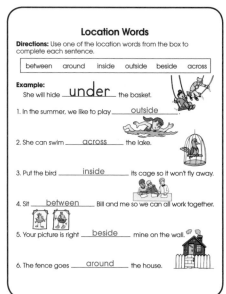

1. In the summer, we like to play _outside_

2. She can swim _across_ the lake.

3. Put the bird _inside_ its cage so it won't fly away.

4. Sit _between_ Bill and me so we can all work together.

5. Your picture is right _beside_ mine on the wall.

6. The fence goes _around_ the house.

Page 340

Location Words

Directions: Draw a line from each sentence to its picture. Then, complete each sentence with the word under the picture.

Example:
He is walking **behind** the tree.

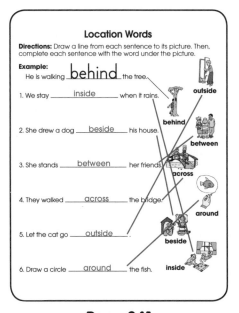

1. We stay _inside_ when it rains.

2. She drew a dog _beside_ his house.

3. She stands _between_ her friends.

4. They walked _across_ the bridge.

5. Let the cat go _outside_ .

6. Draw a circle _around_ the fish.

outside

behind

between

across

around

beside

inside

Page 341

Location Words

Directions: Write the location words that answer the questions.

between	around	inside	outside	beside	across

1. Write all the smaller words you find in the location words.

be, bet, we, a, round, in, side, out, cross

2. Which two words begin with the same sound as 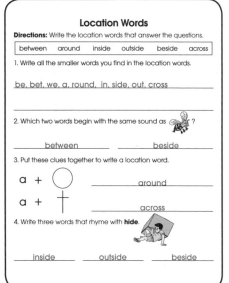 ?

between   beside

3. Put these clues together to write a location word.

a + ◯   _around_

a + ✝   _across_

4. Write three words that rhyme with **hide**.

inside   outside   beside

Page 342

Location Words: Sentences

Directions: Use a location word from the first box and other words from the second box to complete each sentence.

between	around	inside	outside	beside	across
the yard	the house	the table	the school	the box
the hill	the picture	the field	the puddle	the park

Example: Answers will vary. Possible answers:
Our garden grows **outside in the yard.**

1. We like to play _inside the house._

2. The street goes _beside the school._

3. Can you run _across the field?_

4. Let's ride bikes _around the park._

Page 343

Location Words: Sentences

Directions: Join each pair of sentences to make a longer sentence. Use one of the **joining** words **and**, **but**, or **or**.

Example: We play outside when it is sunny.
Today it is raining.

We play outside when it is sunny, but today it is raining.

1. We could walk between the buildings. We could walk around them.

We could walk between the buildings, or we could walk around them.

2. I drew a tree beside the house. I drew flowers beside the house.

I drew a tree beside the house, and I drew flowers beside the house.

Page 344

Location Words: Sentences

Directions: Use a location word to tell where the cat is in each sentence.

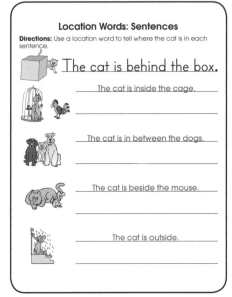

The cat is behind the box.

The cat is inside the cage.

The cat is in between the dogs.

The cat is beside the mouse.

The cat is outside.

Page 345

Short U Words

Short u is the sound you hear in the word **bug**.

Directions: Say each word, and listen for the **short u** sound. Then, write each word, and underline the letter that makes the **short u** sound.

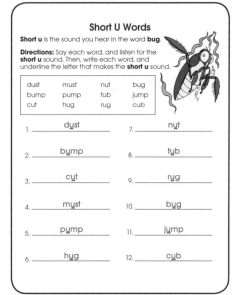

dust	must	nut	bug
bump	pump	tub	jump
cut	hug	rug	cub

1. d<u>u</u>st
2. b<u>u</u>mp
3. c<u>u</u>t
4. m<u>u</u>st
5. p<u>u</u>mp
6. h<u>u</u>g
7. n<u>u</u>t
8. t<u>u</u>b
9. r<u>u</u>g
10. b<u>u</u>g
11. j<u>u</u>mp
12. c<u>u</u>b

Page 346

Short *U* Words: Sentences

Directions: Circle the words in each sentence that are not correct. Then, write the correct **short u** words from the box on the lines.

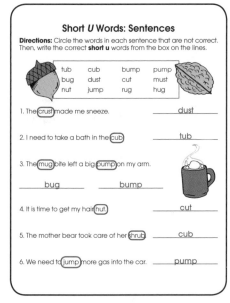

tub	cub	bump	pump
bug	dust	cut	must
nut	jump	rug	hug

1. The ⟨crust⟩ made me sneeze. — dust

2. I need to take a bath in the ⟨cub⟩. — tub

3. The ⟨mug⟩ bite left a big ⟨pump⟩ on my arm.
bug   bump

4. It is time to get my hair ⟨hut⟩. — cut

5. The mother bear took care of her ⟨shrub⟩. — cub

6. We need to ⟨jump⟩ more gas into the car. — pump

Page 347

Long *U* Words

Long u is a vowel sound that says its own name. **Long u** is spelled **u** with a silent **e** at the end, as in **cute**. The letters **oo** make a sound very much like **long u**. They make the sound you hear in the word **zoo**. The letters **ew** also make the **oo** sound, as in the word **grew**.

Directions: Say the words, and listen for the **u** and **oo** sounds. Then, write each word, and underline the letters that make the **long u** and **oo** sounds.

choose	blew	moon	fuse
cube	Ruth	tooth	use
flew	loose	goose	noon

1. ch<u>oo</u>se
2. c<u>u</u>be
3. fl<u>ew</u>
4. bl<u>ew</u>
5. R<u>u</u>th
6. l<u>oo</u>se
7. m<u>oo</u>n
8. t<u>oo</u>th
9. g<u>oo</u>se
10. f<u>u</u>se
11. <u>u</u>se
12. n<u>oo</u>n

Page 348

Long *U* Words: Rhyming Words

Long u is the vowel sound you hear in the word **cube**. Another vowel sound that is very much like the **long u** sound is the **oo** sound you hear in the word **boot**.

Directions: Use the **long u** and **oo** words in the box to write rhyming words.

moon	tooth	use	blew
flew	loose	Ruth	choose
fuse	noon	goose	

1. Write the words that rhyme with **soon**.
moon   noon

2. Write the words that rhyme with **lose**.
fuse   use   choose

3. Write the words that rhyme with **grew**.
flew   blew

4. Write the words that rhyme with **moose**.
loose   goose

5. Write the words that rhyme with **booth**.
tooth   Ruth

Page 349

Long *U* Words: Sentences

Directions: Write the words in the sentences below in the correct order. Begin each sentence with a capital letter, and end it with a period or a question mark.

1. the pulled dentist tooth my loose

    The dentist pulled my loose tooth.

2. ice cubes I choose in my drink to put

    I choose to put ice cubes in my drink.

3. a Ruth fuse blew yesterday

    Ruth blew a fuse yesterday.

4. loose the got in garden goose the

    The goose got loose in the garden.

5. flew the goose winter for the south

    The goose flew south for the winter.

6. is full there a moon tonight

    Is there a full moon tonight?

Page 350

Opposite Words

Directions: Opposites are words that are different in every way. Use the opposite words from the box to complete these sentences.

| hard | hot | bottom | quickly | happy |
| sad | slowly | cold | soft | top |

Example:

My new coat is blue on top and red on the $bottom$.

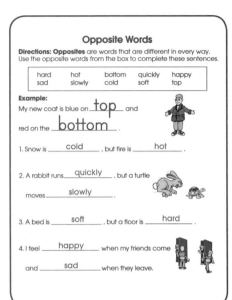

1. Snow is __cold__ , but fire is __hot__ .

2. A rabbit runs __quickly__ , but a turtle moves __slowly__ .

3. A bed is __soft__ , but a floor is __hard__ .

4. I feel __happy__ when my friends come and __sad__ when they leave.

Page 357

Opposite Words

Directions: Draw a line from each sentence to its picture. Then, complete each sentence with the word under the picture.

Example:

She bought a __new__ bat.

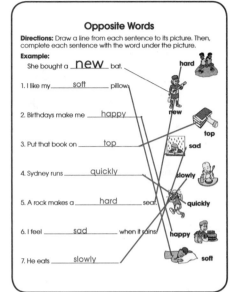

1. I like my __soft__ pillow.

2. Birthdays make me __happy__

3. Put that book on __top__

4. Sydney runs __quickly__

5. A rock makes a __hard__ seat.

6. I feel __sad__ when it rains!

7. He eats __slowly__

Page 358

Opposite Words: Sentences

Directions: Cross out the word in each box that does not tell about the picture. Write a sentence about the picture using the other two words.

Example:

| ~~teeth~~ | garden | digs |

She digs in her garden.

| swims | quickly | ~~sad~~ |

Sentences will vary.

| soft | ~~hard~~ | happy |

| ~~popcorn~~ | bottom | sad |

Page 359

Opposite Words: Sentences

Directions: Look at each picture. Then, write a sentence that uses the word under the picture and tells how something is the same as the picture.

Example:

cold — My hands are as cold as ice.

Answers will vary.

hard

slow

soft

happy

Page 360

Opposite Words: Completing a Story

Directions: Write opposite words in the blanks to complete the story.

| hot | smiled | long | cold |
| huge | quickly | happy | sad |

On Saturday, Dad and I went to the dog park. It was a cold day, but I actually felt __hot__ by the time we walked all the way there. The park was filled with all kinds of dogs! There were tiny dogs with short fur and __huge__ dogs with __long__ fur. They were running and jumping all around. I have never seen a group of dogs look so __happy__ ! I knew I would feel __sad__ when it was time to leave.

A small mutt came up to me and licked my hands. At first, I frowned because his nose was __cold__ and clammy. He was so friendly, though, that I did not really mind. I threw a ball for him, and he __quickly__ ran to fetch it.

I slowly looked at all the joyful dogs around us. "Dad," I said, "I think we're ready to get a dog of our own." Dad __smiled__ . "That's just what I was thinking," he agreed.

Page 361

511

Comprehensive Curriculum - Grade 2

ANSWER KEY

Review

Directions: Tell a story about the picture by following the directions. Write one or two sentences for each answer.

Answers will vary.

1. Write about something that is happening **quickly** or **slowly** in the picture.

2. Use **top** or **bottom** in a sentence about the picture.

3. Tell about something **hard** and something **soft** in the picture. Use the word **but** in your sentence.

Page 362

Learning Words

Directions: Write a learning word to complete each sentence. Use each word only once.

| start | watch | listen | teach | finish | write |

1. You see with your eyes, but you __listen__ with your ears.

2. After you think of an idea, __write__ it on your paper.

3. She will __teach__ you how to write your name.

4. To see what to do, you have to __watch__ the teacher.

5. Show me your picture after you __finish__ drawing it.

6. When you have everything you need, you can __start__ working.

Page 363

Learning Words

Directions: Circle the words in each sentence that are not spelled correctly. Then, write each word correctly on the line.

| start | watch | listen | teach | finish | write |

1. Do you like to (wach) television? __watch__
2. (Right) your name at the bottom. __Write__
3. I will (teech) you to ride a bike. __teach__
4. You have to (lisen) to me. __listen__
5. Did you (finnish) reading your book? __finish__
6. Everyone will (strat) running at the same time. __start__

Change one letter in each word below to make one of the learning words. Write the new word on the line.

reach — __teach__   white — __write__   match — __watch__

Page 364

Learning Words: Verb Endings

Remember: Verbs end with **s** when the sentence tells about only one thing.

Example: One girl **reads**.   Two girls **read**.
But when an action word ends with **ch** or **sh**, add **es**.

Example: We **watch** the baby.   She **watches** the baby.
Jane and Omar **finish** their work. Peter **finishes** his work.

| start | watch | listen | teach | finish | write |

Directions: Write the verb from the box that completes each sentence. Add **s** or **es** to the end of the verb if needed.

Example: Carrie reads the book. She and Chris __read__ it together.

1. Todd listens to the teacher. We all __listen__ to her.
2. Joy finishes the race first. We __finish__ after her.
3. They write letters to our class. Tony __writes__ back to them.
4. We watch the puppet show. She __watches__ with us.
5. He starts at the top of the page. We __start__ in the middle.

Page 365

Learning Words: Completing a Story

Directions: Write learning words to complete this story.

"How can I __teach__ you anything if you don't __listen__?" James asked his little sister, Wendy. He was trying to show her how to __write__ her name. Wendy smiled up at James. "I'll __listen__ now," she said. "Okay. Let's __start__ again. __Watch__ what I do," he said. "First, you make a big **W**." "Up and down," Wendy said. She tried to __write__ a **W** like James, but it looked like a row of upside-down mountains. "That's better," James said. "But you have to know when to stop." He showed her how to __write__ the **e, n,** and **d**. "Now, I'll __teach__ you how to __finish__ your name," he said. He wrote a **y** for her. Wendy made the tail on her **y** go down to the bottom of the page. "I can do it!" she said. "I can __write__ my name from __start__ to __finish__!" She smiled at her brother again. "Would you __teach__ me how to read now, James?" He smiled back at her. "Maybe later, okay?"

Page 366

Time Words

The time between breakfast and lunch is **morning**.
The time between lunch and dinner is **afternoon**.
The time between dinner and bedtime is **evening**.

Directions: Write a time word from the box to complete each sentence. Use each word only once.

| evening | morning | today | tomorrow | afternoon |

1. What did you eat for breakfast this __morning__?
2. We came home from school in the __afternoon__.
3. I help wash the dinner dishes in the __evening__.
4. I feel a little tired __today__.
5. If I rest tonight, I will feel better __tomorrow__.

Page 367

Time Words: Sentences

Directions: Make each pair of short sentences into one long sentence. Use the joining words **and**, **or**, **but**, or **because**.

Example:

This morning, I am sleepy. I stayed up late last night.

This morning I am sleepy because I stayed up late last night.

1. Do you want to go in the morning?
   Do you want to go in the afternoon?

Do you want to go in the morning or in the afternoon?

2. Mom asked me to clean my room today. I forgot.

Mom asked me to clean my room today, but I forgot.

Page 368

Time Words: Sentences

Directions: Write a sentence for these time words. Tell something you do at that time.

Example:

day

Every day, I walk to school.

morning

Answers will vary.

afternoon

evening

Page 369

Review

Directions: Write the story below again, and correct all the mistakes. Watch for words that are not spelled correctly, missing periods and question marks, question marks at the end of telling sentences, and sentences with the wrong joining words.

One mourning, my granmother said I could have a pet mouse. That evenning, we got my mouse at the pet store, or the next afernoon my mouse had babies! Now, I had nyne mouses! I really liked to wach them? I wanted to pick the babies up, and they were too little. When they get bigger, I have to give too mouses to my sisster.

One morning, my grandmother said I could have a pet mouse. That evening, we got my mouse at the pet store, and the next afternoon my mouse had babies! Now, I had nine mice! I really liked to watch them. I wanted to pick the babies up, but they were too little. When they get bigger, I have to give two mice to my sister.

Page 370

Less Than, Greater Than

Directions: The open mouth points to the larger number. The small point goes to the smaller number. Draw the symbol < or > to the correct number.

Example: 5 (>) 3

This means that 5 is greater than 3, and 3 is less than 5.

12 (>) 2   16 (>) 6

16 (>) 15   1 (<) 2

7 (>) 1   19 (>) 5

9 (>) 6   11 (<) 13

Page 372

Counting

Directions: Write the numbers that are:

next in order	one less	one greater
22, 23, _24_, _25_	_15_, 16	6, _7_
674, _675_, _676_	_246_, 247	125, _126_
227, _228_, _229_	_549_, 550	499, _500_
199, _200_, _201_	_332_, 333	750, _751_
329, _330_, _331_	_861_, 862	933, _934_

Directions: Write the missing numbers.

13 14 15 16 17 18

163 164 165 166 167 168

821 822 823 824 825 826

Page 373

Counting by Twos

Directions: Each basket the players make is worth 2 points. Help your team win by counting by twos to beat the other team's score.

2
4
6
8
10
12
14
16
18
20
22
24
26
28
30
32
34

Final Score
Home	Visitor
34	**30**

Winner!
34

Page 374

Comprehensive Curriculum - **Grade 2**

Counting: Twos, Fives, Tens
Directions: Write the missing numbers.

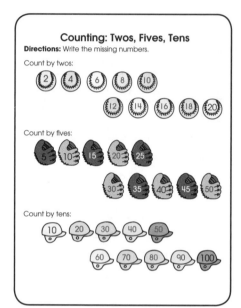

Count by twos:
2, 4, 6, 8, 10, 12, 14, 16, 18, 20

Count by fives:
5, 10, 15, 20, 25, 30, 35, 40, 45, 50

Count by tens:
10, 20, 30, 40, 50, 60, 70, 80, 90, 100

Page 375

Patterns
Directions: Write or draw what comes next in the pattern.

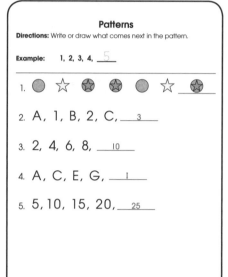

Example: 1, 2, 3, 4, _5_

1. ● ☆ ★ ★ ● ☆ _★_
2. A, 1, B, 2, C, _3_
3. 2, 4, 6, 8, _10_
4. A, C, E, G, _I_
5. 5, 10, 15, 20, _25_

Page 376

Finding Patterns: Numbers
Mia likes to count by twos, threes, fours, fives, tens, and hundreds.

Directions: Complete the number patterns.

1. 5, _10_, _15_, 20, _25_, _30_, 35, _40_, _45_, 50
2. 100, _200_, _300_, 400, _500_, _600_, _700_, 800, _900_
3. _2_, 4, 6, _8_, _10_, 12, _14_, 16, _18_, _20_
4. 10, _20_, _30_, 40, _50_, _60_, 70, _80_, 90
5. 4, _8_, 12, _16_, _20_, 24, _28_, 32, _36_, 40
6. _3_, 6, 9, _12_, _15_, 18, _21_, 24, _27_, 30

Directions: Make up two of your own number patterns.
Answers will vary.

_____ _____ _____ _____ _____ _____

_____ _____ _____ _____ _____ _____

Page 377

Finding Patterns: Shapes
Directions: Complete each row by drawing the correct shape.

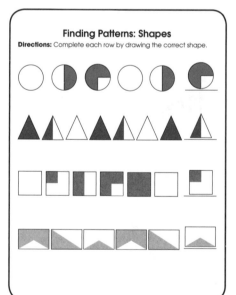

Page 378

Ordinal Numbers
Ordinal numbers indicate order in a series, such as **first**, **second**, or **third**.

Directions: Follow the instructions to color the train cars. The first car is the engine.

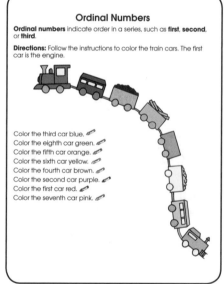

Color the third car blue.
Color the eighth car green.
Color the fifth car orange.
Color the sixth car yellow.
Color the fourth car brown.
Color the second car purple.
Color the first car red.
Color the seventh car pink.

Page 379

Ordinal Numbers
Directions: Follow the instructions.

Draw glasses on the second child.
Put a hat on the fourth child.
Color blonde hair on the third child.
Draw a tie on the first child.
Draw ears on the fifth child.
Draw black hair on the seventh child.
Put a bow on the head of the sixth child.

Page 380

Addition

Addition is "putting together" or adding two or more numbers to find the sum.

Directions: Add.

Example:

$$\begin{array}{r} 2 \\ +5 \\ \hline 7 \end{array}$$

3 +4 7	6 +2 8	7 +1 8	8 +2 10	5 +4 9	3 +1 4
8 +2 10	9 +5 14	10 +3 13	6 +6 12	4 +9 13	7 +7 14
9 +3 12	8 +7 15	6 +5 11	7 +9 16	7 +6 13	9 +9 18

Page 381

Addition: Commutative Property

The **commutative property** of addition states that even if the order of the numbers is changed in an addition sentence, the sum will stay the same.

Example: 2 + 3 = 5
3 + 2 = 5

Directions: Look at the addition sentences below. Complete the addition sentences by writing the missing numerals.

5 + 4 = 9   3 + 1 = 4   2 + 6 = 8
4 + 5 = 9   1 + 3 = 4   6 + 2 = 8

6 + 1 = 7   4 + 3 = 7   1 + 9 = 10
1 + 6 = 7   3 + 4 = 7   9 + 1 = 10

Now, try these:

6 + 3 = 9   10 + 2 = 12   8 + 3 = 11
3 + 6 = 9   2 + 10 = 12   3 + 8 = 11

Answers will vary below. Possible answers:
Look at these sums. Can you think of two number sentences that would show the commutative property of addition?

3 + 4 = 7   5 + 6 = 11   8 + 1 = 9
4 + 3 = 7   6 + 5 = 11   1 + 8 = 9

Page 382

Adding 3 or More Numbers

Directions: Add all the numbers to find the sum. Draw pictures to break up the problem into two smaller problems.

Example:

$$\begin{array}{r} 1 \\ 2 \\ +3 \\ \hline 6 \end{array} \qquad \begin{array}{r} 2 \\ 5 \\ +2 \\ +4 \\ \hline 13 \end{array}$$

3 6 +2 11	8 5 +4 17	3 1 +5 9	8 2 +9 19
2 8 4 +3 17	3 6 5 +2 16	4 1 2 +5 12	6 7 3 +1 17

Page 383

Subtraction

Subtraction is "taking away" or subtracting one number from another to find the difference.

Directions: Subtract.

Example:

$$\begin{array}{r} 4 \\ -3 \\ \hline 1 \end{array}$$

5 -3 2	6 -1 5	4 -3 1	3 -1 2	2 -0 2	1 -1 0
9 -2 7	7 -4 3	10 -5 5	14 -6 8	15 -9 6	12 -3 9
18 -8 10	13 -5 8	14 -7 7	11 -4 7	17 -9 8	16 -8 8

Page 384

Addition and Subtraction

Addition is "putting together" or adding two or more numbers to find the sum. Subtraction is "taking away" or subtracting one number from another to find the difference.

Directions: Add or subtract. Circle the answers that are less than 10.

Examples:

$$\begin{array}{r} 3 \\ +1 \\ \hline 4 \end{array} \qquad \begin{array}{r} 3 \\ -1 \\ \hline 2 \end{array}$$

9 +3 12	6 -2 (4)	12 -1 11	18 +1 19	15 -6 (9)
7 +6 13	16 -9 (7)	10 -3 (7)	14 +5 19	16 -8 (8)
8 +7 15	12 +2 14	13 -4 (9)	17 +2 19	9 +9 18

Page 385

Place Value: Ones, Tens

The **place value** of a digit or numeral is shown by where it is in the number. For example, in the number **23**, **2** has the place value of **tens**, and **3** is **ones**.

Directions: Add the tens and ones, and write your answers in the blanks.

Example:

3 tens   +   3 ones = 33

tens ones		tens ones	
7 tens + 5 ones =	75	4 tens + 0 ones =	40
2 tens + 3 ones =	23	8 tens + 1 one =	81
5 tens + 2 ones =	52	1 ten + 1 one =	11
5 tens + 4 ones =	54	6 tens + 3 ones =	63
9 tens + 5 ones =	95		

Directions: Draw a line to the correct number.

6 tens + 7 ones —— 73
4 tens + 2 ones —— 67
8 tens + 0 ones —— 51
7 tens + 3 ones —— 80
5 tens + 1 one —— 42

Page 386

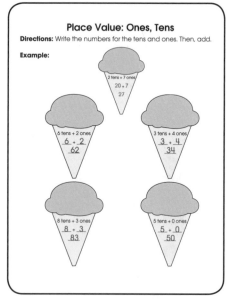

Page 387

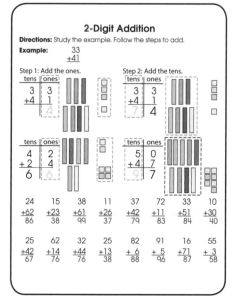

Page 388

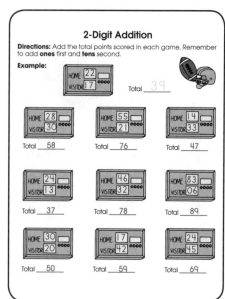

Page 389

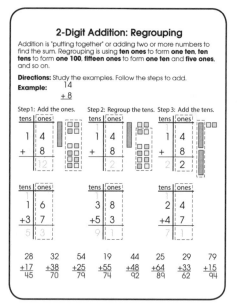

Page 390

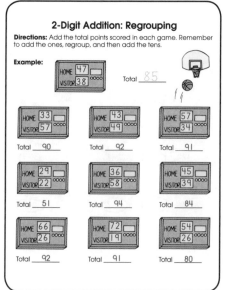

Page 391

2-Digit Subtraction

Directions: Study the example. Follow the steps to subtract.

Page 392

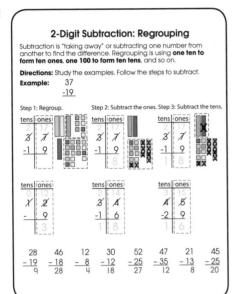

2-Digit Subtraction: Regrouping

Subtraction is "taking away" or subtracting one number from another to find the difference. Regrouping is using **one ten to form ten ones, one 100 to form ten tens**, and so on.

Directions: Study the examples. Follow the steps to subtract.

Example:
```
 37
-19
```

Step 1: Regroup. Step 2: Subtract the ones. Step 3: Subtract the tens.

	28	46	12	30	52	47	21	45
−	19	18	8	12	25	35	13	25
	9	28	4	18	27	12	8	20

Page 393

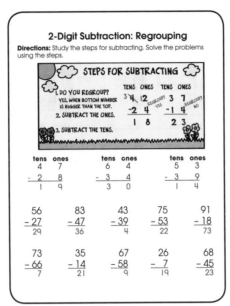

2-Digit Subtraction: Regrouping

Directions: Study the steps for subtracting. Solve the problems using the steps.

tens ones	tens ones	tens ones
4 7	6 4	5 3
− 2 8	− 3 4	− 3 9
1 9	3 0	1 4

	56	83	43	75	91
−	27	47	39	53	18
	29	36	4	22	73

	73	35	67	26	68
−	66	14	58	7	45
	7	21	9	19	23

Page 394

Review

Directions: Add or subtract. Use regrouping when needed. Always do ones first and tens last.

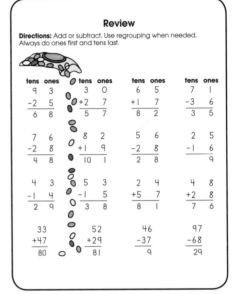

tens ones	tens ones	tens ones	tens ones
9 3	3 0	6 5	7 1
− 2 5	+ 2 7	+ 1 7	− 3 6
6 8	5 7	8 2	3 5

7 6	8 2	5 6	2 5
− 2 8	+ 1 9	− 2 8	− 1 6
4 8	10 1	2 8	9

4 3	5 3	2 4	4 8
− 1 4	− 1 5	+ 5 7	+ 2 8
2 9	3 8	8 1	7 6

33	52	46	97
+47	+29	−37	−68
80	81	9	29

Page 395

2-Digit Addition and Subtraction

Addition is "putting together" or adding two or more numbers to find the sum. Subtraction is "taking away" or subtracting one number from another to find the difference. Regrouping is using **one ten** to form **ten ones, one 100** to form **ten tens**, and so on.

Directions: Add or subtract using regrouping.

Example:
```
tens ones
 2  15
 3   5
-2   7
     8
```

	56	40	35	42	53	97	44	93
	−27	−16	+27	−14	+38	−48	+27	−39
	29	24	62	28	91	49	71	54

	56	44	68	73	33	49	77	27
	−17	+28	−49	−24	+18	+32	−68	+19
	39	72	19	49	51	81	9	46

Page 396

2-Digit Addition and Subtraction

Directions: Add or subtract using regrouping.

23	84	69	41
+48	−56	+29	−17
71	28	98	24

52	73	84	57
−28	+18	−27	−39
24	91	57	18

33	64	37	36
−15	+17	+58	−19
18	81	95	17

65	48	33	25
−28	−30	+18	+35
37	18	51	60

Page 397

Place Value: Hundreds

The place value of a digit or numeral is shown by where it is in the number. For example, in the number **123**, **1** has the place value of **hundreds**, **2** is **tens**, and **3** is **ones**.

Directions: Study the examples. Then, write the missing numbers in the blanks.

Examples:

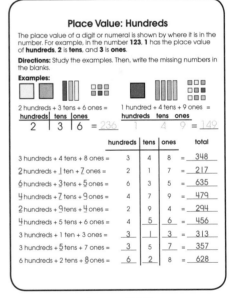

2 hundreds + 3 tens + 6 ones =

hundreds	tens	ones
2	3	6

= 236

1 hundred + 4 tens + 9 ones =

hundreds	tens	ones
1	4	9

= 149

	hundreds	tens	ones	total
3 hundreds + 4 tens + 8 ones =	3	4	8	= 348
2 hundreds + 1 ten + 7 ones =	2	1	7	= 217
6 hundreds + 3 tens + 5 ones =	6	3	5	= 635
4 hundreds + 7 tens + 9 ones =	4	7	9	= 479
2 hundreds + 9 tens + 4 ones =	2	9	4	= 294
4 hundreds + 5 tens + 6 ones =	4	5	6	= 456
3 hundreds + 1 ten + 3 ones =	3	1	3	= 313
3 hundreds + 5 tens + 7 ones =	3	5	7	= 357
6 hundreds + 2 tens + 8 ones =	6	2	8	= 628

Page 398

Comprehensive Curriculum - **Grade 2**

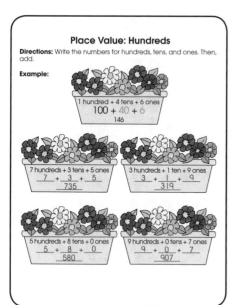

Place Value: Hundreds

Directions: Write the numbers for hundreds, tens, and ones. Then, add.

Example:

1 hundred + 4 tens + 6 ones
100 + 40 + 6
146

7 hundreds + 3 tens + 5 ones
_7_ + _3_ + _5_
_735_

3 hundreds + 1 ten + 9 ones
_3_ + _1_ + _9_
_319_

5 hundreds + 8 tens + 0 ones
_5_ + _8_ + _0_
_580_

9 hundreds + 0 tens + 7 ones
_9_ + _0_ + _7_
_907_

Page 399

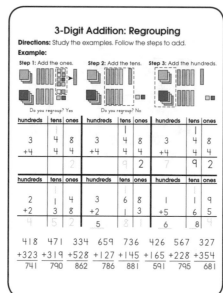

3-Digit Addition: Regrouping

Directions: Study the examples. Follow the steps to add.

Example:

Step 1: Add the ones. **Step 2:** Add the tens. **Step 3:** Add the hundreds.

Do you regroup? Yes   Do you regroup? No

hundreds	tens	ones		hundreds	tens	ones		hundreds	tens	ones
		1				1				1
3	4	8		3	4	8		3	4	8
+4	4	4		+4	4	4		+4	4	4
		2			9	2		7	9	2

hundreds	tens	ones		hundreds	tens	ones		hundreds	tens	ones
	1								1	
2	1	4		3	6	8		1	1	9
+2	3	8		+2	1	3		+5	6	5
4	5	2		5	8	1		6	8	4

418	471	334	659	736	426	567	327
+323	+319	+528	+127	+145	+165	+228	+354
741	790	862	786	881	591	795	681

Page 400

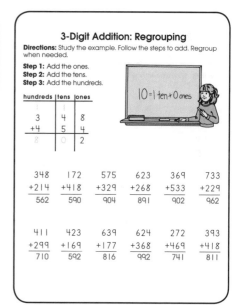

3-Digit Addition: Regrouping

Directions: Study the example. Follow the steps to add. Regroup when needed.

Step 1: Add the ones.
Step 2: Add the tens.
Step 3: Add the hundreds.

10 = 1 ten + 0 ones

hundreds	tens	ones
	1	
3	4	8
+4	5	4
8	0	2

348	172	575	623	369	733
+214	+418	+329	+268	+533	+229
562	590	904	891	902	962

411	423	639	624	272	393
+299	+169	+177	+368	+469	+418
710	592	816	992	741	811

Page 401

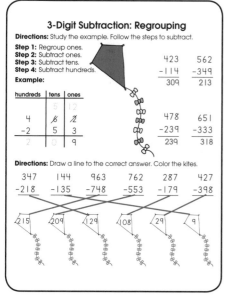

3-Digit Subtraction: Regrouping

Directions: Study the example. Follow the steps to subtract.

Step 1: Regroup ones.
Step 2: Subtract ones.
Step 3: Subtract tens.
Step 4: Subtract hundreds.

423	562
−114	−349
309	213

Example:

hundreds	tens	ones
	5	12
4	6	2
−2	5	3
2	0	9

478	651
−239	−333
239	318

Directions: Draw a line to the correct answer. Color the kites.

347	144	963	762	287	427
−218	−135	−748	−553	−179	−398

215   209   129   108   29   9

Page 402

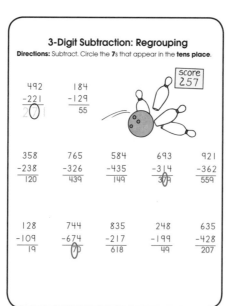

3-Digit Subtraction: Regrouping

Directions: Subtract. Circle the **7**s that appear in the **tens place**.

score 257

492	184
−221	−129
2̶7̶1	55

358	765	584	693	921
−238	−326	−435	−314	−362
120	439	149	3̶7̶9	559

128	744	835	248	635
−109	−674	−217	−199	−428
19	7̶0	618	49	207

Page 403

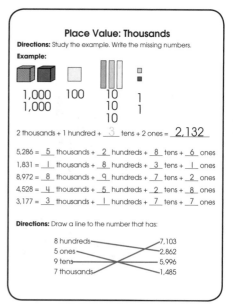

Place Value: Thousands

Directions: Study the example. Write the missing numbers.

Example:

1,000   100   10   1
1,000   10   1
              10

2 thousands + 1 hundred + _3_ tens + 2 ones = _2,132_

5,286 = _5_ thousands + _2_ hundreds + _8_ tens + _6_ ones
1,831 = _1_ thousands + _8_ hundreds + _3_ tens + _1_ ones
8,972 = _8_ thousands + _9_ hundreds + _7_ tens + _2_ ones
4,528 = _4_ thousands + _5_ hundreds + _2_ tens + _8_ ones
3,177 = _3_ thousands + _1_ hundreds + _7_ tens + _7_ ones

Directions: Draw a line to the number that has:

8 hundreds ———— 7,103
5 ones ———— 2,862
9 tens ———— 5,996
7 thousands ———— 1,485

Page 404

Place Value: Thousands

6,431

thousands | hundreds | tens | ones

Directions: Tell which number is in each place.

☆ Thousands place:

2,456 — 2
4,621 — 4
3,456 — 3

☆ Tens place:

4,286 — 8
1,234 — 3
5,678 — 7

☆ Hundreds place:

6,321 — 3
3,210 — 2
7,871 — 8

☆ Ones place:

5,432 — 2
6,531 — 1
9,980 — 0

Page 405

Place Value: Thousands

Directions: Use the code to color the fan.

If the answer has:

9 thousands, color it pink.
6 thousands, color it green.
5 hundreds, color it orange.

8 tens, color it red.
3 ones, color it blue.

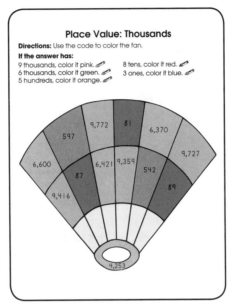

Page 406

Graphs

A **graph** is a drawing that shows information about numbers.

Directions: Count the apples in each row. Color the boxes to show how many apples have bites taken out of them.

Example:

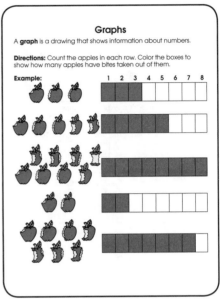

Page 407

Graphs

Directions: Count the bananas in each row. Color the boxes to show how many have been eaten by the monkeys.

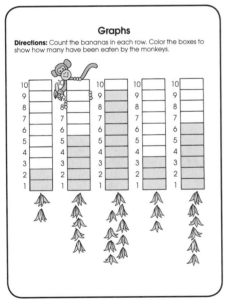

Page 408

Graphs

Directions: Count the fish. Color the bowls to make a graph that shows the number of fish.

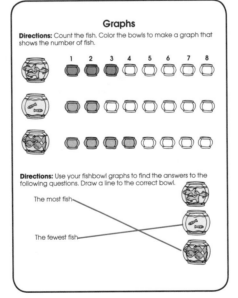

Directions: Use your fishbowl graphs to find the answers to the following questions. Draw a line to the correct bowl.

The most fish

The fewest fish

Page 409

Multiplication

Multiplication is a short way to find the sum of adding the same number a certain amount of times. For example, **4 x 7 = 28** instead of **7 + 7 + 7 + 7 = 28**.

Directions: Study the example. Solve the problems.

Example:

$3 + 3 + 3 = 9$
3 threes = 9
$3 \times 3 = 9$

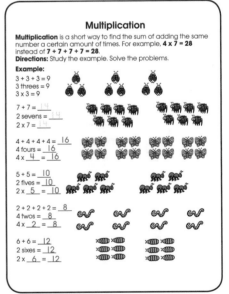

$7 + 7 = \underline{14}$
2 sevens = $\underline{14}$
$2 \times 7 = \underline{14}$

$4 + 4 + 4 + 4 = \underline{16}$
4 fours = $\underline{16}$
$4 \times \underline{4} = \underline{16}$

$5 + 5 = \underline{10}$
2 fives = $\underline{10}$
$2 \times \underline{5} = \underline{10}$

$2 + 2 + 2 + 2 = \underline{8}$
4 twos = $\underline{8}$
$4 \times \underline{2} = \underline{8}$

$6 + 6 = \underline{12}$
2 sixes = $\underline{12}$
$2 \times \underline{6} = \underline{12}$

Page 410

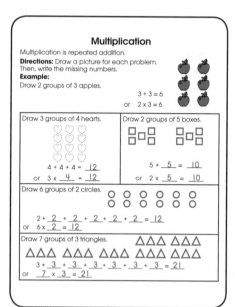

Multiplication

Multiplication is repeated addition.
Directions: Draw a picture for each problem. Then, write the missing numbers.
Example:
Draw 2 groups of 3 apples.

3 + 3 = 6
or 2 x 3 = 6

Draw 3 groups of 4 hearts.
4 + 4 + 4 = 12
or 3 x 4 = 12

Draw 2 groups of 5 boxes.
5 + 5 = 10
or 2 x 5 = 10

Draw 6 groups of 2 circles.
2 + 2 + 2 + 2 + 2 + 2 = 12
or 6 x 2 = 12

Draw 7 groups of 3 triangles.
3 + 3 + 3 + 3 + 3 + 3 + 3 = 21
or 7 x 3 = 21

Page 411

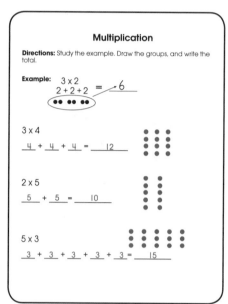

Multiplication

Directions: Study the example. Draw the groups, and write the total.

Example: 3 x 2
2 + 2 + 2 = 6

3 x 4
4 + 4 + 4 = 12

2 x 5
5 + 5 = 10

5 x 3
3 + 3 + 3 + 3 + 3 = 15

Page 412

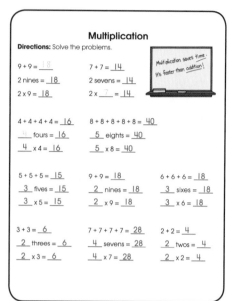

Multiplication

Directions: Solve the problems.

9 + 9 = 18
2 nines = 18
2 x 9 = 18

7 + 7 = 14
2 sevens = 14
2 x 7 = 14

Multiplication saves time. It's faster than addition!

4 + 4 + 4 + 4 = 16
4 fours = 16
4 x 4 = 16

8 + 8 + 8 + 8 + 8 = 40
5 eights = 40
5 x 8 = 40

5 + 5 + 5 = 15
3 fives = 15
3 x 5 = 15

9 + 9 = 18
2 nines = 18
2 x 9 = 18

6 + 6 + 6 = 18
3 sixes = 18
3 x 6 = 18

3 + 3 = 6
2 threes = 6
2 x 3 = 6

7 + 7 + 7 + 7 = 28
4 sevens = 28
4 x 7 = 28

2 + 2 = 4
2 twos = 4
2 x 2 = 4

Page 413

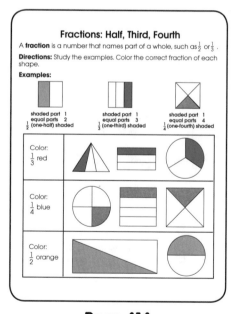

Fractions: Half, Third, Fourth

A **fraction** is a number that names part of a whole, such as $\frac{1}{2}$ or $\frac{1}{3}$.
Directions: Study the examples. Color the correct fraction of each shape.
Examples:

shaded part 1
equal parts 2
$\frac{1}{2}$ (one-half) shaded

shaded part 1
equal parts 3
$\frac{1}{3}$ (one-third) shaded

shaded part 1
equal parts 4
$\frac{1}{4}$ (one-fourth) shaded

Color: $\frac{1}{3}$ red

Color: $\frac{1}{4}$ blue

Color: $\frac{1}{2}$ orange

Page 414

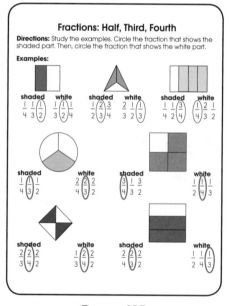

Fractions: Half, Third, Fourth

Directions: Study the examples. Circle the fraction that shows the shaded part. Then, circle the fraction that shows the white part.
Examples:

shaded $\frac{1}{4}$ $\frac{1}{3}$ $\frac{1}{2}$ white $\frac{1}{3}$ $\frac{1}{2}$ $\frac{1}{4}$

shaded $\frac{1}{2}$ $\frac{1}{3}$ $\frac{1}{4}$ white $\frac{1}{2}$ $\frac{1}{3}$ $\frac{1}{4}$

shaded $\frac{1}{4}$ $\frac{1}{2}$ $\frac{1}{3}$ white $\frac{1}{4}$ $\frac{1}{2}$ $\frac{1}{2}$

shaded $\frac{1}{4}$ $\frac{2}{3}$ $\frac{1}{2}$ white $\frac{2}{4}$ $\frac{2}{3}$ $\frac{2}{2}$

shaded $\frac{3}{4}$ $\frac{1}{3}$ $\frac{1}{2}$ white $\frac{1}{2}$ $\frac{1}{4}$ $\frac{1}{3}$

shaded $\frac{2}{3}$ $\frac{2}{4}$ $\frac{2}{2}$ white $\frac{1}{3}$ $\frac{2}{4}$ $\frac{2}{2}$

shaded $\frac{2}{4}$ $\frac{2}{3}$ $\frac{2}{2}$ white $\frac{1}{2}$ $\frac{1}{4}$ $\frac{1}{3}$

Page 415

Fractions: Half, Third, Fourth

Directions: Draw a line from the fraction to the correct shape.

$\frac{1}{4}$ shaded

$\frac{2}{4}$ shaded

$\frac{1}{2}$ shaded

$\frac{1}{3}$ shaded

$\frac{2}{3}$ shaded

Page 416

Geometry

Geometry is mathematics that has to do with lines and shapes.

Directions: Color the shapes.

Color the triangles blue.
Color the circles red.
Color the squares green.
Color the rectangles pink.

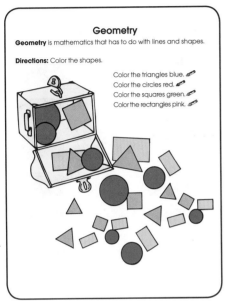

Page 417

Geometry

Directions: Draw a line from the word to the shape.

Use a red line for circles. Use a yellow line for rectangles.
Use a blue line for squares. Use a green line for triangles.

Circle   Square   Triangle   Rectangle

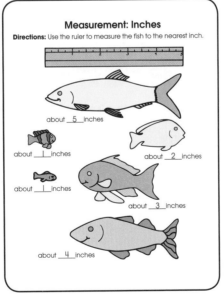

Page 418

Measurement: Inches

Directions: Cut out the ruler. Measure each object to the nearest inch.

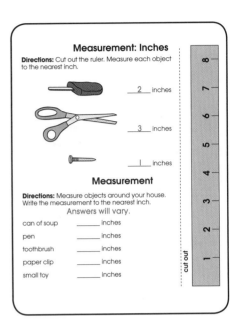

_____2_____ inches

_____3_____ inches

_____1_____ inches

Measurement

Directions: Measure objects around your house. Write the measurement to the nearest inch.

Answers will vary.

can of soup _____ inches

pen _____ inches

toothbrush _____ inches

paper clip _____ inches

small toy _____ inches

Page 421

Measurement: Inches

An **inch** is a unit of length in the standard measurement system.

Directions: Use a ruler to measure each object to the nearest inch.

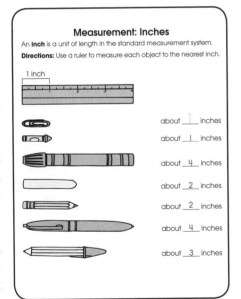

about _1_ inches

about _1_ inches

about _4_ inches

about _2_ inches

about _2_ inches

about _4_ inches

about _3_ inches

Page 423

Measurement: Inches

Directions: Use the ruler to measure the fish to the nearest inch.

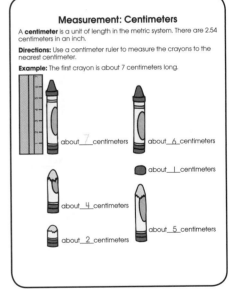

about _5_ inches

about _1_ inches

about _2_ inches

about _1_ inches

about _3_ inches

about _4_ inches

Page 424

Measurement: Centimeters

A **centimeter** is a unit of length in the metric system. There are 2.54 centimeters in an inch.

Directions: Use a centimeter ruler to measure the crayons to the nearest centimeter.

Example: The first crayon is about 7 centimeters long.

about _7_ centimeters   about _6_ centimeters

about _1_ centimeters

about _4_ centimeters

about _2_ centimeters   about _5_ centimeters

Page 425

ANSWER KEY

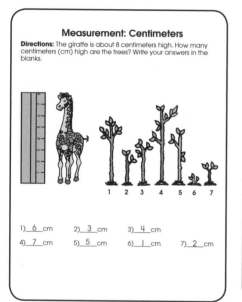

Measurement: Centimeters

Directions: The giraffe is about 8 centimeters high. How many centimeters (cm) high are the trees? Write your answers in the blanks.

1) _6_ cm   2) _3_ cm   3) _4_ cm
4) _7_ cm   5) _5_ cm   6) _1_ cm   7) _2_ cm

Page 426

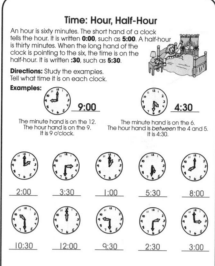

Time: Hour, Half-Hour

An hour is sixty minutes. The short hand of a clock tells the hour. It is written **0:00**, such as **5:00**. A half-hour is thirty minutes. The long hand of the clock is pointing to the six, the time is on the half-hour. It is written **:30**, such as **5:30**.

Directions: Study the examples. Tell what time it is on each clock.

Examples:

9:00 — The minute hand is on the 12. The hour hand is on the 9. It is 9 o'clock.

4:30 — The minute hand is on the 6. The hour hand is *between* the 4 and 5. It is 4:30.

2:00   3:30   1:00   5:30   8:00
10:30   12:00   9:30   2:30   3:00

Page 427

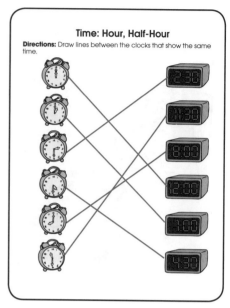

Time: Hour, Half-Hour

Directions: Draw lines between the clocks that show the same time.

2:30 11:30 8:00 12:00 1:00 4:30

Page 428

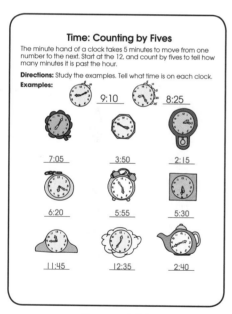

Time: Counting by Fives

The minute hand of a clock takes 5 minutes to move from one number to the next. Start at the 12, and count by fives to tell how many minutes it is past the hour.

Directions: Study the examples. Tell what time it is on each clock.

Examples: 9:10   8:25

7:05   3:50   2:15
6:20   5:55   5:30
11:45   12:35   2:40

Page 429

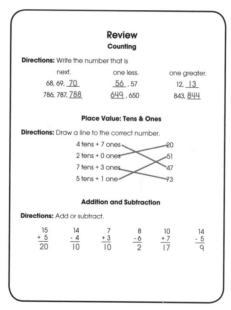

Review
Counting

Directions: Write the number that is

next.   one less.   one greater.
68, 69, _70_   _56_, 57   12, _13_
786, 787, _788_   _649_, 650   843, _844_

Place Value: Tens & Ones

Directions: Draw a line to the correct number.

4 tens + 7 ones — 20
2 tens + 0 ones — 51
7 tens + 3 ones — 47
5 tens + 1 one — 73

Addition and Subtraction

Directions: Add or subtract.

15+5=20 14-4=10 7+3=10 8-6=2 10+7=17 14-5=9

Page 430

Review

2-Digit Addition and Subtraction

Directions: Add or subtract using regrouping, if needed.

66-37=29 38+18=56 87-69=18 52-15=37 40+17=57
84+17=101 65+14=79 99-48=51 61-36=25 56+46=102

Place Value: Hundreds and Thousands

Directions: Draw a line to the correct number.

4 hundreds + 3 tens + 2 ones — 7,201
6 hundreds + 7 tens + 6 ones — 290
5 thousands + 3 hundreds + 7 tens + 2 ones — 432
2 hundreds + 9 tens + 0 ones — 676
7 thousands + 2 hundreds + 0 tens + 1 one — 5,372

3-Digit Addition and Subtraction

Directions: Add or subtract, remembering to regroup, if needed.

458-248=210 793-414=379 822-460=362 528+319=847 697+108=805 569+288=857

Page 431

Review
Multiplication
Directions: Solve the problems. Draw groups if necessary.

$$\begin{array}{c}2\\ \times 8\\ \hline 16\end{array} \qquad \begin{array}{c}6\\ \times 4\\ \hline 24\end{array} \qquad \begin{array}{c}3\\ \times 2\\ \hline 6\end{array} \qquad \begin{array}{c}8\\ \times 4\\ \hline 32\end{array} \qquad \begin{array}{c}5\\ \times 3\\ \hline 15\end{array} \qquad \begin{array}{c}2\\ \times 2\\ \hline 4\end{array}$$

Fractions
Directions: Circle the correct fraction of each shape's white part.

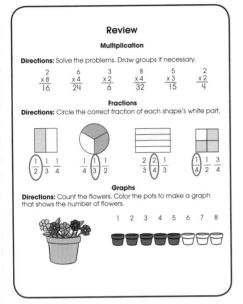

Graphs
Directions: Count the flowers. Color the pots to make a graph that shows the number of flowers.

1 2 3 4 5 6 7 8

Page 432

Review
Geometry
Directions: Match the shapes.

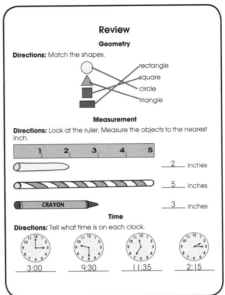

rectangle
square
circle
triangle

Measurement
Directions: Look at the ruler. Measure the objects to the nearest inch.

1 2 3 4 5

_2_ inches

_5_ inches

CRAYON _3_ inches

Time
Directions: Tell what time is on each clock.

3:00   9:30   11:35   2:15

Page 433

Money: Penny, Nickel

Penny 1¢   Nickel 5¢

Directions: Count the coins, and write the amount.

Example:

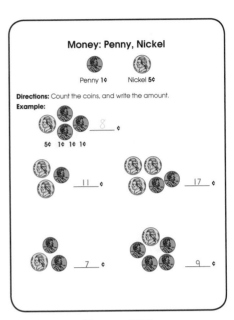

_8_ ¢
5¢ 1¢ 1¢ 1¢

_11_ ¢   _17_ ¢

_7_ ¢   _9_ ¢

Page 434

Money: Penny, Nickel, Dime

Penny 1¢   Nickel 5¢   Dime 10¢

Directions: Count the coins, and write the amount.

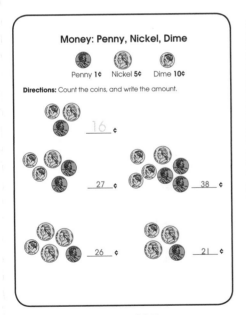

_16_ ¢

_27_ ¢   _38_ ¢

_26_ ¢   _21_ ¢

Page 435

Money: Penny, Nickel, Dime
Directions: Draw a line from the toy to the amount of money it costs.

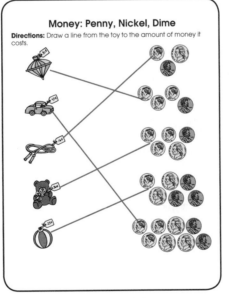

Page 436

Money: Penny, Nickel, Dime
Directions: Draw a line to match the amounts of money.

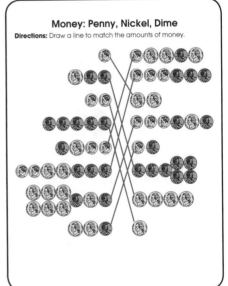

Page 437

Money: Quarter

A quarter is worth 25¢.
Directions: Count the coins, and write the amounts.

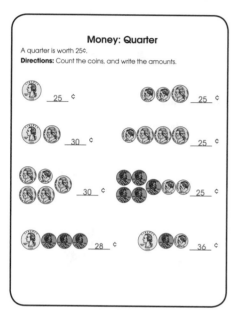

Money: Decimals

A **decimal** is a number with one or more places to the right of a decimal point, such as 6.5 or 2.25. Money amounts are written with two places to the right of the decimal point.

25¢	10¢	5¢	1¢
$.25	$.10	$.05	$.01

Directions: Count the coins, and circle the amount shown.

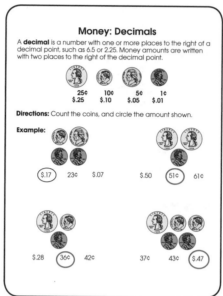

Money: Decimals

Directions: Draw a line from the coins to the correct amount in each column.

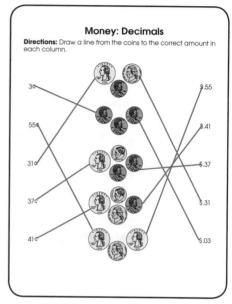

Page 438   **Page 439**   **Page 440**

Money: Dollar

One dollar equals 100 cents. It is written $1.00.
Directions: Count the money, and write the amounts.

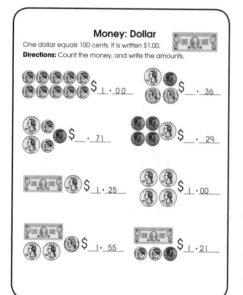

Adding Money

Directions: Write the amount of money using decimals. Then, add to find the total amount.

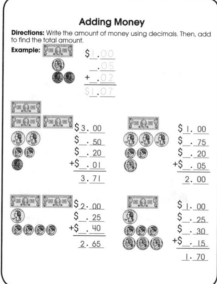

Review

Directions: Add the money, and write the total.

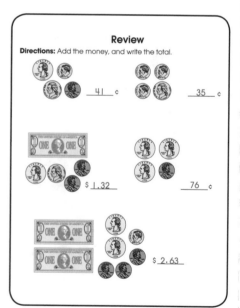

Page 441   **Page 442**   **Page 443**

Problem Solving

Directions: Tell whether you should add or subtract. **In all** is a clue to add. **Left** is a clue to subtract. Draw pictures to help you.

Example:
Jane's dog has 5 bones. He ate 3 bones. How many bones are left?

subtract

$$\begin{array}{r} 5 \\ -\ 3 \\ \hline 2 \end{array}$$ bones

Lucky the cat had 5 mice. She got 4 more for her birthday. How many mice did she have in all?

add

$$\begin{array}{r} 5 \\ +\ 4 \\ \hline 9 \end{array}$$ mice

Sam bought 6 fish. She gave 2 fish to a friend. How many fish does she have left?

subtract

$$\begin{array}{r} 6 \\ -\ 2 \\ \hline 4 \end{array}$$ fish

Page 445

Problem Solving: Addition, Subtraction, Multiplication

Directions: Tell if you add, subtract, or multiply. Then, write the answer.

Example:
There were 12 frogs sitting on a log by a pond, but 3 frogs hopped away. How many frogs are left?

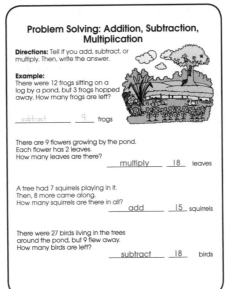

subtract ___9___ frogs

There are 9 flowers growing by the pond. Each flower has 2 leaves. How many leaves are there?

multiply ___18___ leaves

A tree had 7 squirrels playing in it. Then, 8 more came along. How many squirrels are there in all?

add ___15___ squirrels

There were 27 birds living in the trees around the pond, but 9 flew away. How many birds are left?

subtract ___18___ birds

Page 446

Problem Solving: Fractions

A fraction is a number that names part of a whole, such as $\frac{1}{2}$ or $\frac{1}{3}$.

Directions: Read each problem. Use the pictures to help you solve the problem. Write the fraction that answers the question.

Simon and Jessie shared a pizza. Together they ate $\frac{3}{4}$ of the pizza. How much of the pizza is left?

$\frac{1}{4}$

Sylvia baked a cherry pie. She gave $\frac{1}{3}$ to her grandmother and $\frac{1}{3}$ to a friend. How much of the pie did she keep?

$\frac{1}{3}$

Ahmad erased $\frac{1}{2}$ of the blackboard before the bell rang for recess. How much of the blackboard does he have left to erase?

$\frac{1}{2}$

Directions: Read the problem. Draw your own picture to help you solve the problem. Write the fraction that answers the question.

Yoko mowed $\frac{1}{4}$ of the yard before lunch. How much does she have left to mow?

$\frac{3}{4}$

Page 447

Problem Solving: Time

Directions: Solve each problem.

Addy wakes up at 7:00. She has 30 minutes before her bus comes. What time does her bus come?

___7___ : ___30___

Vera walks her dog for 15 minutes after supper. She finishes supper at 6:30. When does she get home from walking her dog?

___6___ : ___45___

Diego practices the piano for 30 minutes when he gets home from school. He gets home at 3:30. When does he stop practicing?

___4___ : ___00___

Tanya starts mowing the grass at 4:30. She finishes at 5:00. For how many minutes does she mow the lawn?

___30___ minutes

Aiden does his homework for 45 minutes. He starts his work at 7:15. When does he stop working?

___8___ : ___00___

Page 448

Problem Solving: Money

Directions: Read each problem. Use the pictures to help you solve the problems.

Ben bought a ball. He had 11¢ left. How much money did he have at the start?

___40___ ¢

Tara has 75¢. She buys a car. How much money does she have left?

___30___ ¢

Leah wants to buy a doll and a ball. She has 80¢. How much more money does she need?

___8___ ¢

Jacob has 95¢. He buys the car and the ball. How much more money does he need to buy a doll for his sister?

___38___ ¢

Pilar paid three quarters, one dime, and three pennies for a hat. How much did it cost?

___88___ ¢

Page 449

Alphabetical (ABC) order

Have your child alphabetize her word cards from the "Spelling Concentration" game on.

Have your child list all the rain forest animals (or forest or ocean animals) that she can. Ask her to alphabetize the list on another sheet of paper. Give her extra help with words that begin with the same letter if needed.

Write the ABCs in a column down the left-hand side of a sheet of paper. As you read a story with your child, have her find and write words that begin with each letter.

Select a category. Then, help your child find a word for each letter of the alphabet that fits that category. Example: Animals—*anteater*, *bear*, *cow*, etc.

Help your child create tongue twisters using words in ABC order. Examples: A big cat danced elegantly. Frank gave Harry icky jellybeans.

Classifying

Have your child choose a topic and write a word list related to it. Example: Summer—*hot, sun, bare feet, shorts*, etc. She can create sentences using these words.

Help your child classify and list animals in groups: mammals, reptiles, fish, birds, amphibians, etc.

Creative Writing

Challenge your child to use his spelling words to create a "word find" for you to do.

Have your child make a list of rhyming words.

Have your child practice the spelling words by using all of them to create a story.

Have your child choose a topic, and write as many words as possible that fit the category. Example: volleyball: *net, ball, uniform, serve, spike, bump, set, time out, sand, court*, etc.

Expose your child to words with multiple meanings, and have him look up the words in a dictionary. Have your child practice using the words in both written and spoken forms.

Encourage your child to form similes with spelling words. A simile is a comparison using *like* or *as*. Examples: He is as light as a feather. She is like a quiet little mouse.

Help your child create a Family Book. Have your child add photos, draw pictures, and write captions for an original family scrapbook.

Teach your child to write limericks. A limerick is a five-line humorous rhymed verse. Example: There once was a cat that was fat/ Who ate on a little red mat./ She said with a smile,/ "I've been here a while,/ So you just go on now and scat!"

Create a story jar for your child. Write several tantalizing story starters on slips of paper. Some examples might be "If I found $100 . . ." or "What was that creaking sound I heard from the attic?" When your child needs a good idea for a story, he/she can draw a slip from the jar.

Dictionary Skills

Create a personal dictionary or a "Word Wall" poster for your child to keep track of each new word she learns.

Have a family "word of the week." Challenge family members to look up the word, to learn its spelling, and to use it as much as possible during the week.

Make an alphabet book. Have your child cut big letters from magazines and glue each letter on a separate page. She can arrange the pages in ABC order. Then, have your child draw pictures of objects that start with each letter.

Choose a new word each day for your child to look up in the dictionary. Discuss the word's meaning. Have your child write a sentence using the new word. She can keep a list of the words in a word journal.

Help your child find new words on the Internet, in newspapers, on signs, etc. Have your child look them up in the dictionary. Make a collage using the words.

Following Directions

Have your child read and follow directions for constructing a model, playing a game, preparing a recipe, and so on. Ask your child to write her own directions for making a simple recipe or playing a simple game.

Geometry

Help your child cut out various geometric shapes and make a shape mobile to hang up.

Use construction paper to create prisms and three-dimensional objects, such as a party hat, a cube, etc.

Grammar

Have your child practice creating plurals by adding *s* to the original word to make it mean more than one.

Write sentences for your child to proofread. Include both punctuation and spelling errors. Example: The bair went over the mountain?

Use your computer to write sentences for your child to correct. For example: The boys name is jim. Your child can gain valuable practice with both English skills and the computer by moving the arrow and delete keys to correct the sentence.

Graphs

Graph the birthdays of the people in your family. Ask your child questions based on the graph, such as "In which month are there the most birthdays?" The fewest number? In which months are there no birthdays?

Graph the people in your family, using criteria such as boys, girls, pets, etc.

Inferences

Make riddle cards using clues for different fairy tale or cartoon characters. Play a guessing game with the cards. Let your child read the clues and name the character. Example: What little bear went hungry because a young girl ate his porridge? If you make these ahead of time, they can help pass the time on a long trip.

Put the pieces of a 12-to-20-piece puzzle in a bag. Let your child look at the pieces and make inferences about what the picture will be. Then, put the puzzle together.

Making Deductions

Put an object in a box, and write clues for it. Have your child read the clues and guess what the object may be.

Measurement

Ask your child what tools we use for measuring things (calendars and clocks to measure time, thermometer to measure temperature, etc.). Brainstorm a list of different measuring tools.

Show your child how to measure the circumference of cylindrical objects. For example, have your child predict the distance around a tree trunk. Pull a length of string around a tree trunk until the two ends meet. Cut the string. Then, measure the length of the string in inches and centimeters. Compare the actual measurement with your child's prediction.

Present a math word problem for your child to solve. Have her explain and write in sequence how to solve the problem.

Multiple-Meaning Words

Talk with your child about multiple-meaning words when opportunities present themselves in conversation. For example: "Did you hear the phone **ring**?" and "What a beautiful diamond **ring**!" Ask your child to brainstorm other examples of multiple-meaning words.

Parts of Speech

Play a fun "parts of speech" word game with your child. Write nouns, verbs, and adjectives on index cards, and have your child illustrate them. Then, let your child choose a noun card, a verb card, and an adjective card, and put them together to form fun sentences.

Have your child select a section of the newspaper and circle as many nouns and underline as many verbs as possible. You might ask her to circle plural nouns in a different color.

Patterns

Help your child find shape patterns as you drive or go for a walk together. Look for patterns in clothing, in billboards, or on store signs.

Watch for word patterns as you read together. In the book *Too Much Noise* by Ann McGovern, your child can easily identify phrases that are repeated, and often, based on the story, predict the next phrase in the pattern.

Point Of View

Read a chapter in a chapter book with your child. Then, ask your child to draw a picture of what happened in that chapter. You could also ask your child to draw a picture of what he thinks might happen next.

Read fairy tales like "The Three Little Pigs," "Cinderella," "The Three Billy Goats Gruff," "Hansel and Gretel," etc. Then, ask your child to retell the story from the point of view of the villain. Have him build a case explaining why the character did what he did.

Predicting Outcomes

While reading a story, stop periodically and have your child predict what he thinks will happen next.

Before reading a book with your child, ask him questions about the story, and scan the illustrations. Ask questions beginning with *who, what, why, when, where,* and *how.* For example: What do you think this book is about? What do you think the title means? Who is this on the cover of the book? What is he/she doing? Do you think this is a true story or a make-believe story?"

Write an incomplete sentence using descriptive words, but leave off the ending. Ask your child to finish the sentence. Example: The slinky, slimy lizard crept slowly into Marco's new, shiny bookbag and ____.

Recalling Details

Have your child choose a character from a story and write or tell about the character. Ask him to draw a picture of the character.

Read a fairy tale with your child. Ask him to tell or write the story from a different point of view. For example: Make the troll the good character in "Three Billy Goats Gruff" and the goats the bad characters.

Have your child make a story chart for a book, displaying the important events that happened at the beginning, middle, and end of the story.

Your child can create a shoebox diorama displaying a scene from a favorite story, book, play, poem, and so on. A diorama is a three-dimensional scene that includes characters and objects from a story, displayed in an open box, similar to a stage. Encourage your child to be creative!

Relating to the Known

Choose a topic of interest to your child, such as insects, planets, sports, etc. Then, discuss what she knows and what she wants to learn about the topic. Formulate questions that will help your child learn new information based upon past knowledge. Example: How does a bee protect itself?

Retell

Read a book together. Then, ask your child to retell the story emphasizing what happened in the beginning, middle, and end.

Rhymes

Make up silly sentences with your child to practice rhyming skills. For example, "I saw a paper star when I cleaned out the ___." You may also want to say a series of words and have your child tell you which one doesn't rhyme: *coat, float, dish, goat.*

Same and Different

Choose two animals, sports, toys, TV programs, etc., and ask your child to tell you how they are the same or how they are different.

Have your child compare three rooms in your home. Ask her to tell you how they are the same and how they are different.

Sentences

Create word or sentence "dot-to-dots." Instead of numbers, write letters or words. Have your child connect the dots in the correct sequence to write a word or to correctly order a sentence.

Play a game that helps your child learn to use words in context. Write several words on index cards. Take turns drawing a card and using the word on the card in a sentence.

Print sentences, or copy a story on a sheet of paper. Leave blanks for key words. Have your child read the story and supply the missing words.

Write descriptive sentences on long cardboard strips. Have your child read the sentences. Then, cut the sentences into word sections, and have your child put the sentences back in order.

Sequencing

Invite your child to recreate a story as a comic strip. List six or more important events or scenes from a story in sequence. Then, have your child write each event on a separate sheet of paper and draw an accompanying picture. Glue the pages in order on large sheets of colorful construction paper.

Write or tell a story together. Begin the story. After a few sentences, have your child continue the story. Take turns until you get to the end.

Use the comics to help your child practice sequence. Select comics that show a simple sequence, and read the comic strip with your child. Cut the comic strip apart, and challenge your child to rearrange it in the correct order. You could also draw simple pictures in a series, and have your child draw a picture to show what would happen next. Pictures from the family photo album are also fun to sequence. Your child can use the visual clues of growth to help arrange them in sequential order.

Spelling

Create a deck of cards with letters and letter teams. Have your child try to make words from the cards drawn.

Write each of your child's spelling words on an index card. Cut apart the cards at the syllables. Mix up the cards, and have your child try to put the original words back together.

Play "Spell-o" with your child. Write each word in a box on a 5 x 5 grid. As you name a spelling word, have your child spell it back to you. He can then cover the square. When the card has five in a row covered, your child has "Spell-o!"

Fill a squirt bottle with water, and let your child spell words by squirting water on dry pavement.

Challenge your child to think of as many words as possible with letter teams such as *oy*. Try other letter teams such as *au*, *aw*, *ee*, and *ow*. Allow your child to check a dictionary if he needs to.

Synonyms, Antonyms, Homophones

Encourage your child to create more varied and interesting sentences by substituting synonyms for words he uses repeatedly. As your child reads his writing to you, point out places where a synonym might be used, such as the use of the words *tiny* or *small* instead of *little*.

Teach your child how to use a thesaurus to find synonyms (words that have almost the same meaning) of each spelling word. A thesaurus organized like a dictionary is the easiest to use.

Make a synonym memory game with your child. Write ten words on index cards. Then, write synonyms for the words on additional index cards. Mix up the cards, and place them facedown to play. Let your child turn over two cards at a time. If he matches two words that are synonyms, he gets to keep the cards. If the two words do not match, he must return the cards to their position. Then, the next player takes his turn. Play continues until all of the cards are gone. This game may also be played with words and their antonyms.

Act out a word (such as *hello*) from your list of antonyms, and ask your child to act out the antonym (*goodbye*).

Create a list of antonyms or homophones with your child. Then, ask your child to write a poem or limerick using the words.

Using the list of homophones, ask your child to write and illustrate sentences using a pair of homophones. Examples: I have a pair of pears. The bear had bare feet.

Time

Help your child create a paper plate clock. Use a paper fastener to attach the minute and hour hands. Suggest different hour and half-hour times for your child to show on the clock face.

Tracking

Draw a map of your home or neighborhood. Have your child draw paths from your home to other places in the area. Go for a walk or a drive, following one of the paths your child drew.

Have your child write, in order, how to escape from your home in case of an emergency. Then, follow the path with your family.

Visualizing

Ask your child to form a picture of a memory in her mind. Then, ask her to write or draw a description of what she sees.

Cut out pictures of scenery from old magazines. Share the pictures with your child. Ask her to tell you what images come to mind as she views them.

INDEX

INDEX